GATE PREP SERIES

GATE

Graduate Aptitude Test in Engineering

2022

Polymer Science & Engineering

Solved Papers

(2008-2021)

G. K. PUBLICATIONS (P) LTD.

Title : GATE 2022 - Polymer Science & Engineering - Solved Papers (2008-2021)

Language : English

Editor's Name : Vinit Garg

Typeset & Published by :

Career Launcher Infrastructure (P) Ltd.

A-45, Mohan Cooperative Industrial Area, Near Mohan Estate Metro Station, New Delhi - 110044

Marketed by :

G.K. Publications (P) Ltd.

Plot No. 9A, Sector-27A, Mathura Road, Faridabad, Haryana-121003

ISBN : **978-93-91061-58-6**

Printer's Details : Made in India, New Delhi.

For product information :

Visit ***www.gkpublications.com*** or email to ***gkp@gkpublications.com***

GATE
Polymer Science & Engineering

Contents

PREVIOUS YEARS SOLVED PAPERS

GATE

Graduate Aptitude Test in Engineering

IIT Institutes

GATE 2021 conducted by
Indian Institute of Technology, Mumbai

GATE 2022 will be conducted by
Indian Institute of Technology, Kharagpur

Indian Institute of Technology, Delhi

Indian Institute of Technology, Chennai

Indian Institute of Technology, Guwahati

Indian Institute of Technology, Roorkee

Indian Institute of Technology, Kanpur

Preface

The Graduate Aptitude Test in Engineering (GATE) is an online exam conducted by the IITs for admissions to PG courses in IITs, IISc Bangalore, NITs and many state run universities as well as private universities. Also there are more than 37 PSUs that use GATE score for recruitments. A large number of corporates are also using GATE score as a tool to screen students for placements.

GK Publications is well known as the "publisher of choice" to students preparing for GATE and other technical examinations in the country. We published the first set of books in 1994 when GATE exam, both objective and conventional, was conducted in the paper and pencil environment, and used as a check point for entry to post graduate courses in IITs and IISCs. At that time, students had little access to technology and relied mainly on instructor led learning followed by practice with books available for these examinations.

A lot has changed since then!

Today, GATE is conducted in an online only mode with multiple choice and numerical based questions. The score is valid for three years and is used not only for post graduate courses but is also used by major PSUs for recruitment. Today's students have easy access to technology and the concept of a monologue within the classroom has changed to dialogue where students come prepared with concepts and then discuss topics. They learn a lot of things on the go with their mobile devices and practice for mock tests online.

We, as a leading publisher of GATE books, have also embraced change. Today, our books are no more guides and papers only but come with a fully supported mobile app and a web portal. The mobile app provides access to video lectures, short tests and regular updates about the exam. The web portal in additional to what is available on the app provides full length mock tests to mimic the actual exam and help you gauge your level of preparedness. The combination of practice content in print, video lectures, and short and full length tests on mobile and web makes this product a complete courseware for GATE preparation.

This book includes previous years GATE questions along with detailed solution of each question for better understanding. It will help the GATE aspirants to know an idea about the pattern of questions asked in GATE examination.

We also know that improvement is a never ending process and hence we welcome your suggestions and feedback or spelling and technical errors if any. Please write to us at gkp@gkpublications.com

We hope that our small effort will help you prepare well for the examination.

We wish you all the best!

GK Publications Pvt. Ltd.

About GATE

The Graduate Aptitude Test in Engineering (GATE) conducted by IISc and IITs has emerged as one of the bench mark tests for engineering and science aptitude in facilitating admissions for higher education (M.Tech./Ph.D.) in IITs, IISc and various other Institutes/Universities/Laboratories in India. With the standard and high quality of the GATE examination in 27 disciplines of engineering and science, Humanities and Social Sciences subjects, it identifies the candidate's understanding of a subject and aptitude and eligibility for higher studies. During the last few years, GATE score is also being used as one of the criteria for recruitment in Government Organizations such as Cabinet Secretariat, and National/State Public Sector Undertakings in India. Because of the importance of the GATE examination, the number of candidates taking up GATE exams has increased tremendously. GATE exams are conducted by the IITs and IISc as a computer based test having multiple choice questions and numerical answer type questions. The questions are mostly fundamental, concept based and thought provoking. From 2017 onwards GATE Exam is being held in Bangladesh, Ethiopia, Nepal, Singapore, Sri Lanka and United Arab Emirates. An Institute with various nationalities in its campus widens the horizons of an academic environment. A foreign student brings with him/her a great diversity, culture and wisdom to share. Many GATE qualified candidates are paid scholarships/assistantship, especially funded by Ministry of Human Resources Development, Government of India and by other Ministries. IIT, Kharagpur is the Organizing Institute for GATE 2022.

Why GATE?

Admission to Post Graduate and Doctoral Programmes

Admission to postgraduate programmes with MHRD and some other government scholarships/ assistantships in engineering colleges/institutes is open to those who qualify through GATE. GATE qualified candidates with Bachelor's degree in Engineering/Technology/Architecture or Master's degree in any branch of Science/Mathematics/Statistics/Computer Applications are eligible for admission to Master/Doctoral programmes in Engineering/Technology/Architecture as well as for Doctoral programmes in relevant branches of Science with MHRD or other government scholarships/ assistantships. Candidates with Master's degree in Engineering/Technology/Architecture may seek admission to relevant Ph.D programmes with scholarship/assistantship without appearing in the GATE examination.

Financial Assistance

A valid GATE score is essential for obtaining financial assistance during Master's programs and direct Doctoral programs in Engineering/Technology/Architecture, and Doctoral programs in relevant branches of Science in Institutes supported by the MHRD or other Government agencies. As per the directives of the MHRD, the following procedure is to be adopted for admission to the post-graduate programs (Master's and Doctoral) with MHRD scholarship/assistantship. Depending upon the norms adopted by a specific institute or department of the Institute, a candidate may be admitted directly into a course based on his/her performance in GATE only **or** based on his/her performance in GATE **and** an admission test/interview conducted by the department to which he/she has applied **and/or** the candidate's academic record. If the candidate is to be selected through test/interview for post-graduate programs, a minimum of 70% weightage will be given to the performance in GATE and the remaining 30% weightage will be given to the candidate's performance in test/interview and/or academic record, as per MHRD guidelines. The admitting institutes could however prescribe a minimum passing percentage of marks in the test/interview. Some colleges/institutes specify GATE qualification as the mandatory requirement even for admission without MHRD scholarship/assistantship.

To avail of the financial assistance (scholarship), the candidate must first secure admission to a program in these Institutes, by a procedure that could vary from institute to institute. Qualification in GATE is also a minimum requirement to apply for various fellowships awarded by many Government organizations. Candidates are advised to seek complete details of admission procedures and availability of MHRD scholarship/assistantship from the concerned admitting institution. The criteria for postgraduate admission with scholarship/assistantship could be different for different institutions. The management of the post-graduate scholarship/assistantship is also the responsibility of the admitting institution. Similarly, reservation of seats under different categories is as per the policies and norms prevailing at the admitting institution and Government of India rules. *GATE offices will usually not entertain any enquiry about admission, reservation of seats and / or award of scholarship / assistantship.*

PSU Recruitments

As many as 37 PSUs are using GATE score for recruitment. It is likely that more number of PSUs may start doing so by next year. Below is the list of PSUs:

MDL, BPCL, GAIL, NLC LTD, CEL, Indian Oil, HPCL, NBPC, NECC, BHEL, WBSEDCL, NTPC, ONGC, Oil India, Power Grid, Cabinet Secretariat, Govt. of India, BAARC, NFL, IPR, PSPCL, PSTCL, DRDO, OPGC Ltd., THDC India Ltd., BBNL, RITES, IRCON, GHECL, NHAI, KRIBHCO, Mumbai Railway Vikas Corporation Ltd. (MRVC Ltd.), National Textile Corporation, Coal India Ltd., BNPM, AAI, NALCO, EdCIL India.

Important :

1. Admissions in IITs/IISc or other Institutes for M.Tech./Ph.D. through GATE scores shall be advertised separately by the Institutes and GATE does not take the responsibility of admissions.
2. Cabinet Secretariat has decided to recruit officers for the post of Senior Field Officer (Tele) (From GATE papers of EC, CS, PH), Senior Research Officer (Crypto) (From GATE papers of EC, CS, MA), Senior Research Officer (S&T) (From GATE papers EC, CS, CY, PH, AE, BT) in the Telecommunication Cadre, Cryptographic Cadre and Science & Technology Unit respectively of Cabinet Secretariat. The details of the scheme of recruitment shall be published in National Newspaper/Employment News by the concerned authority.
3. Some PSUs in India have expressed their interest to utilize GATE scores for their recruitment purpose. The Organizations who intend to utilize GATE scores shall make separate advertisement for this purpose in Newspapers etc.

Who Can Appear for GATE?

Eligibility for GATE

Before starting the application process, the candidate must ensure that he/she meets the eligibility criteria of GATE given in Table.

Eligibility Criteria for GATE 2022

Degree/Program	Qualifying Degree/Examination	Description of Eligible Candidates	Expected Year of Completion
B.E. / B.Tech. / B.Pharm.	Bachelor's degree in Engineering / Technology (4 years after 10+2 or 3 years after B.Sc. / Diploma in Engineering / Technology)	Currently in the 3rd year or higher grade or already completed	2022
B. Arch.	Bachelor's degree of Architecture (5- year course) / Naval Architecture (4- year course) / Planning (4- year course)	Currently in the 3rd year or higher grade or already completed	2023 (for 5-year program), 2022 (for 4-year program)
B.Sc. (Research) / B.S.	Bachelor's degree in Science (Post-Diploma/4 years after 10+2)	Currently in the 3rd year or higher grade or already completed	2022
Pharm. D. (after 10+2)	6 years degree program, consisting of internship or residency training, during third year onwards	Currently in the 3rd/4th/5th/6th year or already completed	2024
M.B.B.S.	Degree holders of M.B.B.S. and those who are in the 5th/6th/7th semester or higher semester of such programme.	5th, 6th, 7th or higher semester or already completed	2022
M. Sc. / M.A. / MCA or equivalent	Master's degree in any branch of Arts/Science/Mathematics/Statistics/ Computer Applications or equivalent	Currently in the first year or higher or already Completed	2022
Int. M.E./ M.Tech. (Post-B.Sc.)	Post-B.Sc Integrated Master's degree programs in Engineering/ Technology (4-year program)	Currently in the 1st / 2nd/3rd/4th year or already completed	2024
Int. M.E./ M.Tech. or Dual Degree (after Diploma or 10+2)	Integrated Master's degree program or Dual Degree program in Engineering/Technology (5-year program)	Currently in the 3rd /4th/5th year or alreadycompleted	2023
B.Sc. / B.A. / B.Com.	Bachelor degree in any branch of Science / Arts / Commerce (3 years program)	Currently in the 3rd year or already completed	2021
Int. M.Sc. / Int. B.S. / M.S.	Integrated M.Sc. or 5-year integrated B.S.-M.S. program	Currently in the 3rd year or higher or already completed	2022
Professional Society Examinations (equivalent to B.E. / B.Tech. / B.Arch.)	B.E./B.Tech./B.Arch. equivalent examinations of Professional Societies, recognized by MoE/UPSC/AICTE (e.g. AMIE by Institution of Engineers-India, AMICE by the Institute of Civil Engineers-India and so on)	Completed Section A or equivalent of such professional courses	NA

In case a candidate has passed one of the qualifying examinations as mentioned above in 2020 or earlier, the candidate has to submit the degree certificate / provisional certificate / course completion certificate / professional certificate / membership certificate issued by the society or institute. In case, the candidate is expected to complete one of the qualifying criteria in 2022 or later as mentioned above, he/she has to submit a certificate from Principal or a copy of marks card for section A of AMIE.

Certificate From Principal

Candidates who have to submit a certificate from their college Principal have to obtain one from his/her institution beforehand and upload the same during the online submission of the application form.

Candidates With Backlogs

Candidates, who have appeared in the final semester/year exam in 2022, but with a backlog (arrears/failed subjects) in any of the papers in their qualifying degree should upload a copy of any one of the mark sheets of the final year,

OR

obtain a declaration from their Principal along with the signature and seal beforehand and upload the same during the online submission of the application form.

GATE Structure

Structure of GATE

GATE 2022 will be conducted on 27 subjects (papers). Table below shows the list of papers and paper codes for GATE 2022. A candidate is allowed to appear in ANY ONE or UP TO TWO papers of the GATE examination. However, note that the combination of TWO papers in which a candidate can appear MUST be from the pre-defined list as given in Table. Also note that for a paper running in multiple sessions, a candidate will be mapped to appear for the examination in one of the sessions ONLY.

List of GATE Papers and Corresponding Codes

GATE Paper	Code	GATE Paper	Code
Aerospace Engineering	AE	Instrumentation Engineering	IN
Agricultural Engineering	AG	Mathematics	MA
Architecture and Planning	AR	Mechanical Engineering	ME
Bio-medical Engineering	BM	Mining Engineering	MN
Biotechnology	BT	Metallurgical Engineering	MT
Civil Engineering	CE	Petroleum Engineering	PE
Chemical Engineering	CH	Physics	PH
Computer Science and Information Technology	CS	Production and Industrial Engineering	PI
Chemistry	CY	Statistics	ST
Electronics and Communication Engineering	EC	Textile Engineering and Fibre Science	TF
Electrical Engineering	EE	Engineering Sciences	XE*
Environmental Science & Engineering	ES	Humanities & Social Sciences	XH**
Ecology and Evolution	EY	Life Sciences	XL***
Geology and Geophysics	GG		

Note: *Environmental Science and Engineering (ES) and Humanities and Social Sciences (XH) are two new papers introduced in GATE 2022.*

*XE Paper Sections	Code	**XH Paper Sections	Code	***XL Paper Sections	Code
Engineering Mathematics (Compulsory) (15 marks)	A	Reasoning and Comprehension (Compulsory) (25 marks)	B1	Chemistry (Compulsory) (25 marks)	P
Any TWO optional Sections (2x35 = 70 marks)		Any ONE optional Section (60 marks)		Any TWO optional Sections (2x30 = 60 marks)	
Fluid Mechanics	B	Economics	C1	Biochemistry	Q
Materials Science	C	English	C2	Botany	R
Solid Mechanics	D	Linguistics	C3	Microbiology	S
Thermodynamics	E	Philosophy	C4	Zoology	T
Polymer Science and Engineering	F	Psychology	C5	Food Technology	U
Food Technology	G	Sociology	C6		
Atmospheric and Oceanic Sciences	H				

*XE (Engineering Sciences), **XH (Humanities & Social Sciences), ***XL (Life Sciences), papers are of general nature and will be comprised of Sections listed in the above table

Note: *Each subject/paper is of total 100 marks. General Aptitude (GA) section of 15 marks is common for all papers. Hence remaining 85 marks are for the respective subject/paper code.*

Combination of Two Papers Allowed to Appear in GATE 2022 (subject to availability of infrastructure and schedule)

Code of The First (Primary) Paper	Codes of Papers Allowed as The Second Paper
AE	XE
AG	ES
AR	CE
BM	BT / XL
BT	BM / XL
CE	AR / ES
CH	CY / PE / XE
CS	MA
CY	CH / XL
EC	IN / PH
EE	IN
ES	AG / CE
EY	XL
GG	MN / PE / PH
IN	EC / EE / PH
MA	CS / PH / ST
ME	XE
MN	GG / XE
MT	PH / XE
PE	CH / GG / XE
PH	EC / GG / IN / MA / MT / ST
PI	XE
ST	MA / PH
TF	XE
XE	AE / CH / ME / MN / MT / PE / PI / TF
XH	----
XL	BM / BT / CY / EY

General Aptitude Questions

All the papers will have a few questions that test the General Aptitude (Language and Analytical Skills), apart from the core subject of the paper.

Duration and Examination Type

All the papers of the GATE 2022 examination will be for 3 hours duration and they consist of 65 questions for a total of 100 marks. Since the examination is an ONLINE computer based test (CBT), at the end of the stipulated time (3-hours), the computer screen will automatically close the examination inhibiting any further action.

Candidates will be permitted to occupy their allotted seats 40 minutes before the scheduled start of the examination. Candidates can login and start reading the instructions 20 minutes before the start of examination. The late login time (if any) recorded by the computer system MUST NOT be beyond 30 minutes from the actual starting time of the examination. Under NO circumstances, will a candidate be permitted to login after 30 minutes from the actual examination starting time. Candidates will NOT be permitted to leave the examination hall before the end of the examination.

Pattern of Question Papers

GATE 2022 may contain questions of THREE different types in all the papers:

(i) **Multiple Choice Questions (MCQ)** carrying 1 or 2 marks each, in all the papers and sections. These questions are objective in nature, and each will have choice of four answers, out of which ONLY ONE choice is correct.

Negative Marking for Wrong Answers: For a wrong answer chosen in a MCQ, there will be negative marking. For 1-mark MCQ, 1/3 mark will be deducted for a wrong answer. Likewise, for 2-mark MCQ, 2/3 mark will be deducted for a wrong answer.

(ii) **Multiple Select Questions (MSQ)** carrying 1 or 2 marks each in all the papers and sections. These questions are objective in nature, and each will have choice of four answers, out of which ONE or MORE than ONE choice(s) is / are correct.

Note: There is NO negative marking for a wrong answer in MSQ questions. However, there is NO partial credit for choosing partially correct combinations of choices or any single wrong choice.

(iii) **Numerical Answer Type (NAT)** Questions carrying 1 or 2 marks each in most of the papers and sections. For these questions, the answer is a signed real number, which needs to be entered by the candidate using the virtual numeric keypad on the monitor (keyboard of the computer will be disabled). No choices will be shown for these types of questions. The answer can be a number such as 10 or –10 (an integer only). The answer may be in decimals as well, for example, 10.1 (one decimal) or 10.01 (two decimals) or –10.001 (three decimals). These questions will be mentioned with, up to which decimal places, the candidates need to present the answer. Also, for some NAT type problems an appropriate range will be considered while evaluating these questions so that the candidate is not unduly penalized due to the usual round-off errors. Candidates are advised to do the rounding off at the end of the calculation (not in between steps). Wherever required and possible, it is better to give NAT answer up to a maximum of three decimal places.

Note: *There is NO negative marking for a wrong answer in NAT questions.*
Also, there is NO partial credit in NAT questions.

Marking Scheme – Distribution of Marks and Questions

General Aptitude (GA) Questions

In all papers, GA questions carry a total of 15 marks. The GA section includes 5 questions carrying 1-mark each (sub-total 5 marks) and 5 questions carrying 2-marks each (sub-total 10 marks).

Question Papers other than GG, XE, XH and XL

These papers would contain 25 questions carrying 1-mark each (sub-total 25 marks) and 30 questions carrying 2-marks each (sub-total 60 marks) consisting of some MCQ type questions, while the remaining may be MSQ and / or NAT questions.

GG (Geology and Geophysics) Paper

Apart from the General Aptitude (GA) section, the GG question paper consists of two parts: Part A and Part B. Part A is compulsory for all the candidates. Part B contains two sections: Section 1 (Geology) and Section 2 (Geophysics). Candidates will have to attempt questions in Part A and questions in either Section 1 or Section 2 of Part B. The choice of Section 1 OR Section 2 of Part B has to be made at the time of online registration in GOAPS. At the examination hall, candidate cannot request for change of section.

Part A consists of 25 questions carrying 1-mark each (sub-total 25 marks and some of these will be MSQ and/or numerical answer type questions while remaining questions will be MCQ type). Either section of Part B (Section 1 and Section 2) consists of 30 questions carrying 2-marks each (sub-total 60 marks and some of these will be MSQ and/or numerical answer type questions while remaining questions will be MCQ type).

XE Paper (Engineering Sciences)

A candidate appearing in the XE paper has to answer the following:

- GA – General Aptitude carrying a total of 15 marks.
- Section A – Engineering Mathematics (Compulsory): This section contains 11 questions carrying a total of 15 marks: 7 questions carrying 1-mark each (sub-total 7 marks), and 4 questions carrying 2-marks each (sub-total 8 marks). Some questions will be of numerical answer type while remaining questions will be MCQ type.
- Any two of XE Sections B to H: The choice of two sections from B to H can be made during the examination after viewing the questions. Only TWO optional sections can be answered at a time. A candidate wishing to change midway of the examination to another optional section must first choose to deselect one of the previously chosen optional sections (B to H). Each of the optional sections of the XE paper (Sections B through H) contains 22 questions carrying a total of 35 marks: 9 questions carrying 1-mark each (sub-total 9 marks) and 13 questions carrying 2-marks each (sub-total 26 marks). Some questions will be of MSQ and/or numerical answer type while remaining questions will be MCQ type.

XH Paper (Humanities and Social Sciences)

A candidate appearing in the XH paper has to answer the following:

- **GA - General Aptitude** carrying a total of 15 marks.
- **Section B1 - Reasoning and Comprehension (Compulsory):** This section contains 15 questions carrying a total of 25 marks: 5 questions carrying 1-mark each (sub-total 5 marks) and 10 questions carrying 2-marks each (sub-total 20 marks). Some questions will be of MSQ and/or numerical answer type while remaining questions will be MCQ type.
- **Any ONE of XH Sections C1 to C6:** The ONE choice of section from C1 to C6 has to be made at the time of online registration in GOAPS. At the examination hall, candidate cannot request for change of section. Each of the optional sections of the XH paper (Sections C1 through C6) contains 40 questions carrying a total of 60 marks: 20 questions carrying 1-mark each (sub-total 20 marks) and 20 questions carrying 2-marks each (sub-total 40 marks). Some questions will be of MSQ and/or numerical answer type while remaining questions will be MCQ type.

XL Paper (Life Sciences)

A candidate appearing in the XL paper has to answer the following:

- **GA – General Aptitude** carrying a total of 15 marks.
- **Section P–Chemistry (Compulsory):** This section contains 15 questions carrying a total of 25 marks: 5 questions carrying 1-mark each (sub-total 5 marks) and 10 questions carrying 2-marks each (sub-total 20 marks). Some questions will be of MSQ and/or numerical answer type while remaining questions will be MCQ type.
- **Any two of XL Sections Q to U:** The choice of two sections from Q to U can be made during the examination after viewing the questions. Only TWO optional sections can be answered at a time. A candidate wishing to change midway of the examination to another optional section must first choose to deselect one of the previously chosen optional sections (Q to U). Each of the optional sections of the XL paper (Sections Q through U) contains 20 questions carrying a total of 30 marks: 10 questions carrying 1-mark each (sub-total 10 marks) and 10 questions carrying 2-marks each (sub-total 20 marks). Some questions will be of MSQ and/or numerical answer type while remaining questions will be MCQ type.

GATE Score

After the evaluation of the answers, the actual (raw) marks obtained by a candidate will be considered for computing the GATE Score. For multi-session papers (subjects), raw marks obtained by the candidates in different sessions will be converted to Normalized marks for that particular subject. Thus, raw marks (for single session papers) or normalized marks (for multi-session papers) will be used for computing the GATE Score, based on the qualifying marks.

Calculation of Normalized Marks for Multi-Session Papers

In GATE 2022 examination, some papers may be conducted in multi-sessions. Hence, for these papers, a suitable normalization is applied to take into account any variation in the difficulty levels of the question papers across different sessions. The normalization is done based on the fundamental assumption that "in all multi-session GATE papers, the distribution of abilities of candidates is the same across all the sessions". This assumption is justified since the number of candidates appearing in multi-session papers in GATE 2022 is large and the procedure for allocation of session to candidates is random. Further, it is also ensured that for the same multi-session paper, the number of candidates allotted in each session is of the same order of magnitude.

Based on the above, and considering various normalization methods, the committee arrived at the following formula for calculating the normalized marks for the multi-session papers.

Nsormalization mark of jth candidate in the ith session $\widehat{M_{ij}}$ is given by

$$\widehat{M_{ij}} = \frac{\bar{M}_t^g - M_q^g}{\bar{M}_{ti} - M_{iq}}(M_{ij} - M_{iq}) + M_q^g$$

where

M_{ij} : is the actual marks obtained by the jth candidate in i^{th} session

$\bar{M}_t^g$: is the average marks of the top 0.1% of the candidates considering all sessions

M_q^g : is the sum of mean and standard deviation marks of the candidates in the paper considering all sessions

$\bar{M}_{ti}$: is the average marks of the top 0.1% of the candidates in the ith session

M_{iq} : is the sum of the mean marks and standard deviation of the ith session

Calculation of GATE Score for All Papers

For all papers for which there is only one session, actual marks obtained by the candidates will be used for calculating the GATE 2022 Score. For papers in multi-sessions, normalized marks will be calculated corresponding to the raw marks obtained by a candidate and the GATE 2022 Score will be calculated based on the normalized marks.

The GATE 2022 score will be computed using the formula given below.

$$\text{GATE Score} = S_q + (S_t - S_q)\frac{(M - M_q)}{(\bar{M}_t - M_q)}$$

where

M : marks obtained by the candidate (actual marks for single session papers and normalized marks for multi-session papers)

M_q : is the qualifying marks for general category candidate in the paper

$\bar{M}_t$: is the mean of marks of top 0.1% or top 10 (whichever is larger) of the candidates who appeared in the paper (in case of multi-session papers including all sessions)

S_q : 350, is the score assigned to M_q

S_t : 900, is the score assigned to $\bar{M}_t$

In the GATE 2022 the qualifying marks (M_q) for general category student in each subject will be 25 marks (out of 100) or $\mu + \sigma$, whichever is larger. Here μ is the mean and σ is the standard deviation of marks of all the candidates who appeared in the paper.

After the declaration of results, GATE Scorecards can be downloaded by the GATE qualified candidates ONLY.

The GATE 2022 Committee has the authority to decide the qualifying mark/score for each GATE paper. In case of any claim or dispute with respect to GATE 2022 examination or score, the Courts and Tribunals in Mumbai alone will have the exclusive jurisdiction to entertain and settle them.

GATE Syllabus

Section 1: Chemistry of High Polymers

Monomers, functionality, degree of polymerizations, classification of polymers, glass transition, melting transition, criteria for rubberiness, polymerization methods: addition and condensation; their kinetics, metallocene polymers and other newer methods of polymerization, copolymerization, monomer reactivity ratios and its significance, kinetics, different copolymers, random, alternating, azeotropic copolymerization, block and graft copolymers, techniques for polymerization-bulk, solution, suspension, emulsion. Concept of intermolecular order (morphology) – amorphous, crystalline, orientation states. Factor affecting crystallinity. Crystalline transition. Effect of morphology on polymer properties.

Section 2: Polymer Characterization

Solubility and swelling, Concept of molecular weight distribution and its significance, concept of average molecular weight, determination of number average, weight average, viscosity average and Z-average molecular weights, polymer crystallinity, analysis of polymers using IR, XRD, thermal (DSC, DMTA, TGA), microscopic (optical and electronic) techniques, Molecular wt. distribution: Broad and Narrow, GPC, mooney viscosity.

Section 3: Synthesis, Manufacturing and Properties

Commodity and general purpose thermoplastics: PE, PP, PS, PVC, Polyesters, Acrylic, PU polymers. Engineering Plastics: Nylon, PC, PBT, PSU, PPO, ABS, Fluoropolymers Thermosetting polymers: Polyurethane, PF, MF, UF, Epoxy, Unsaturated polyester, Alkyds. Natural and synthetic rubbers: Recovery of NR hydrocarbon from latex; SBR, Nitrile, CR, CSM, EPDM, IIR, BR, Silicone, TPE, Speciality plastics: PEK, PEEK, PPS, PSU, PES etc. Biopolymers such as PLA, PHA/PHB.

Section 4: Polymer Blends and Composites

Difference between blends and composites, their significance, choice of polymers for blending, blend miscibility-miscible and immiscible blends, thermodynamics, phase morphology, polymer alloys, polymer eutectics, plastic-plastic, rubber-plastic and rubber-rubber blends, FRP, particulate, long and short fibre reinforced composites. Polymer reinforcement, reinforcing fibres – natural and synthetic, base polymer for reinforcement (unsaturated polyester), ingredients / recipes for reinforced polymer composite.

Section 5: PolymerTechnology

Polymer compounding-need and significance, different compounding ingredients for rubber and plastics (Antioxidants, Light stabilizers, UV stabilizers, Lubricants, Processing aids, Impact modifiers, Flame retardant, antistatic agents. PVC stabilizers and Plasticizers) and their function, use of carbon black, polymer mixing equipments, cross-linking and vulcanization, vulcanization kinetics.

Section 6: Polymer Rheology

Flow of Newtonian and non-Newtonian fluids, different flow equations, dependence of shear modulus on temperature, molecular/segmental deformations at different zones and transitions. Measurements of rheological parameters by capillary rotating, parallel plate, cone-plate rheometer. Visco-elasticitycreep and stress relaxations, mechanical models, control of rheological characteristics through compounding, rubber curing in parallel plate viscometer, ODR and MDR.

Section 7: Polymer Processing

Compression molding, transfer molding, injection molding, blow molding, reaction injection molding, filament winding, SMC, BMC, DMC, extrusion, pultrusion, calendaring, rotational molding, thermoforming, powder coating, rubber processing in two-roll mill, internal mixer, Twin screw extruder.

Section 8: Polymer Testing

Mechanical-static and dynamic tensile, flexural, compressive, abrasion, endurance, fatigue, hardness, tear, resilience, impact, toughness. Conductivity-thermal and electrical, dielectric constant, dissipation factor, power factor, electric resistance, surface resistivity, volume resistivity, swelling, ageing resistance, environmental stress cracking resistance, limiting oxygen index. Heat deflection temperature –Vicat softening temperature, Brittleness temperature, Glass transition temperature, Coefficient of thermal expansion, Shrinkage, Flammability, dielectric constant, dissipation factor, power factor, Optical Properties - Refractive Index, Luminous Transmittance and Haze, Melt flow index

Section 9: Polymer Recycling and Waste Management

Polymer waste, and its impact on environment, Sources, Identification and Separation techniques, recycling classification, recycling of thermoplastics, thermosets and rubbers, applications of recycled materials. Life cycle assessment of polymer products (case studies like PET bottles, packaging bags)

SOLVED PAPER - 2021

Q. 1 – Q. 9 carry one mark each

1. Linear low density polyethylene (LLDPE) is a copolymer of ethylene and a small fraction of ________ .

(*a*) butadiene (b) isoprene

(*c*) butene (*d*) hexadiene

2. Binary polymer blends of polypropylene and polyamide 6 are immiscible. From a thermodynamic viewpoint this is due to _______.

(*a*) low enthalpy of mixing

(*b*) higher entropy of mixing

(*c*) high enthalpy of mixing

(*d*) low entropy of mixing

3. Which one of the following is an elastomer ?

(*a*) Polyamide 6, 6

(*b*) Poly(ethylene terepthalate)

(*c*) Vulcanized polybutadiene

(*d*) Higher density polyethylene

4. Compression moulded isotropic polypropylene film exhibits ________ in X-ray diffraction analysis.

(*a*) spot pattern

(*b*) circular ring pattern

(*c*) circular ring and spot pattern

(*d*) arc pattern

5. Which one of the following is an example of a biodegradable polymer ?

(*a*) Polyethylene (*b*) Polyamide 6, 6

(c) Polypropylene (*d*) Polylactic acid

6. Polymer crystals show a range of melting points in contrast to single melting point of crystals of small molecules, because ______.

(*a*) there is an absence of intermolecular interactions

(*b*) there is an absence of long range ordering

(*c*) the polymer chains are not in thermodynamic equilibrium in a metastable state

(*d*) the melting behavior of polymer crystal is independent of sample thermal history

7. When the rate of cooling is increased during the solidification process, the glass transition temperature of a polymer ______ .

(*a*) decreases

(*b*) increases

(*c*) stays unaltered

(*d*) shows a non-monotonic dependence

8. Equal and opposite forces of a constant magnitude F are applied at the two ends of a thin elastomeric rod, which is held at a temperature $T_1 (T_g < T_1 < T_m)$, where T_g and T_m are the glass transition temperature and melting temperature respectively. If the temperature is increased to T_2 ($T_g < T_2 < T_m$ and $T_2 > T_1$), the rod will __________ .

(*a*) expand along the loading direction and the transverse direction

(*b*) shrink along the loading direction

(*c*) remain dimensionally unaltered

(*d*) expand only along the loading direction

9. The size of coiled polymer chain in a dilute solution is R_G in a good solvent, R_I in an ideal solvent and R_P in a poor solvent. Select the correct ordering of sizes.

(*a*) $R_G > R_I > R_P$

(*b*) $R_G < R_I < R_P$

(*c*) $R_P > R_G > R_I$

(*d*) $R_P < R_G < R_I$

Q. 10 – Q. 12 carry two marks each

10. Match the Additive of its Function.

Additive	**Function**
P. Tritolyl phosphate	1. Coupling Agent
Q. Triethoxy vinyl silane	2. Antioxidant
R. Azoisobutyronitrile	3. Plasticizer
S. 4-Methyl-2, 6-di-t-butyl phenol	4. Blowing Agent

(*a*) P-3, Q-2, R-1, S-4

(*b*) P-3, Q-1, R-4, S-2

(*c*) P-4, Q-1, R-3, S-2

(*d*) P-1, Q-2, R-4, S-3

11. Match the polymer processing operating with respect to its typical range of shear rate.

Processing Operation	Shear rate (s^{-1})
P. Compression Moulding	1. 1000 - 10000
Q. Extrusion	2. 100 - 1000
R. Calendering	3. 1 - 10
S. Injection Moulding	4. 10 - 100

(*a*) P-3, Q-4, R-2, S-1
(*b*) P-1, Q-3, R-2, S-4
(*c*) P-2, Q-4, R-3, S-1
(*d*) P-3, Q-2, R-1, S-4

12. Shear stress (σ) and shear viscosity (η) are plotted as functions of the shear rate, $\dot{\gamma}$, for idealized "solid-like with yielding (1)" and "liquid-like (2)" materials.

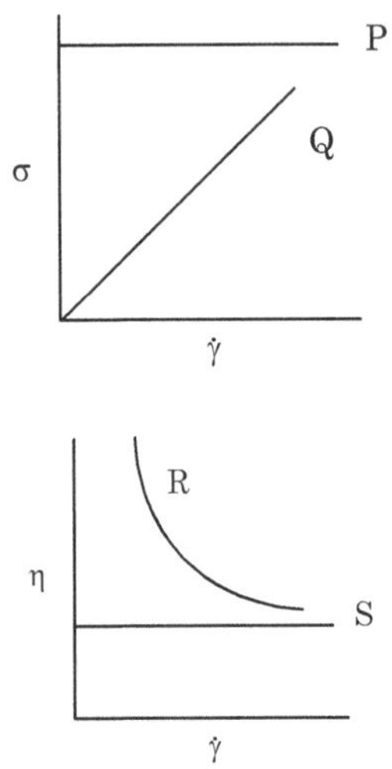

Associate the shear stress and viscosity plots with the appropriate material responses.

(*a*) P-2, Q-1, R-2, S-1 (*b*) P-1, Q-2, R-1, S-2
(*c*) P-1, Q-2, R-2, S-1 (*d*) P-2, Q-1, R-1, S-2

Q. 13 – Q. 22 carry two marks each

13. The plateau modulus of polystyrene has a value of 0.2×10^6 Pa at 150°C. Given, the density of polystyrene is 1.05 g/cm^3, the universal gas constant, R = 8.3 J K^{-1} mol^{-1}, and the monomer molecular weight is 104 g/mol. The molecular weight between entanglements (rounded off to the nearest integer) of polystyrene chains is ______ g/mol.

14. A unidirectional composite of epoxy and carbon fiber of 50% by volume is made. The elastic modulus of epoxy and carbon fiber are 3.5 GPa and 350 GPa, respectively. The ratio (rounded off to one decimal place) of the modulus of the composite to the matrix modulus is ________.

15. A single screw extruder is operating at a rotational speed of 2 revolutions per second for the extrusion of a Newtonian polymer under open-discharge conditions (in absence of a die, the pressure drop, $\Delta p = 0$). The extruder has a screw diameter, D = 5 cm, a channel depth, H = 0.4 cm, distance between flights, W = 1 cm, and a helix angle, $\theta = 20°$. Assume the value of $\pi = 3.14$. The volumetric flow rate (rounded off to 2 decimal places) is ________ cm^3/s.

16. At 215°C, the viscosity of a polystyrene of molecular weight 250×10^3 g/mol is 8.0×10^3 Pa.s. The critical molecular weight of polystyrene, $M_c = 35 \times 10^3$ g/mol. For a similar polystyrene of molecular weight 50×10^3 g/mol, the viscosity (rounded off to nearest integer) will be ________ $\times 10^3$ Pa.s.

17. There are two different PTFE polymer specimens of the following density (ρ) and % crystallinity. For PTFE-specimen-1, is 2.144 g/cm^3 and % crystallinity is 50. For PTFE-specimen-2, p is 2.215 g/cm^3 and % crystallinity is 75. Assuming the polymer is pure and defect free, the density (rounded off to 3 decimal places) of 100% amorphous PTFE specimen will be _____ g/cm^3.

18. The behavior of a polymer is described by a Maxwell model consisting of a spring element of modulus to 10^{10} Pa in series with a dashpot of viscosity 10^{12} Pa.s. In the solid, 50 s after the sudden application of a fixed strain of 1%, the strees (rounded off to 2 decimal places) will be ________ $\times 10^7$ Pa.

19. A particular free radical polymerization process yields a polymer with a number averaged degree of polymerization, $\bar{x}_n = 100$. The monomer concentration is doubled and the initiator concentration is increased by four times. Assuming that all rate coefficients and other parameters remain unchanged, the value of $\bar{x}_n$ (rounded off to the nearest integer) is ________.

20. A polymer is synthesized from 2 moles of terephthalic acid (molecular weight of the repeat unit, ($-OCC_6H_4CO-$), is 132 g/mol), 1 mol of ethylene glycol (molecular weight of the repeat unit, ($-OCH_2CH_2O-$), is 60 g/mol), and 1 mol of butylene glycol (molecular weight of the repeat unit, ($-O(CH_2)_4O-$), is 88 g/mol). The reaction is terminated at 99% conversion of the acid. The reaction is terminated at 99% conversion of the acid. The number averaged molecular weight, $\overline{M}_n$ (rounded off the nearest integer) is ___ g/mol.

21. A sample of natural rubber (cis-1,4-polyisoprene) is vulcanized such that one of every 240 chain carbon atoms is cross-linked. The formula unit of the isoprene monomer is C_5H_8 (molecular weight = 68 g/mol). The average molecular weight (rounded off to the nearest) between cross-links is ______ g/mol.

22. A sample of an oriented semi-crystalline polymer is subjected to uniaxial tensile stress, σ, in an X-ray diffractometer. The wavelength of X-ray radiation (Cu K_α) is $\lambda = 1.542$ Å. The position of the (002) peak, which was found initially at a Bragg angle of 37.50° at $\sigma = 160$ MPa. Assuming elastic deformation, the strain (rounded off to three decimal places) in the sample along the direction of applied stress is ________ $\times 10^{-3}$.

ANSWERS

1. (*c*)	**2.** (*d*)	**3.** (*c*)	**4.** (*b*)	**5.** (*d*)	**6.** (*c*)	**7.** (*b*)
8. (*b*)	**9.** (*a*)	**10.** (*b*)	**11.** (*a*)	**12.** (*b*)	**13.** (18000 to 19000)	
14. (50.4 to 50.6)		**15.** (5.00 to 7.00)		**16.** (62 to 99)	**17.** (1.980 to 2.040)	
18. (6.00 to 7.00)		**19.** (100 to 100)		**20.** (10000 to 10500)		**21.** (4000 to 4200)
22. (1.000 to 1.500)						

EXPLANATIONS

1. **Linear low-density polyethylene** (LLDPE) is a substantially linear polymer (polyethylene), with significant numbers of short branches, commonly made by copolymerization of ethylene with longer-chain olefins.

2.
$$\Delta G = \Delta H - T\Delta S$$

ΔG = change in Gibbs Free Energy

ΔH = change in enthalpy

T = temperature in Kelvin

ΔS = change in entropy

$\Delta G_m > 0$ miscible

$\Delta G_m > 0$ immiscible

$$\Delta H - T\Delta S > 0$$

$$\frac{\Delta H}{T.\Delta S} > 0$$

Low entropy and low temperture is the favourable condition for immiscibility of blends.

3. Elastomer – Polybutadiene

Plastics – PA66, PET and HDPE

4.

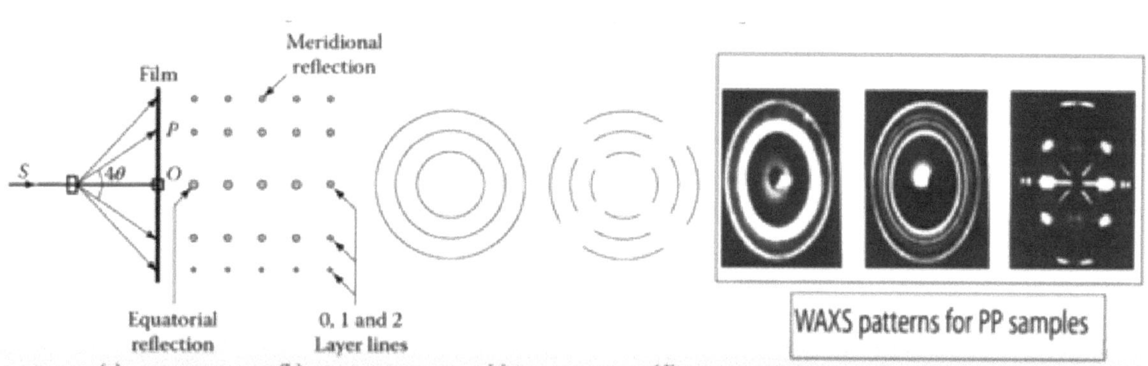

Registration of X-ray diffraction with flat film: (a) the scattered beams meet the film, (b) diffraction pattern of perfect crystals, (c) diffraction pattern of crystalline isotropic (non-oriented) polymer, (d) diffraction pattern of crystalline oriented (drawn) polymer.

X-ray diffraction patterns of un-oriented semi-crystalline polymers are characterized by a series of concentric rings. As the specimen is oriented, these ring break up into arcs and spots. From the intensity and the size of these arcs, the degree of orientation of the crystalline can be determined.

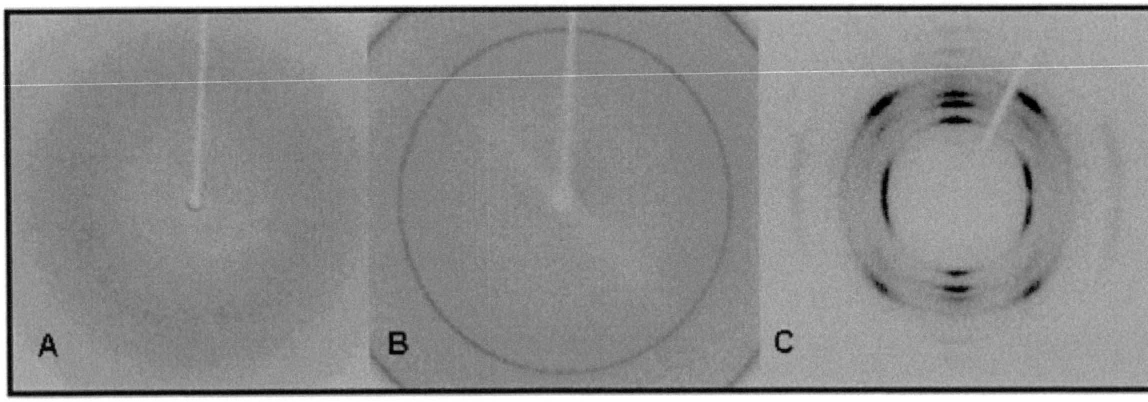

A. amorphous scattering,
B. unoriented polycrystalline scattering,
C. oriented polycrystalline and amorphous scattering

5. Esdegradable polymers (BPs) disposed in bioactive environments degrade by the enzymatic action of microorganisms such as bacteria, fungi, and algae. Their polymer chains may also be broken down by nonenzymatic processes such as chemical hydrolysis. BPs are often derived from plant processing of atmospheric CO_2. Biodegradation converts them to CO_2, CH_4, water, biomass, humic matter, and other natural substances. These polymers are found both naturally and synthetically made, and largely consist of ester, amide, and ether functional groups. An example of biodegradable polymers are: Poly β-hydroxybutyrate–co-β-hydroxy valerate (PHBV). It is formed by combining 3-hydroxy butanoic acid and 3-hydroxy pentanoic acid. Other examples include polyglycolic acid (PGA), Polyhydroxy butyrate (PHB), Polycaprolactone (pcl), Nylon-2-nylon-6.

List of Biodegradable Polymers

- Polylactic acid (PLA)
- Polycarprolactones (PCL)
- Polyglycolic acid (PGA)
- Polyhydroxybutarate (PHB)
- Polyethylene oxide (PEO)
- Polyanhydride (PA)
- Polyvinyl alcohol (PVA)
- Polyalkyls

6. Melting is a transition between crystalline solid and liquid state. Small molecules like water has sharp melting point at 0?C at 1 tam presuure. Whereas in polymer crystalline regions does not melt at a fixed temperature but rather over a temperature range. The melting point of crystallites depends on their size. Small crystallites melt at lower temperatures than large crystallites. Since crystallites of different size are present, polymers always melt over a temperature range.

7. During very fast cooling the chain does not get enough time to rearrange themselves in an efficient manner and tends to appear hard/glassy at a earlier stage and showing Higher Tg.

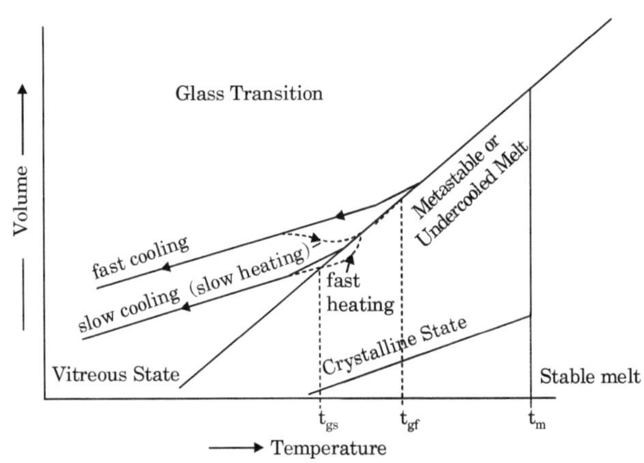

8.

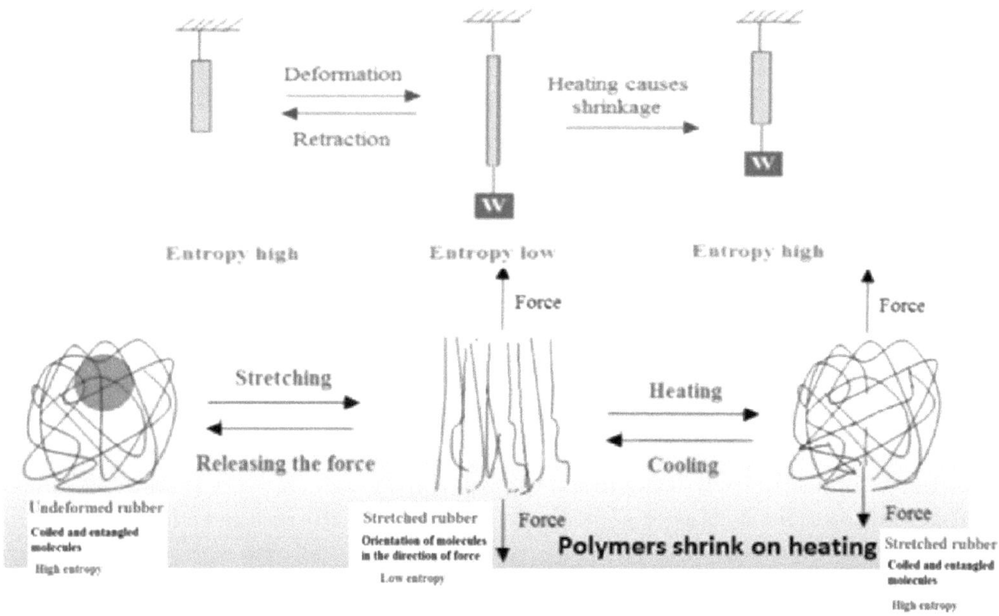

When stretched rubber is heated, molecules undergo chaotic movement, and thus a random state is formed. The enhanced thermal energy of the chains increases the molecular conformation and accelerates its recovery. Hence under a constant load, rubber pieces shrink at high temperatures.

9.

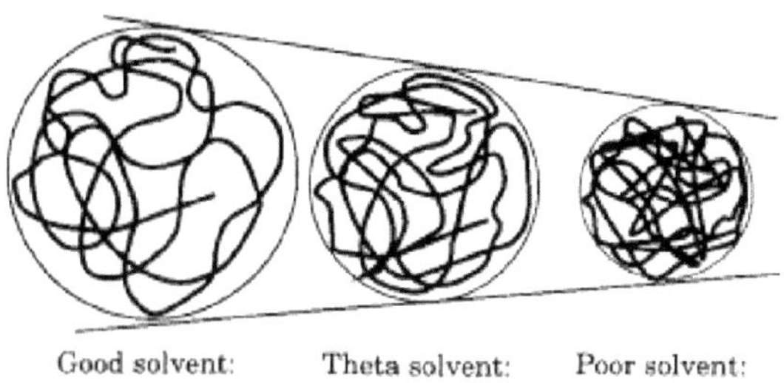

Good, Bad and θ solvents;

Solvent quaity : Interaction monomer – solvent

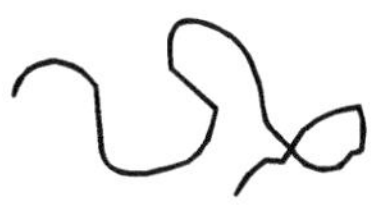

Good solvent : maximization of monomer-solvent contacts

→ chain expansion, "swollen chain"

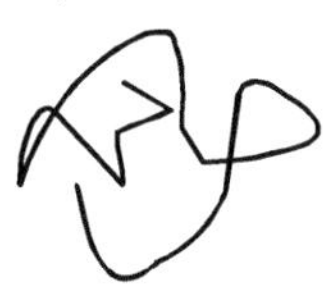

Theta solvent : balanced interactions

→ unperturbed (ideal chain

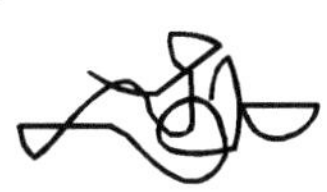

Poor solvent : minimization of monomer-solvent contact

→ chain collapse, clustering, precipitation

10. 1. Antioxidants are used to prevent thermal degradation and inhibit oxidation (i.e. degradation). Hindered Amine, Hindered Phenol, Thioesters, Phosphites, Hydroxylamines, dithiopropionate, phenyl salisylate etc.

2. Chemical blowing agents are added to the polymer either prior to or during plasticization. They consist of organic or inorganic compounds that dissociate gas due to a reaction during processing. Chemical blowing agents include isocyanate and water for polyurethane, azodicarbonamide for vinyl, hydrazine and other nitrogen-based materials for thermoplastic and elastomeric foams, and sodium bicarbonate for thermoplastic foams.

3. Plasticizer is necessary in rubber formulations for improving the processing of the rubber by lowering the compound's viscosity, and also for aiding in low temperature flexibility of the formulated rubber. The most common plasticisers include esters such as adipates, azelates, citrates, benzoates, ortho-phthalates, terephthalates, sebacates, and trimellitates.

4. Coupling agents are chemicals which improve the interfacial properties of mineral fillers and polymers (they reduce the interfacial tension which is diadvnatageous rather than advantageous, but simultaneously they reduce the agglomeration tendency of filler particles, thus improving their accessibility to polymer molecules). Example -Silane

11.

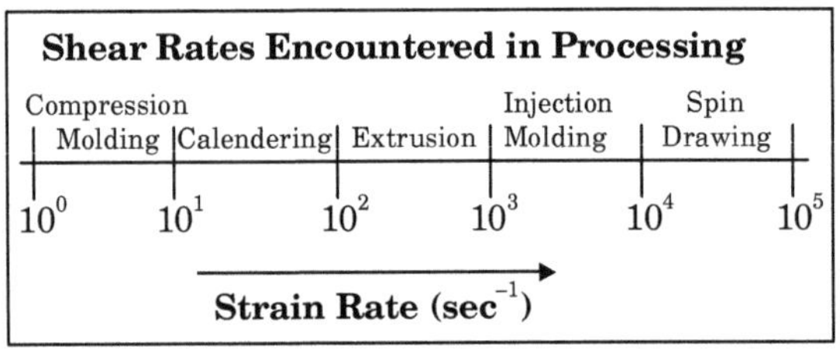

12. Viscous fluids follow the Newton's law; Stress is proportional to the strain rate.

$$\sigma = \alpha\frac{dy}{dt}, \qquad \sigma = \eta\frac{dy}{dt}$$

Where η is viscosity and $\frac{dy}{dt}$ is strain rate.

Viscosity is independent on the shear rate in case of Newtonian fluid. Liquid generally comes in the category of Newtonian fluid. Curve Q & S represents the liquid like fluid.

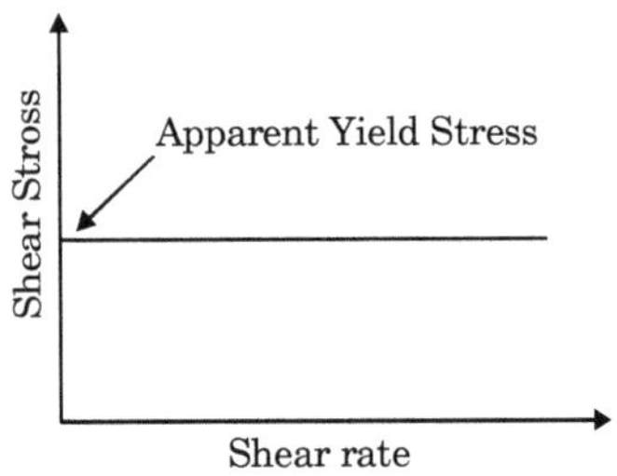

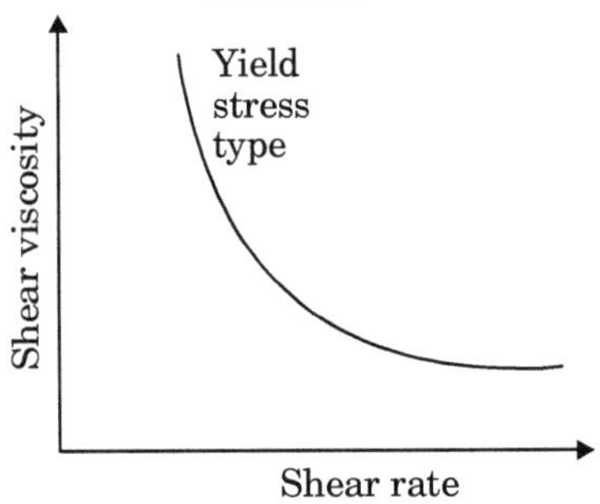

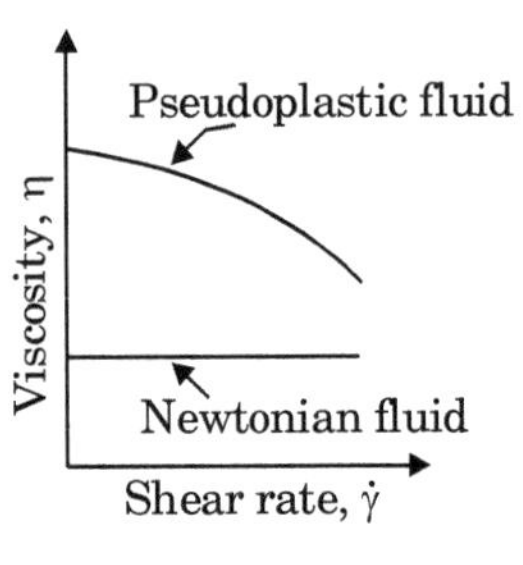

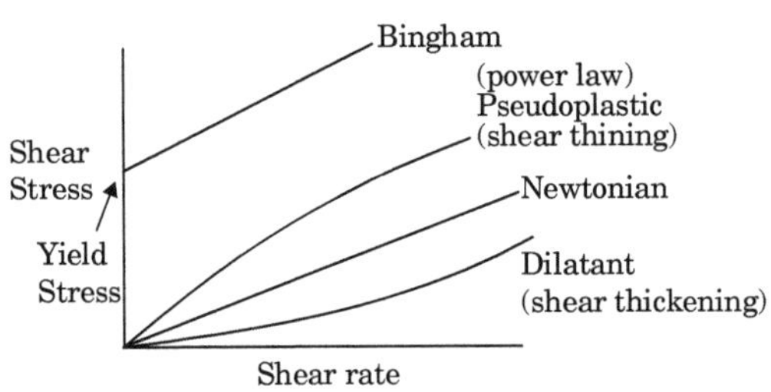

Viscosity is independent on the shear rate in case of Newtonian fluid. Liquid generally comes in the category of Newtonian fluid. Curve Q & S represents the liquid like fluid.

13.
$$G_p = \frac{\rho RT}{M_e}$$
$$M_e = \frac{\rho RT}{G_p}$$

G_p = Plateau modulus

M_e = molecular weight between entanglements of polystyrene chains

$G_p = 0.2 \times 10^6$, $p = 1.05\frac{g}{cm^3}$, $R = 8.314\ jK^{-1}mol^{-1}$, $T = 423$ K

$$= \frac{1.05 \times 10^6 \times 8.314 \times 423}{0.2 \times 10^6} = 18360\ \frac{g}{mol}$$

14. Ratio of the modulus of composite to the matrix modulus $= \frac{E_c}{E_m}$

E_c – modulus of composite; E_f – modulus of filler & E_m – modulus of matrix

V_m & V_f volume fraction of matrix and filler respectively in the composite.

$$E_c = E_m V_m + E_f V_f$$
$$E_c = 3.5 \times 0.5 + 350 \times 0.5 = 176.75$$

Ratio of the modulus of composite to the matrix modulus

$$= \frac{E_c}{E_m} = \frac{176.75}{3.5} = 50.5$$

15.

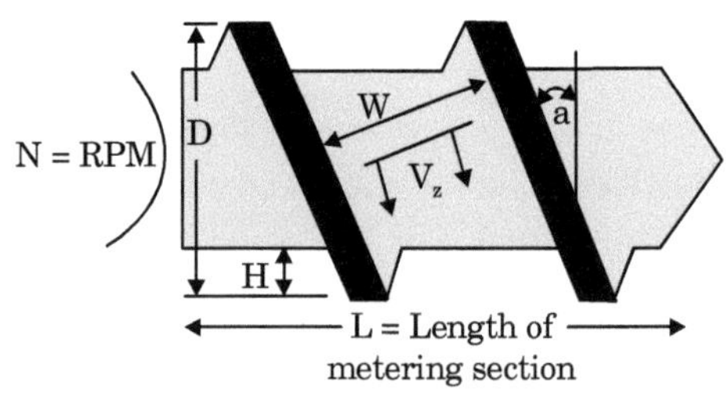

In the absence of a die in a single screw extruder $\Delta P = 0$ & Q is equal to drag flow

D (diameter) = 5cm; W(channel width) = 1cm; H (channel depth) = 0.4cm; N(screw rotation speed) = 2;

Θ helix angle = 20°

$$Q = \frac{1}{2}\pi\ WHND\cos\theta$$

$$Q_D = \frac{1}{2} \times 3.14 \times 1 \times 0.4 \times 2 \times 5 \times \cos 20$$

$$Q_D = 5.90\ cm^3/s$$

16.

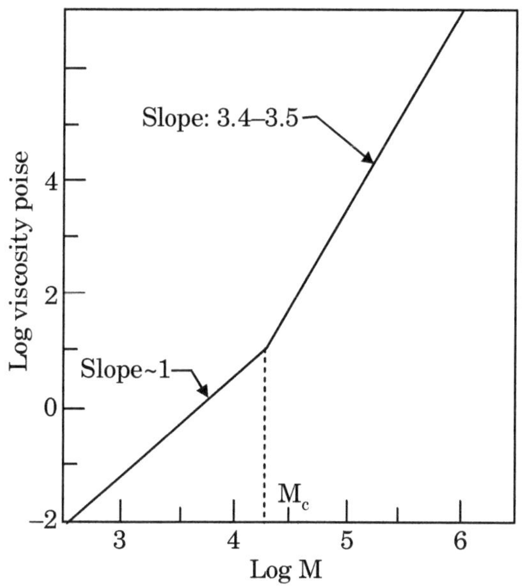

Dependence of polymer (melt) viscosity on molecular weight (M): a typical plot of log viscosity against log M.

$[\eta] = K[M]^1$ when $M < M_c$

$[\eta] = K[M]^{3.4}$ when $M > M_c$

M_c = critical molecular weight = 35×10^3 g/mol

$M_1 = 250 \times 10^3$ g/mol

$M_2 = 500 \times 10^3$ g/mol

Both the molecular weight is higher than the critical molecular weight. Hence, we have to use:

$[\eta] = K[M]^{3.4}$ when $M > M_c$

Condition 1 :

$$8 \times 10^3 = K[250 \times 10^3]^{3.4}$$

$$K = \frac{8 \times 10^3}{[250 \times 10^3]^{3.4}}$$

Condition 2 :

$$[\eta] = K[500 \times 10^3]^{3.4}$$

K value put in the equation from condition 1

$$[\eta] = \frac{8 \times 10^3}{[250 \times 10^3]^{3.4}} \times [500 \times 10^3]^{3.4}$$

$$= 84.45 \times 10^3 \text{ Pa.s}$$

17. $$\%\text{Crystallinity} = \frac{\rho_c(\rho_s - \rho_a)}{\rho_s(\rho_c - \rho_a)} \times 100$$

Where, ρ_s : Density of specimen

ρ_a : Density of the totally amorphous polymer.

ρ_c : Density of the perfectly crystalline polymer

$$\% \text{ crysatllinity} = \frac{\frac{1}{\rho_a} - \frac{1}{\rho_s}}{\frac{1}{\rho_a} - \frac{1}{\rho_c}}$$

PTFE - Specimen 1

$$0.5 = \frac{\frac{1}{\rho_a} - \frac{1}{2.215}}{\frac{1}{\rho_a} - \frac{1}{\rho_c}} \quad ...(1)$$

PTFE Specimen 2

$$0.75 = \frac{\frac{1}{\rho_a} - \frac{1}{2.215}}{\frac{1}{\rho_a} - \frac{1}{\rho_c}} \quad ...(2)$$

Put the value of $\frac{1}{\rho_a} - \frac{1}{\rho_c}$ from equation 1 to 2

$$0.75 = \frac{1/\rho_a - 1/2.215}{\dfrac{1/\rho_a - 1/2.144}{0.5}}$$

Density of 10% amorphous = 2.013 g/cm³.

18. Use Maxwell model equation

$\therefore$ Given, $E = 10^{10}$, $\eta = 10^{12}$, $\varepsilon = 1\%$ $t = 50$ s

$$\boxed{\varepsilon(t) = \sigma_0\left[\frac{1}{E} + \frac{t}{\eta}\right]}$$

$$0.01 = \sigma\left[\frac{1}{10^{10}} + \frac{50}{10^{12}}\right]$$

$$\Rightarrow \quad \sigma = 6.66 \times 10^7 \text{ Pa}$$

19. $$\nu = \frac{K_p[M]}{2(K_d K_t f[I])^{1/2}}$$

Degree of polymerization is equal to kinetic chain length, Hence

$$x_n \alpha \frac{[M]}{[I]^{1/2}}$$

Condition 1 :

$$100 = \frac{[M]}{[I]^{1/2}}$$

Condition 2 :

$$x_n = \frac{[2M]}{[4I]^{1/2}} = \frac{[M]}{[I]^{1/2}} = 100$$

$$x_n = 100$$

20. p = extent of reaction = 0.99; then degree of polymerization is given by

$$X_n = \frac{1}{1-p} = \frac{1}{1-0.99} = 100$$

$$M_n = M_o X_n$$

M_n = number average molecular weight of Polymer & M_0 = monomer weight

Average monomer weight

$$M_0 = \frac{\sum M_i N_i}{\sum N_i}$$

$$= \frac{132 \times 2 + 60 \times 1 + 88 \times 1}{2 + 1 + 1}$$

$$= 103$$

$$M_n = 103 \times 100 = 10300$$

21. 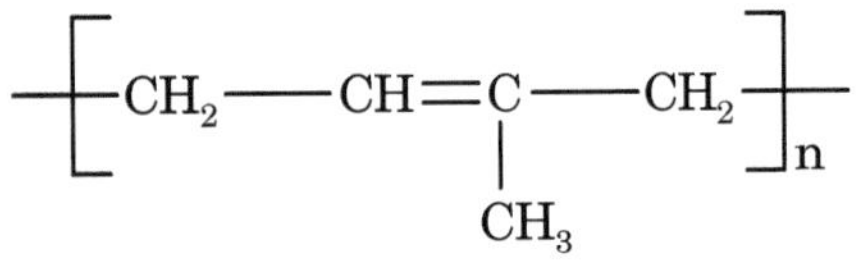

As there are 240 chain c atoms and in one isoprene unit there are 5 c atoms but out of these 4 C atoms are contributing to chain only and remaining 1 C atoms remains in side.

240 number of carbon atom requires how much monomer $= \frac{240}{4} = 60.$

Molecular weight between crosslinks

$$= 60 \text{ units} \times 68 \frac{g}{mol} = 4080 \frac{g}{mol}$$

22. $\text{strain} = \frac{\text{change in lattice parameter}}{\text{original lattice parameter}}$

$$= \frac{a_2 - a_1}{a_1}$$

According to Bragg s law.

$$\Rightarrow \quad n\lambda = 2d \sin\theta$$

$$\Rightarrow \quad \lambda = \frac{2a}{\sqrt{h^2 + k^2 + l^2}} \sin\theta$$

$$\Rightarrow \quad a = \frac{\left(\lambda\sqrt{h^2 + k^2 + l^2}\right)}{2\sin\theta}$$

where θ is the usual Bragg angle, λ is the radiation wave length = 1.542, d = Inter planner spacing & n = an integer, order of reflection

Lattice planes is determined by three integers h, k, and ?, the Miller indices. Peak = (002) mean; h = 0, k = 0 and l = 2

$$\text{strain} = \frac{\text{change in lattice parameter}}{\text{original lattice parameter}}$$

$$= \frac{a_2 - a_1}{a_1}$$

$$= \frac{\dfrac{\left(\lambda\sqrt{h^2 + k^2 + l^2}\right)}{2\sin\theta_2} - \dfrac{\left(\lambda\sqrt{h^2 + k^2 + l^2}\right)}{2\sin\theta_1}}{\dfrac{\left(\lambda\sqrt{h^2 + k^2 + l^2}\right)}{2\sin\theta_1}}$$

$$\Rightarrow \text{Strain} = \frac{\dfrac{1}{\sin 37.45°} - \dfrac{1}{\sin 37.50°}}{\dfrac{1}{\sin 37.50°}}$$

$$= 1.138 \times 10^{-3}$$

SOLVED PAPER - 2020

Q 1 - Q 9 carry one mark each.

1. The solvent in which chain transfer is maximum in a radical polymerization is

(*a*) Benzene (*b*) Chloroform

(*c*) Carbon tetrachloride (*d*) Toluene

2. The monomer that can NOT be polymerized by anionic polymerization is

(*a*) Styrene (*b*) Ethyl vinyl ether

(*c*) Butadiene (*d*) Methyl methacry late

3. The elastomer retaining flexibility at the lowest temperature is

(*a*) Styrene butadine rubber

(*b*) Nitrile rubber

(*c*) Silicone rubber

(*d*) Butyl rubber

4. The polymer with minimum number of branches is

(*a*) LDPE (*b*) LLDPE

(*c*) HDPE (*d*) VLDPE

5. The nearest value of conductivity of Nylon 6 is

(*a*) 10^6 S/m (*b*) 10^0 S/m

(*c*) 10^{-13} S/m (*d*) 10^{-21} S/m

6. Aramid is

(*a*) Polyamide

(*b*) Polyether

(*c*) Polyester

(*d*) Polyimide

7. A miscible blend in 1 : 1 (by weight) composition is formed with

(*a*) Polystyrene and polybutadiene

(*b*) Polystyrene and poly (phenylene oxide)

(*c*) Polystyrene and poly (methyl methacrylate)

(*d*) Polystyrene and poly (dimethyl siloxane)

8. Dicumyl peroxide is

(*a*) Plasticizer

(*b*) Cross-linking agent

(*c*) Mold release agent

(*d*) Peptizer

9. The change in stress of a polymer as a function of time at a fixed strain is known as

(*a*) Fatigue

(*b*) Creep

(*c*) Stress relaxation

(*d*) Fracture toughness

Q 10 - Q 22 carry two marks each.

10. Match the polymers in Column A with their corresponding polymerization methods in Column B

Column A	**Column B**
P. Bisphenol A polycarbonate	1. Cationic
Q. Polyethylene	2. Step-growth
R. Poly (Styrene-b-butadiene)	3. Coordination
S. Butyl rubber	4. Anionic

(*a*) P-3, Q-2, R-4, S-1 (*b*) P-3, Q-3, R-2, S-1

(*c*) P-2, Q-3, R-4, S-1 (*d*) P-1, Q-3, R-4, S-2

11. Match the appropriate processing technique in Column A to fabricate the product in Column B

Column A	**Column B**
P. Blow molding	1. Plastic buckets
Q. Rotational molding	2. PVC sheet
R. Injection molding	3. Basket ball
S. Calendering	4. Plastic bottles

(*a*) P-2, Q-3, R-4, S-1 (*b*) P-3, Q-4, R-2, S-1

(*c*) P-4, Q-2, R-1, S-3 (*d*) P-4, Q-3, R-1, S-2

12. Match the appropriate characterization technique in Column A used to determine the polymer attributes in Column B

Column A	**Column B**
P. Gel permeation chromatography	1. Functional group
Q. FT-IR spectroscopy	2. Crystal structure
R. Differential scanning calorimetry	3. Glass transition temperature
S. X-ray diffraction	4. Molecular weight

(*a*) P-2, Q-3, R-4, S-1 (*b*) P-3, Q-4, R-1, S-2

(*c*) P-2, Q-4, R-1, S-3 (*d*) P-4, Q-1, R-3, S-2

13. Match each additive in Column A with its function given in Column B

Column A	**Column B**
P. Azodiformamide	1. Curing agent
Q. Di-octyl phthalate	2. UV stabilizer
R. Benzoyl peroxide	3. Blowing agent
S. 2-(2′-hydroxy phenyl) benzotriazole	4. Plasticizer

(*a*) P-2, Q-3, R-1, S-2 (*b*) P-3, Q-4, R-1, S-2

(*c*) P-4, Q-3, R-2, S-1 (*d*) P-1, Q-3, R-4, S-2

14. Plot of shear stress against shear rate for various types of fluids is given below. The appropriate assignment for P, Q, R and S is

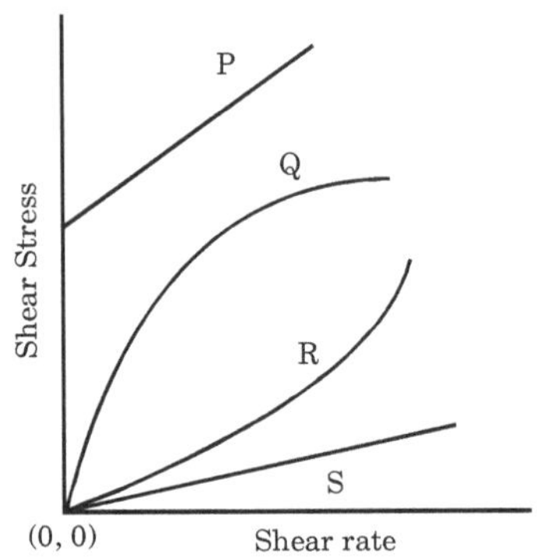

(*a*) P-Dilatant, Q-Bingham plastic, R-Pseudoplastic, S-Newtonian

(*b*) P-Bingham plastic, Q-Pseudoplastic, R-Dilatant, S-Newtonian

(*c*) P-Pseudoplastic, Q-Bingham plastic, R-Newtonian, S-Dilatant

(*d*) P-Newtonian, Q-Dilatant, R-Pseudoplastic, S-Bingham plastic

15. The number average molecular weight of a polyster formed from equimolar mixture of adipic acid and ethylene glycol at a conversion of 99.5% will be (*round off to nearest integer*).

16. For a freely jointed linear polyethylene chain with molar mass of 1.4×10^5 gmol^{-1}, the value of root mean square end-to-end distance in nanometer is _________ (*round off to 1 decimal place*). [Given : C-C bond length = 0.154 nanometer]

17. Viscosity measurements were performed for a set of PMMA solutions of different concentrations in toluene at 25°C. The plot of reduced viscosity against concentration (c) of the PMMA solutions produced an intercept of 21.0 cm^3 g^{-1} on the ordinate at $c = 0$. The value of viscosity average molecular weight of PMMA in toluene at 25°C is _________ (*round off to nearest integer*). [Given : Mark-Houwink constants K = 7.5×10^{-3} cm^3 g^{-1} and $a = 0.72$ for PMMA in toluene at 25°C]

18. Glass fibre reinforced PP composite is to be prepared with 20 volume % of glass fibre. The densities of glass fibre and PP are 2540 kg m^{-3} and 900 kg m^{-3}, respectively. The mass of glass fibre required to produce 1 kg of the composite in kg is _____ (*round off to 2 decimal places*).

19. A polymer solution flows through a cylindrical tube with a diameter of 4 mm at a volumetric flow rate of 10^{-9} m^3 s^{-1}. Under laminar flow condition and assuming the polymer solution to be a Newtonian fluid with viscosity 10^2 N s m^{-2}, the value of pressure drop per unit length of the tube in N m^{-3} is _________ (*round off to nearest integer*). [Consider the value of π as 3.14]

20. A molten polymer with a bulk modulus of 1 GPa is pressurized to 200 MPa during injection molding. The fractional decrease in volume of the molten polymer at this pressurized condition is _________ (*round off to 1 decimal place*).

21. Assume that each cross-link produced by vulcanization of polyisoprene contains an.average of two sulphur atoms and that the sulphur is present only in the cross-links. If 40% of the isoprene units are cross-linked, the sulphur content in weight percentage is ________ (*round off to 2 decimal places*).

22. A tensile force of 160 N is applied to a piece of vulcanized rubber of dimension 30 mm × 4 mm × 4 mm. Assuming the vulcanized rubber to be incompressible, if the sample is elongated to 150% of its original length under the same applied force, the true stress in N mm^{-2} will be _______ (*round off to 1 decimal place).*

ANSWERS

1. (*c*)	**2.** (*b*)	**3.** (*c*)	**4.** (*c*)	**5.** (*c*)	**6.** (*a*)	**7.** (*b*)
8. (*b*)	**9.** (*c*)	**10.** (*c*)	**11.** (*d*)	**12.** (*d*)	**13.** (*b*)	**14.** (*b*)

15. (17150 to 17250) **16.** (15.3 to 15.5) **17.** (60000 to 62000) **18.** (0.40 to 0.42)

19. (15800 to 16000) **20.** (0.2 to 0.2) **21.** (15.75 to 15.95) **22.** (14.9 to 15.1)

EXPLANATIONS

1. **Chain transfer** is a polymerization reaction by which the activity of a growing polymer chain is transferred to another molecule. Chain transfer reactions occur in most forms of addition polymerization including radical polymerization, ring-opening polymerization, coordination polymerization, and cationic polymerization, as well as anionic polymerization. Common chain transfer agents include thiols, especially dodecyl mercaptan (DDM), and halocarbons such as carbon tetrachloride.

2. Anionic polymerization is a form of chain-growth polymerization that encompasses the polymerization of vinyl monomers with strong electronegative groups. This type of polymerization is often employed to produce synthetic polydiene rubbers, solution styrene-butadiene rubbers (SBR), and thermoplastic styrenic elastomers.

   All monomers with (strong) electronegative substituents polymerize readily in the presence of carbanions. Some electron-withdrawing substituents that stabilize the negative charge through charge delocalization, and hence permit anionic polymerization include – CN, – COOR, $-C_6H_5$, and $-CH = CH_2$, to name only a few. Therefore, monomers such as styrenes, dienes, acrylates and methacrylates, aldehydes, epoxides, acrylonitriles and cyanoacrylates readily undergo anionic polymerization reactions.

3. When it comes to selecting the most suitable base elastomer when low temperature flexibility must be a key characteristic of a product or component, we can clearly see that, silicone is the most attractive option, offering an excellent level of flexibility when operating at low temperatures.

   Silicone stays flexible at the lowest temperatures of all elastomers, without noticeable change in its properties. When silicone is compared to other elastomers, it is clearly seen that it stays elastic at lower operating temperatures whilst other such materials become brittle.

4. HDPE (High Density Polyethylene) has minimal branching of its' **polymer** chains. Because it is denser it is more rigid and less permeable than the LDPE. It has a density of 0.941-0.965g/cm^3.

5. The nearest value of conductivity of nylon 6 is $10^{(-13)}$ S/m.

6. **Aramid**, also known as **aromatic polyamide**, any of a series of synthetic polymers (substances made of long chainlike multiple-unit molecules) in which repeating units containing large phenyl rings are linked together by amide groups. Amide groups (CO-NH) form strong bonds that are resistant to solvents and heat.

7. A miscible blend in 1:1 (by weight) composition is formed with polystyrene and poly(phenylene oxide) .

8. Dicumyl peroxide is mainly used as cross-linking agent for polymers and elastomers. Polymers which can be cross-linked with organic peroxides are used to produce hose, wires, tires, rubber seals, etc. Dicumyl peroxide can also be used as flame-retardant synergist in expanded polystyrene(EPS). In that case, the peroxide is incorporated in small quantities in EPS, and will catalyse the flame retardant action in case of heating.

9. Stress relaxation is a time-dependent decrease in stress under a constant strain. This characteristic behaviour of the polymer is studied by applying a fixed amount of deformation to a specimen and measuring the load required to maintain it as a function of time.

10.

Polymers	Polymerization Method
Bisphenol A Polycarbonate	Step- growth
Polyethylene	Coordination
Poly(styrene-b-butadiene)	Anionic
Butyl rubber	Cationic

Step-growth polymerization refers to a type of **polymerization mechanism** in which bi-functional or multifunctional monomers react to form first dimers, then trimers, longer oligomers and eventually long **chain polymers.**

Coordination polymerisation is a form of **polymerization** that is catalyzed by transition metal salts and complexes.

Anionic polymerization is a form of chain-growth **polymerization** that encompasses the **polymerization** of vinyl monomers with strong electronegative groups.

Cationic polymerization is a type of chain growth **polymerization** in which a **cationic** initiator transfers charge to a monomer which then becomes reactive.

11.

Processing Technique	Products
Blow molding	Plastic bottles
Rotational Molding	Basket ball
Injection molding	Plastic buckets
Calendering	PVC sheet

Blow molding is a molding process used in the manufacturing industry to create hollow objects made of plastic.

Rotational Molding is used mainly for producing hollow parts by adding plastic powder to a shell-like mold, and then rotating and heating it at the same time.

Injection molding is a manufacturing process commonly used for fabricating items from plastic trinkets and toys to automotive body parts, cell phone cases, water bottles, and containers.

Calendering is a speciality process for high-volume, high quality plastic film and sheet, mainly used for PVC as well as for certain other modified thermoplastics.

12.

Characterization Technique	**Polymer Attributes**
Gel permeation chromatography	Molecular weight
FT- IR spectroscopy	Functional group
Differential Scanning calorimetry	Glass transition temperature
X- ray diffraction	Crystal structure

13.

Additive	**Functions**
Azodiformamide	Blowing agent
Di- octyl phthalate	Plasticizer
Benzoyl peroxide	Curing agent
2-(2'-hydroxy phenyl) benzotriazole	UV Stabilizer

14. P-Bingham Plastic, Q- Pseudoplastic, R- Dilatant, S- Newtonian

The four basic types of time-independent fluids are shown in the figures below:

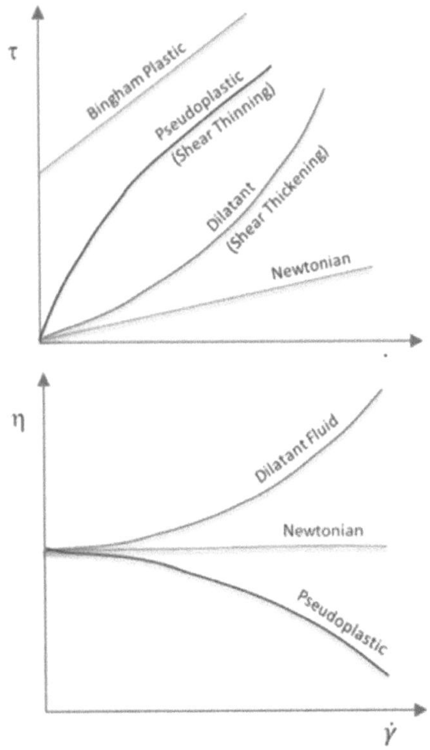

15. The reaction 46of adipic acid and ethylene glycol

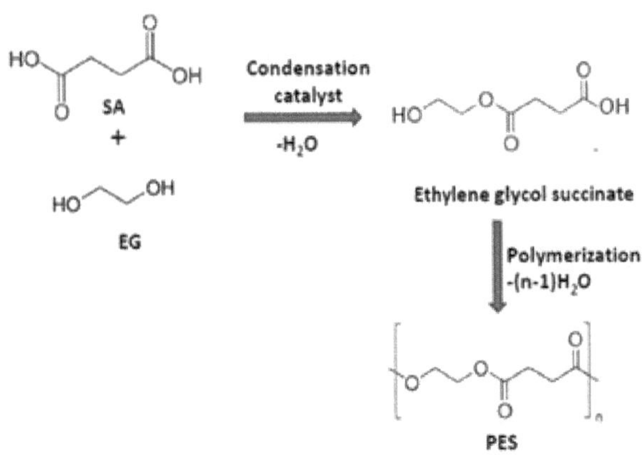

Number average molecular weight:

$$M_n = \frac{M_o}{(1-p)}$$

$$P = 0.995$$

M_o = molecuar weight of the monomer

$$= \frac{\text{Mole of monomer } 1 \times \text{Mol. wt. monomer } 1 + \text{mole of monomer } 2 \times \text{Mol. wt. of monoer } 2 - \text{water molecules weight}}{\text{Total mole}}$$

$$M_o = \frac{1 \times 62 + 1 \times 146 - 36}{2} = 86$$

$$M_n = \frac{86}{(1-0.995)} = 17200$$

16. Root mean square end to end distance $<R^2>^{1/2} = l<2n>^{1/2}$

n = number of segment, & l = bond length = 0.154 nanometer.

Polyethylene ($CH_2 - CH_2$) monomer weight $= 12 * 2 + 1 * 4 = 28$

Number of segment (n) = 140000/28 = 5000

Root mean square end to end distance $<R^2>^{1/2}$ $= 0.154 \text{ x } (2 \text{ x } 5000)^{1/2} = 15.4$ nanometer

17. Mark-Houwink equation

$$[\eta] = KM^a$$

Where $[\eta]$ = viscosity = 21.0 cm^3/g

M is Molecular weight

k and a are constants for polymer solvent system.

$K = 7.5 \times 10^{-3} cm^3/g$ & $a = 0.72$

$21 = 7.5 \times 10^{-3} \times [M]^{0.72}$

$[M]^{0.72} = 2800$

M = 61336.5703 g/mol

18. Assume Total volume of composite = $1m^3$

Total volume fraction = 1= volume fraction of matrix + volume fraction of fibre

Volume of fraction of fiber = 0.2; volume of fiber $= 0.2 \times 1 = 0.2$

Volume fraction of matrix = 0.8; volume of matrix $= 0.8 \times 1 = 0.8$

Mass of fiber = density × volume = 2540 × 0.2 = 508 kg

Mass of Polypropylene = 900 × 0.8 = 720 kg

Total composite mass = 720 + 508 = 1228 kg

Mass fraction of the fibre

$$= \frac{\text{Mass of fibre}}{\text{Total mass of composite}} = \frac{508}{1228} = 0.4137$$

1 kg of composite requires 0.4137 Kg fiber.

19. Hagen poseuille equation: flow rate is given by:

$$Q = \frac{\pi \Delta P}{128 \mu L} D^4$$

Equation is valid Reynolds number < 2000 i.e. laminar flow.

Q = flow rate;

ΔP = pressure drop;

μ = viscosity of the fluid;

L = length of the path

D = diameter of pipe = 2 × radius

$Q = 10^{-9}\ m^3/s$;

$D = 2R = 2 \times 2 \times 10^{-3}\ m$;

$\mu = 10^2\ Nsm^{-2}$

$$\frac{\Delta P}{L} = \frac{128 Q_\mu}{\pi D^4} = \frac{128 \times 10^{-9} \times 10^2}{3.14 \times (2 \times 2 \times 10^{-3})^4} = 15923.57$$

20. Bulk modulus (β)

$$\beta = \frac{\Delta P}{\frac{\Delta V}{V}}$$

Bulk modulus (β) = 1 GPa; applied pressure = 200 MPa

$$\frac{\Delta V}{V} = \frac{\text{pressure applied}}{\beta} = \frac{200}{1 \times 10^3} = 0.2$$

21. Isoprene monomer weight = 68 g/mol &

And Sulphur molecular weight = 32 g/mol

Assume weight of isoprene = 100gm

And Number of moles of isoprene = 100/68 = 1.47 mol

The mass of sulphur required for 40 percent cross-linking is therefore

Mass of sulphur = 0.40 × 1.47 × 32

= 18.816 gm

Total weight of isoprene & sulphur

= 100+ 18.816

= 118.816 gm

Weight fraction of the sulphur

= (18.816/118.816) × 100

= 15.84 %

22. True stress, S, will actually occur at y = strain

$$S = \frac{S_o L}{L_o} = S_o(1 + \gamma);$$

$$\gamma = \frac{L - L_o}{L_o} = \frac{150 - 100}{100} = 0.5$$

F = 160N;

A = 4 * 4

= $16\ mm^2$

S_o = F/A

= 160/(16) = $10\ N/mm^2$

S = 10 × (1 + 0.5)

= $15\ N/mm^2$

SOLVED PAPER - 2019

Q. 1 – 9 carry one mark each

1. The functionality of allyl alcohol (CH_2 = CH –CH_2OH) for condensation reaction with terephlhalic acid is

(*a*) 0 (*b*) 1

(*c*) 2 (*d*) 3

2. Which of the following polymers can be synthesized by ring opening polymerization?

(*a*) Po1y(viny1 alcohol)

(*b*) Nylon 66

(*c*) Poly(ethylene terephthalate)

(*d*) Poly(ε-caprolactone)

3. The weather resistant polymer among the following is

(*a*) natural rubber

(*b*) styrene butadiene rubber

(*c*) nitrile rubber

(*d*) silicone rubber

4. If a combination of sodium and naphthalene is used to initiate polymerization of styrene, then the most likely mechanism of polymerization is

(*a*) free radical (*b*) cationic

(*c*) anionic (*d*) olefin metathesis

5. Hypalon is the trade name for

(*a*) chlorosulfonatcd polyethylene

(*b*) chlorinated polyethylene

(*c*) ultra high molecular weight polyethylene

(*d*) cross-linked polyethylene

6. The copolymer(s) among high density polyethylene (HDPE), low density polyethylene (LDPE) and linear low density polyethylene (LLDPE) is/are

(*a*) LDPE only

(*b*) LLDPE only

(*c*) LDPE and LLDPE

(*d*) HDPE and LDPE

7. The polymer which lacks the ability to exhibit, tacticity among the following is

(*a*) polypropylene

(*b*) polystyrene

(*c*) polyisobutylene

(*d*) poly(methyl methacrylate)

8. The correct order of glass transition temperature (T_g) for the polymers listed below is (PC = polycarbonate; PET = poly(ethylene terephthalate); PE = polyethylene; PP = polypropylene)

(*a*) PC > PET > PP > PE (*b*) PC > PET > PE > PP

(*c*) PET > PC > PE > PP (*d*) PET > PC > PP > PE

9. Polystyrene coffee cup can be most economically manufactured by

(*a*) thermoforming

(*b*) injection molding

(*c*) compression molding

(*d*) blow molding

Q. 10 – 22 carry two marks each

10. Match the following rubber additives to their function:

Additive

P. Tetramethyl thiuram disulfide

Q. Xylyl mercaptan

R. Sulfur

S. Microcrystalline wax

Function

1. Peptizer
2. Antiozonant
3. Accelerator
4. Cross-linking agent

(*a*) P-4,Q-1,R-3,S-2 (*b*) P-3, Q-1, R-4, S-2

(*c*) P-3, Q-2, R-4, S-1 (*d*) P-4, Q-2, R-3, S-1

11. Match the following polymers with their characteristic infrared (IK) stretching frequency:

Polymer	IR stretching frequency (cm^{-1})
P. Polystyrene	1. ~2242
Q. Polyacrylonitrile	2. ~1733
R. Poly(elhylene terephthalate)	3. ~3392
S. Poly(vinyl alcohol)	4. ~3100

(*a*) P-2, Q-3, R-1, S-4 (*b*) P-2, Q-1, R-4, S-3

(*c*) P-4, Q-2, R-3, S-1 (*d*) P-4, Q-1, R-2, S-3

12. Match the following products to Hie most suitable polymer for their manufacture:

Product

P. Electrical cables

Q. Electrical switches

R. Optical lenses

S. Shoe soles

Polymer

1. Polyurethane
2. Poly(methyl methacrylate)
3. Cross-linked polyethylene
4. Phenol formaldehyde resin

(*a*) P-3, Q-2, R-1, S-4 (*b*) P-3, Q-4, R-2, S-1

(*c*) P-4, Q-3, R-1, S-2 (*d*) P-2, Q-3, R-1, S-4

13. The order of limiting oxygen index for the following polymers is (polypropylene = PP; PTFE = polytetrafluoroethylene; PVC = poly (vinyl chloride))

(*a*) PP < PTFE < Nylon 6 < PVC

(*b*) PP < PVC < Nylon 6 < PTFE

(*c*) PP < Nylon 6 < PVC < PTFE

(*d*) PP < Nylon 6 < PTFE < PVC

14. Match the following plastic additives to their function:

Additive

P. Molybdenum disulfide

Q. Glycerol monostearate

R. Tribasic lead sulphate

S. 2-Hydroxybenzophenone

Function

1. Heat stabilizer
2. UV-absorber
3. Antistatic agent
4. Solid layer lubricant

(*a*) P-3, Q-1, R-2, S-4 (*b*) P-3, Q-4, R-1, S-2

(*c*) P-4, Q-3, R-2, S-1 (*d*) P-4, Q-3, R-1, S-2

15. Match the material classification in Column A with the appropriate one in Column B: (PS = polystyrene, PPO = polyphenylene oxide, PDMS = poly(dimethyl siloxane), PP = polypropylcnc, PE = polyethylene, PP-g-MA- malcic anhydride grafted PP)

Column A

P. Miscible blend

Q. Immiscible blend

R. Compatibilizcd blend

S. Polymer composite

Column B

1. PDMS + Fumed silica
2. Nylon 6 + PP-g-MA + PP
3. PS + PPO
4. PE + PP

(*a*) P-3, Q-4, R-2, S-1 (*b*) P-4, Q-3, R-2, S-1

(*c*) P-3, Q-4, R-1, S-2 (*d*) P-4, Q-3, R-1, S-2

16. A lineal' amorphous polymer has a T_g of + 10 °C. At 28 °C, it has a melt viscosity of 4×10^8 poise. The viscosity of the polymer at its T_g is ______ $\times 10^{13}$ poise (round off to one decimal place).

17. A polypropylene (PP) bar with a 10 mm × 10 mm square section is 225 mm long. The modulus of PP bar is 861 MN m^{-2}. It is pinned at both ends and an axial compressive load of 140 N is applied. The strain due to the applied load experienced by the PP bar is ______ % (round off to two decimal places).

18. In a unidirectional carbon fibre/vinyl ester composite, the ratio of the moduli of the carbon fibre to that of vinyl ester is 35 and the fibres take up 50% of the cross-section. The percentage of applied force taken up by the fibres is _____ % (round off to one decimal place).

19. A 3 mm thick layer of softened poly(methyl methacrylate) at 190 °C is sandwiched between two flat parallel plates. A shear stress of 100 kPa is applied to the softened polymer. Assuming the softened polymer as a Newtonian fluid with an apparent viscosity of 3.9×10^4 Pa s, the relative sliding velocity between the two plates is ______ mm s^{-1} (round off to one decimal place).

20. For AIBN initialed polymerization of styrene, if both the monomer and initiator concentration are doubled, then the rate of polymerization increases by a factor of ______ (round off to two decimal places).

21. If 49 moles of hcxamcthylene diamine is reacted with 50 moles of adipic acid to prepare Nylon 66, then the number average molecular weight, $\overline{M}_n$ of the resulting polymer at 99.5% conversion (ignoring contribution from end groups) is g mol^{-1} (round off to 2 decimal places).

22. A single screw extruder is to be used to manufacture a nylon rod of 0.5 cm diameter at a production rate of 2.5 cm s^{-1}. The density of solid nylon and nylon melt are 1.140 g cm^{-3} and 0.790 g cm^3, respectively. The melt flow rate through the die is ______ cm^3 s^{-1} (round off to two decimal places).

ANSWERS

1. (b)	**2.** (d)	**3.** (d)	**4.** (c)	**5.** (a)	**6.** (b)	**7.** (c)
8. (a)	**9.** (a)	**10.** (b)	**11.** (d)	**12.** (b)	**13.** (c)	**14.** (d)
15. (a)	**16.** (1.2 to 1.4)	**17.** (0.15 to 0.17)		**18.** (97.0 to 97.5)		**19.** (7.6 to 7.8)
20. (2.80 to 2.84)		**21.** (7497.72 to 7517.72)		**22.** (0.69 to 0.73)		

EXPLANATIONS

1. The functionality of a monomer is the number of sites it has for bonding to other monomers under the given conditions of the polymerization reaction. Thus, a bifunctional monomer, i.e., monomer with functionality two, can link to two other molecules under suitable conditions. A polyfunctional monomer is one that can react with more than two molecules under the conditions of the polymerization reactions. Presence of no. of reactive functional group like –OH, –COOH, –NH2, –SH, –NCO, double bond and triple bond etc shows the functionality of a polymer. Ally alcohol has presence of one –OH reactive functional group for bonding with other molecules. So, ally alcohol has functionality of one.

CH_2=CH-CH_2-OH +

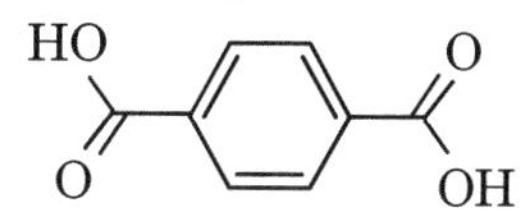

↓

Product + H_2O

2. A polymerization in which a cyclic monomer yields a monomeric unit which is acyclic or contains fewer cycles than the monomer.

Note : If the monomer is polycyclic, the opening of a single ring is sufficient to classify the reaction as ring-opening polymerization.

Modified from the earlier definition.

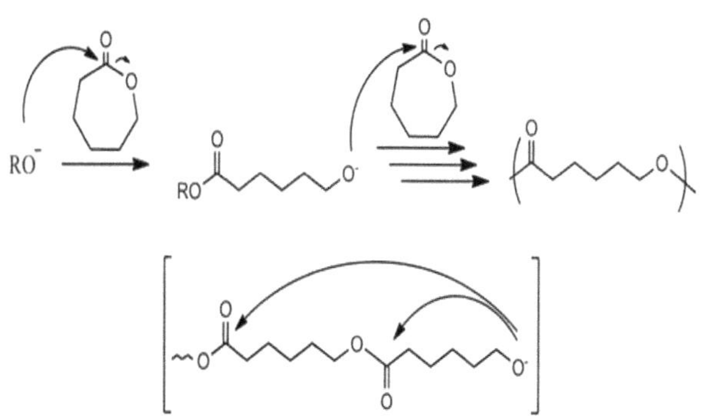

3. Silicone – Silicone is an extremely versatile material. It features excellent elastomeric properties at both low and high temperatures. Silicone is **highly resistant to oxygen, ozone, UV** light, aging, weather, and extreme temperatures. It works in temperatures that range from -67°F to +400°F, and intermittent to +450°F. Syntehtic rubbers are more wetaher and heat resitacne than natureal rubber. The high bonding energy of the silicon to oxygen (Si-O) backbone provides stability against breakdown by UV irradiation. For example, the bonding energy of Si-O bonds is 444 kJ/mol versus only 348 kJ/mol for C-C bonds. silicone elastomers exhibit low surface energy that does not allow water to spread out over their surface, i.e. a hydrophobic or water repellancy property.

Elastomer	Weather Resistance
Butyl	Excellent
EPDM	Excellent
Hypalon	Excellent
Natural Rubber	Poor/Fair
Neoprene	Good
Nitrile	Fair
Polyurethane	Excellent
SBR	Poor/Fair
Silicone	Excellent
Thermoplastic Elastomer	Excellent
Vamac	Excellent
Viton	Excellent

4. Anionic polymerization takes place with monomers having electron-withdrawing groups such as nitrile, carboxyl, phenyl, and vinyl. These polymerizations are initiated by nucleophilic addition to the double bond of the monomer through the formation of carbanion. Styrene has benzene ring in the side group. Benzene usually acts as electron withdrawing group as it is electron rich. For polymerization of Styrene use anionic catalyst.

5. In polymer science, Hypalon is a trademark for chlorosulfonated polyethylene (CSPE) synthetic rubber (CSM) noted for its resistance to chemicals, temperature extremes, and ultraviolet light. It was a product of DuPont Performance Elastomers, a subsidiary of DuPont.

6. LLDPE is structurally similar to LDPE. It is made by copolymerizing ethylene with 1-butene and smaller amounts of 1-hexene and 1-octene, using Ziegler-Natta or metallocene catalysts. The resultant structure has a linear backbone, but it has short, uniform branches that, like the longer branches of LDPE, prevent the polymer chains from packing closely together. Overall, LLDPE has similar properties to LDPE and competes for the same markets.

7. 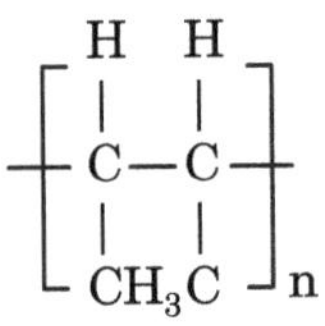

Polypropylene (PP)

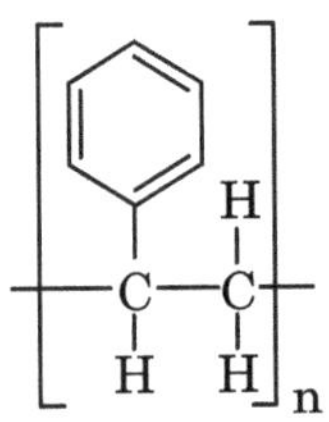

Polystyrene

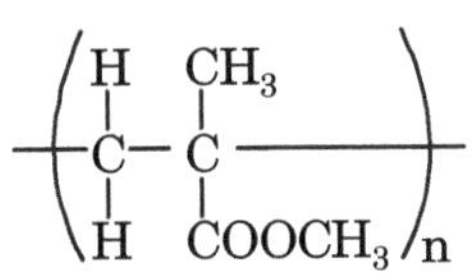

Polymethyl methacrylate : PMMA

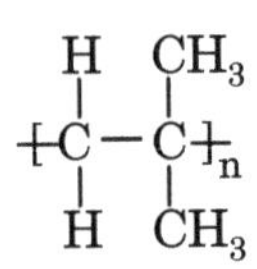

polyisobutylene

Tacticity (arrangement or order) is **the relative stereochemistry of adjacent chiral centers within a macromolecule**. Tacticity have different arrangement of the side group.

In polyisobutylene has similar type of arrangement due to present of identical side groups in the structure. Hence, Polyisobutylene does not show tacticity.

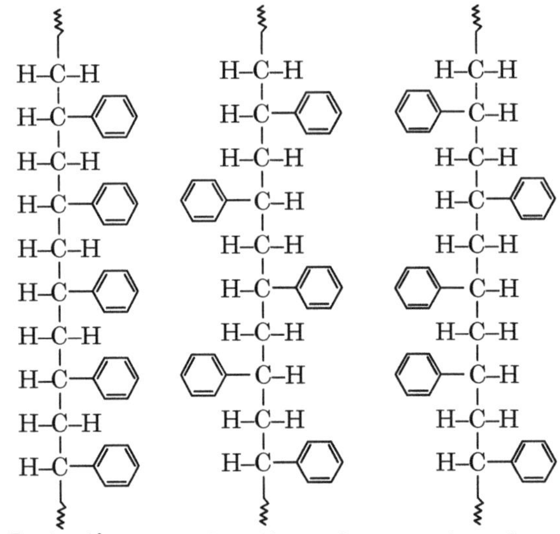

Isotactic **Syndiotactic** **Atactic**

8. Presence jfo side group increases the glass transition temperature. PP has ($-CH_3$) side group enhance the glass transition value.

Presence of aromatic ring in the structure gives the rigidity to the main chain and reduces the flexibility. It increases the Tg value.

PC have higher aromatic content

PE $(-CH_2-CH_2-)_n$

PP $(-CH_2-CH(CH_3)-)_n$

PET 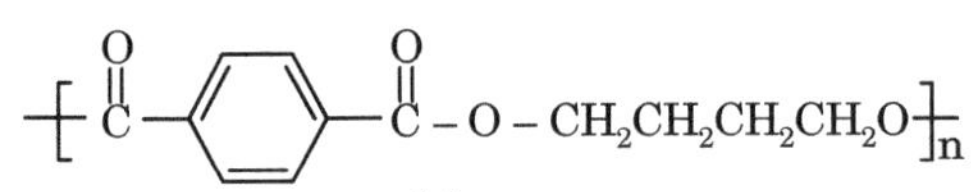

(a)

PP 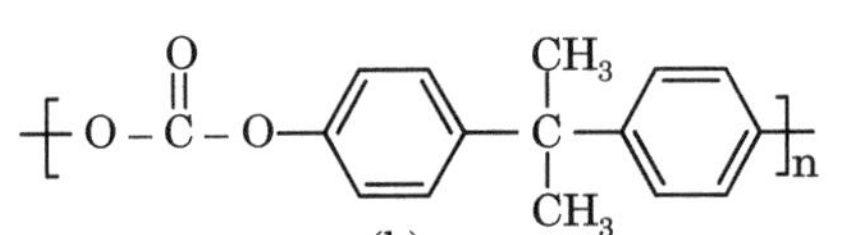

(b)

9. The disposable plastic cups are manufactured by thermoforming technique.

10. 1. The cross-linking or curing agent is the formulation component that causes this reaction to take place. These terms are generally used with all polymeric materials that are capable of forming a thermosetting structure. Example- amines, sulfur, metal oxide and peroxides.

2. Antiozonants – are chemicals and / or waxes that "bleed" to the surface of a rubber article, **to protect it against attack from ozone (O3)**. For long-term storage protection, some rubber articles are sealed with an exterior coating of wax or similar substance for additional protection against attack from

ozone. Paraffin Wax & microcrystalline wax are commonly use in rubber industry.

3. An accelerator is defined as the chemical added into a rubber compound to increase the speed of vulcanization and to permit vulcanization to proceed at lower temperature and with greater efficiency. Thiazoles and Sulfenamide accelerators play a role of being Primary Accelerators & accelerators such as Guanidines, Thiurams, and Dithiocarbamates etc are used as Secondary accelerators to activate the primary accelerators.

4. Peptizers are used in the mastication of natural rubber to optimize its processing. They reduce the molecular weight of the polymers by breaking down the molecule chains. In contrast to the mechanical mastication of rubber, chemical peptizers shorten the mastication time and lower the energy consumption, with the result that productivity in compounding improves. Examples of peptizers are pentachlorothiophenol, phenylhydrazine, certain diphenylsulfides, and xylyl mercaptan.

11. Summary:

O–H stretch from 3300-2500 cm^{-1}

C=O stretch from 1760-1690 cm^{-1}

C–O stretch from 1320-1210 cm^{-1}

O–H bend from 1440-1395 and 950-910 cm^{-1}

12.

Product	**Polymer**
P. Electrical cables	3. Cross-linked polyethylene
Q. Electrical switches	4. Phenol formaldehyde resin
R. Optical lenses	2. Poly(methyl methacrylate)
S. Shoe soles	1. Polyurethane

Cross-linked polyethylene, commonly abbreviated PEX, XPE or XLPE, is a form of polyethylene with cross-links. It is used predominantly in building services pipework systems, hydronic radiant heating and cooling systems, domestic water piping, and insulation for high tension (high voltage) electrical cables.

Then later, Bakelite, which was an early form brittle plastic, made from formaldehyde and phenol. Baekeland developed the plastic by combining phenolic resin, formaldehyde, and heat. It is a polymer which becomes irreversibly hardened upon being cured. A cured thermosetting polymer is called a thermoset.

Poly(methyl methacrylate) (PMMA), also known as acrylic, acrylic glass, or plexiglass as well as by the trade names Crylux, Plexiglas, Acrylite, Lucite, and Perspex among several others (see below), is a transparent thermoplastic often used in sheet form as a lightweight or shatter-resistant alternative to glass.

Polyurethane (PU) is one of the most common polymers used in shoes, and for good reason - it's lightweight, durable, and waterproof. PU is also remarkably oil-resistant, which makes it a great ingredient in boots designed for construction or industrial use. Thermoplastic polyurethane (TPU) is a subset of PU.

13.

Plymer	**LOI**
Polyethylene	17
Polypropylene	17
Polystyrene	18
Poly(butylene terephthalate	18
Vinyl ester	22
Epoxy	25
Poly (ethylene terephthalate)	26
Nylon 6	26
Nylon 6, 6	26
Polycarbonate	26
Poly(vinyl chloride)	29
Polysulfone	30
Acrylonitrile butacliene-styrene	32
Poly(ether sulfone)	35
Polyamide-imide	46
Polyether-imide	46
Poly(phenylene sulfide)	49
Poly(vinyliclene chloride)	60
Polytetrafluoroethylene	90

14. 1. Addition of light stabilizers / UV absorbers can extend the life and improve the appearance of the plastic. The most commonly used light stabilizers in plastics are hindered amine light stabilizers (HALS); the most common UV absorbers are benzotriazoles, benzophenones and organic nickel compounds. Phenyl salicylate & o-Hydroxybenzophenone.

2. Solid layer lubricant-Molybdenum disulfide & graphite.
3. An antistatic agent is a compound used for treatment of materials or their surfaces in order to reduce or eliminate buildup of static electricity. Glycerol monostearate (GMS); ethoxylated fatty acid amines; and diethanolamides & quaternary ammonia.
4. Heat stabilizer - TMQ, $BaSO_4$ & Tribasic lead sulphate.

15. 1. Immiscible Blend- PC-PS, PET-PBT, PE-PP & PP-PS
2. Miscible blend- SAN/PMMA, PS-PPO
3. Polymer composite – Polymer + filler
4. Compatibilizied blend- Requires external additive to make compatibility between the immiscible blend. Example – Maleic anhydride and Silane

16. From WLF equation, we have

$$\log\left(\frac{\eta}{\eta_g}\right) = -\left(\frac{17.44(T - T_g)}{51.6 + T - T_g}\right)$$

$$\log\left(\frac{\eta}{\eta_g}\right) = -\left(\frac{17.44(18)}{51.6 + 18}\right)$$

$$\log\left(\frac{4 \times 10^8}{\eta_g}\right) = -\left(\frac{17.44(18)}{51.6 + 18}\right)$$

$$\eta_g = 1.2954 \times 10^{13}$$

17. $\varepsilon = \dfrac{\delta l}{l} = \dfrac{P}{AE}$

$$\varepsilon = \frac{140}{861 \times 10^6 \times 100 \times 10^{-6}}$$

$$\varepsilon = .001626$$

$$\varepsilon = .1626 \,(\text{in } \%)$$

18. Pf = force by fiber & Pm = force by matrix

$$\frac{P_f}{P_c} = \frac{\sigma_f A_f}{\sigma_f A_f + \sigma_m A_m}$$

$$P_C = P_f + P_m$$

the ratio of the moduli of the carbon fibre to that of vinyl ester is = 35

Ratio of the fiber and matrix area= 0.5/0.5 = 1

$$\frac{P_f}{P_c} = \frac{1}{1 + \dfrac{\sigma_m A_m}{\sigma_f A_f}}$$

$$\frac{P_f}{P_c} = \frac{1}{1 + \dfrac{1}{35}}$$

$$= \frac{36}{36} = 0.9722$$

The percentage of applied force taken up by the fibres is 97.22 %

19. $\tau = \mu \dfrac{du}{dy}$

$$100 \times 10^3 = 3.9 \times 10^4 \times \frac{du}{3 \times 10^{-3}}$$

$$du = .007692 \text{ m/s}$$

$$du = 7.692 \text{ mm/s}$$

20. Rate of polymerization (R_p) α [M]. √[I]

Rp = K. [M]. √[I].....(1)

Rp_2 = K. [2M]. √[2I] = 2√2. K. [M]. "[I] = 2.82 Rp

21. $$X_n = \frac{1 + r}{1 + r - 2Pr}$$

$r = N_A/N_B$ = 49/50;' & P = 0.995

$$X_n = \frac{1 + \dfrac{49}{50}}{1 + \dfrac{49}{50} - 2 \times 0.995 \times \dfrac{49}{50}} = 66.443$$

Number average molecular weight:

$$Mn = M_o.X_n$$

M_o = molecuar weight of the repeated unit

$$= \frac{49 \times 98 + 50 \times 128}{49 + 50} = 113.15$$

M_n = 113.15 × 66.44 = 7517.72

22.

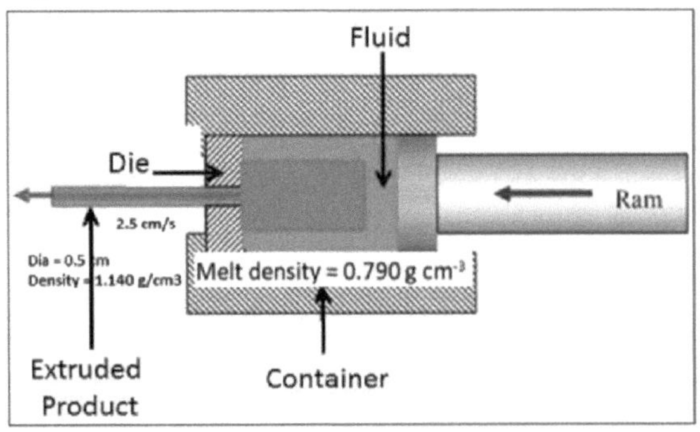

Solid rod

Volumetric flow rate V = Area (A) × Velocity (V)

$A = \pi r^2 = 3.14 \times 0.5/2^2 = 0.19625$

V = 2.5 cm/s

Q = 0.19625 × 2.5 = 0.490625 cm^3/s

Mass flow rate = Q × Density

= 0.490625 × 1.14 = 0.56 g/s

Mass flow rate of solid nylon rod is equal to mass flow rate of nylon melt.

Mass of melt flow = Mass of rod

Volumetric melt flow rate X density = 0.56

Volumetric melt flow rate X 0.79 = 0.56

Volumetric melt flow rate = 0.71 cm^3/s

SOLVED PAPER - 2018

Q. 1 – Q. 9 carry one mark each.

1. Which one of the following polymers occurs naturally?

(*a*) Bakelite

(*b*) Teflon

(*c*) Cellulose

(*d*) Perspex

2. The order of average molecular weights of a polymer is

(*a*) $M_z > M_w > M_v > M_n$

(*b*) $M_w > M_z > M_n > M_v$

(*c*) $M_n > M_w > M_v > M_z$

(*d*) $M_z > M_v > M_n > M_w$

3. Rubbers are a class of polymer known for

(*a*) High intermolecular forces

(*b*) High T_g polymers

(*c*) Crystalline polymers

(*d*) Low intermolecular forces

4. Nylon 6 is manufactured from

(*a*) Sebacic acid and hexamethylene diamine

(*b*) Caprolactam

(*c*) Adipic acid and hexamethylene diamine

(*d*) Caprolactone

5. Storage modulus and tan δ of a polymer are experimentally measured by

(*a*) Differential scanning calorimetry

(*b*) Thermogravimetric analysis

(*c*) Thermomechanical analysis

(*d*) Dynamic mechanical thermal analysis

6. A plastic bucket is manufactured by

(*a*) Compression moulding

(*b*) Injection moulding

(*c*) Extrusion

(*d*) Blow moulding

7. The monomers, A and B with reactivity ratios r_A and r_B, form alternate copolymers when

(*a*) $r_A = r_B = 0$ (*b*) $r_A = r_B = 1$

(*c*) $r_A > 1, r_B > 1$ (*d*) $r_A < 1, r_B < 1$

8. The degree of polymerization of a poly(methyl methacrylate) sample having number average molecular weight of 1,50,000 g/mol is__________. (C = 12, H = 1, O = 16 g/mol).

9. If the heat of fusion of 100 % crystalline polyethylene is 290 mJ/mg, a sample of polyethylene with heat of fusion of 141 mJ/mg will have _______ % crystallinity.

Q. 10 – Q. 22 carry two marks each.

10. Match the following:

P. Butyl rubber	1. Metallocene polymerization
Q. Cold SBR	2. Cationic polymerization
R. Poly(ethylene terephthalate)	3. Redox polymerization
S. Polypropylene	4. Condensation polymerization

(*a*) P-3; Q-1; R-2; S-1 (*b*) P-2; Q-3; R-1; S-4

(*c*) P-4; Q-3; R-1; S-2 (*d*) P-2; Q-3; R-4; S-1

11. Match the following:

P. Polyaramid	1. Baby-feeding nipple
Q. Polytetrafluoroe-thylene	2. Optical glasses
R. Polycarbonate	3. Non-stick cookware
S. Poly(dimethyl siloxane)	4. Bullet-proof jacket

(*a*) P-4; Q-3; R-2; S-1 (*b*) P-2; Q-3; R-4; S-1

(*c*) P-4; Q-1; R-2; S-3 (*d*) P-3; Q-4; R-2; S-1

12. Flexible PVC tubes are used for watering. If some organic solvents are passed through this tube, it becomes stiff. This is due to the fact that the organic solvents

(*a*) plasticize PVC and raise T_g.

(*b*) remove plasticizer and raise T_g.

(*c*) remove plasticizer and lower T_g.

(*d*) react with PVC and increase T_g

13. Match the following:

P. Plastic egg container	1. Injection moulding
Q. Water tank	2. Extrusion
R. Chair	3. Rotational moulding
S. Cable	4. Thermoforming

(*a*) P-3; Q-1; R-4; S-2

(*b*) P-4; Q-3; R-2; S-1

(*c*) P-2; Q-3; R-4; S-1

(*d*) P-4; Q-3; R-1; S-2

14. Match the following:

P. Flame retardant	1. 4-Methyl-2,6-di-t-butyl phenol
Q. UV absorber	2. Azocarbonamide
R. Blowing agent	3. Phenyl salisylate
S. Antioxidant	4. Aluminium trihydrate

(*a*) P-4; Q-1; R-2; S-3 (*b*) P-4; Q-3; R-2; S-1
(*c*) P-3; Q-4; R-2; S-1 (*d*) P-2; Q-4; R-1; S-3

15. A plot of strain (%) versus time of a polymer is given below. Based on this plot and the properties as mentioned below, find out the correct combination.

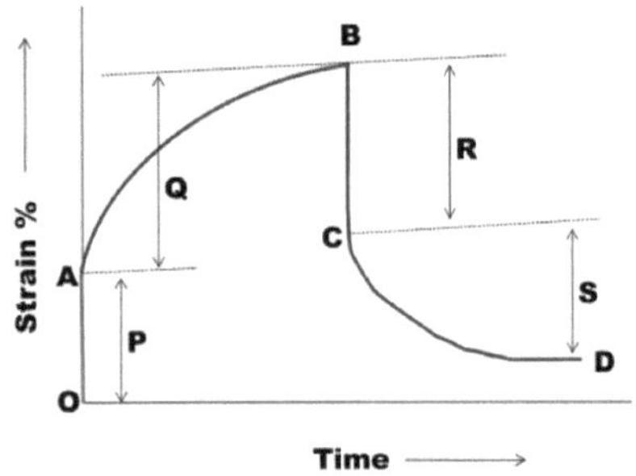

1 = Viscoelastic deformation;
2 = Elastic deformation
3 = Viscoelastic recovery;
4 = Elastic recovery

(*a*) P-1; Q-4; R-2; S-3 (*b*) P-2; Q-3; R-4; S-1
(*c*) P-3; Q-1; R-2; S-4 (*d*) P-2; Q-1; R-4; S-3

16. The plot shows apparent viscosity versus shear rate of Newtonian, Dilatent and Pseudoplastic fluids. Based on this plot and the fluid behaviour as mentioned below, find out the correct combination.

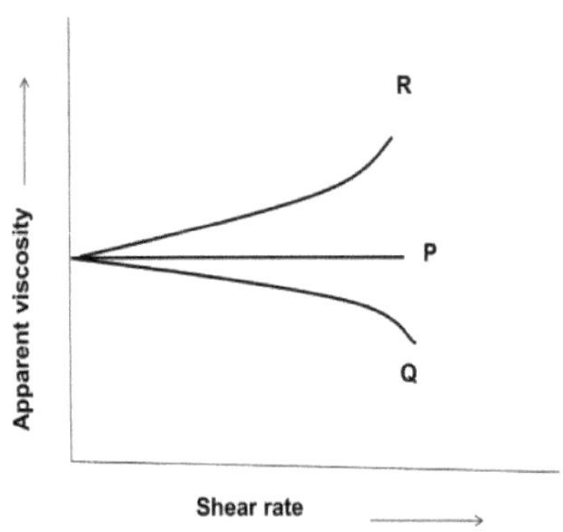

1 = Dilatent fluid;
2 = Newtonian fluid,
3 = Pseudoplastic fluid

(*a*) P-1; Q-2; R-3 (*b*) P-3; Q-1; R-2
(*c*) P-2; Q-3; R-1 (*d*) P-2; Q-3; Q-1

17. Plot of the modulus versus temperature of different types of polymers is given below.

Based on this plot and the nature of the polymers as mentioned below, find out the correct combination.

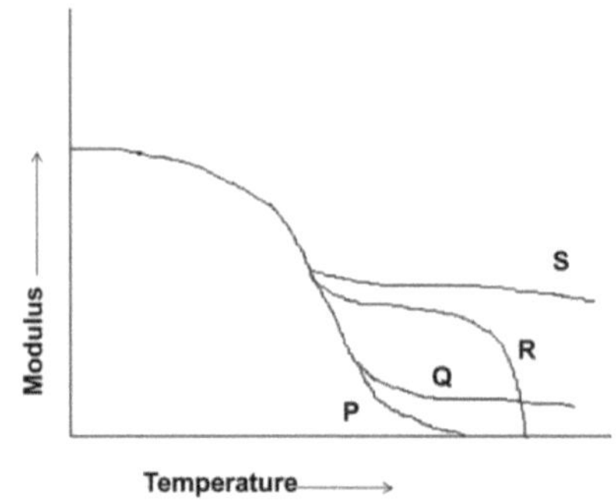

1 = An amorphous polymer of high molecular weight having entanglements
2 = An amorphous polymer of moderate molecular weight
3 = Highly crosslinked polymer
4 = Semi-crystalline polymer

(*a*) P-2; Q-1; R-3; S-4
(*b*) P-1; Q-2; R-3; S-4
(*c*) P-2; Q-1; R-4; S-3
(*d*) P-1; Q-3; R-4; S-2

18. The T_g of homopolymers of A and B are +100°C and –70°C respectively. The T_g of a random copolymer of A and B having 40 wt% A and 60 wt% B is ________°C.

19. The number average molecular weight of a polymer prepared from $HO(CH_2)_{14}COOH$ is 24,000 g/mol. The conversion of the monomer required to reach the above molecular weight is ________%. (C = 12, H = 1, O = 16 g/mol).

20. Glass fibers in nylon provide reinforcement. The modulus of elasticity for each component of the composite is; $E_{glass} = 10.5 \times 10^6$ psi; $E_{nylon} = 0.4 \times 10^6$ psi. If the nylon contains 30 vol % E-glass, the fraction of the applied force is carried by the glass fiber is________. (Assume that both glass fiber and nylon have equal strain).

21. The solubility parameter of a polymer having cohesive energy density (E_{coh}) 43870 J/mol and molar volume (V) 136 cm^3/mol is ________ (J/cm^3)$^{1/2}$.

22. The heat of polymerization of styrene is 20 Kcal/mol. Heat of 5×10^5 Kcal will be released on polymerization of ________ Kg of styrene (C = 12 and H = 1 g/mol).

ANSWERS

1. (c) **2.** (a) **3.** (d) **4.** (b) **5.** (d) **6.** (b) **7.** (a)
8. (1500 to 1500) **9.** (48.52 to 48.72) **10.** (d) **11.** (a) **12.** (b) **13.** (d)
14. (b) **15.** (d) **16.** (c) **17.** (c) **18.** (–25.00 to –24.50)
19. (98.80 to 99.10) **20.** (0.90 to 0.93) **21.** (17.91 to 18.00) **22.** (2600 to 2600)

EXPLANATIONS

1. (c) Cellulose : A naturally occurring carbohydrate polymer. Cellulose is a largely indigestible polysaccharide (a complex carbohydrate), composed of thousands of glucose molecules. Cellulose is naturally present in plants. It is an important structural component of the primary cell wall of green plants, many forms of algae and the oomycetes.

2. (a)

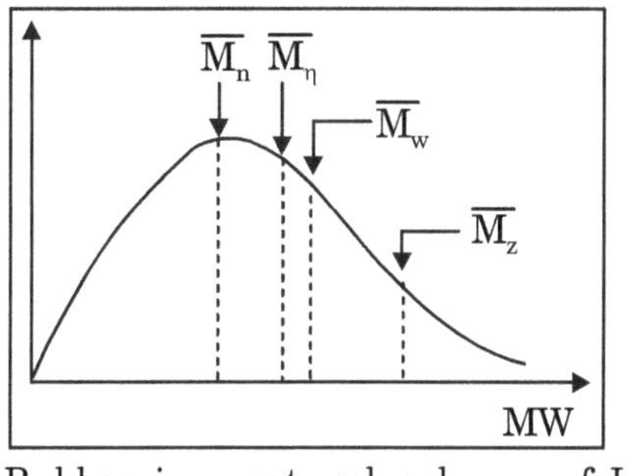

3. (d) Rubber is a natural polymer of Isoprene (2-Methyl -1, 3 – Butadiene). It is a linear, 1, 4 – addition polymer of Isoprene.

Natural rubber has elastic properties and it undergoes long range of reversible extension even if relatively small forces are applied on it. Therefore, it is also known as Elastomer. Natural rubber is prepared from latex which is a Colloidal Solution of Rubber in Water.

4. (b)

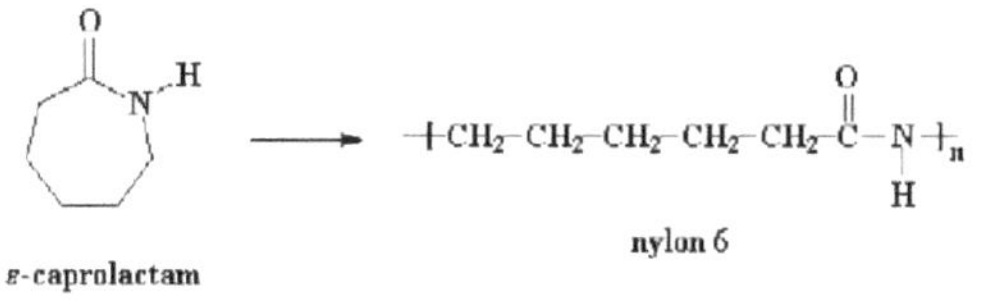

5. (d) Dynamic mechanical analysis (DMA), also called as dynamic mechanical spectroscopy is a technique used to study and characterize materials. It is most useful for studying the viscoelastic behavior of polymers. A sinusoidal stress is applied and the strain in the material is measured, allowing one to determine the complex modulus.

6. (b) Plastic injection molding is the process used for manufacturing plastic parts. Injection molding is used to develop many things such as electronic housings, containers, bottle caps, combs,automotive interiors, and most other plastic products available today. It is ideal for producing high volumes of plastic parts due to the reason that several parts can be produced in each cycle by using multi-cavity injection molds. Some of the advantages of injection molding are high tolerance precision, repeatability, large material selection, low labor cost, minimal scrap losses, and little need to finish parts after molding. Some disadvantages of this process are expensive upfront tooling investment and process limitations.

7. (a) An alternating copolymer consists of two different repeat units that alternate in sequence in the polymer chain. A regularity in repetition of structural units is only possible if the two monomers M_1 or M_2 are unable to hompolymerize or have a strong preference to react with each other (quasi alternating copolymer). This is only the case if the reactivity ratios defined by

$$r_1 = \frac{k_{11}}{k_{12}}$$

$$r_2 = \frac{k_{22}}{k_{21}}$$

approach zero,

$$r_1 = r_2 \approx 0,$$

It means K_{11} & $K_{22} = 0$; Monomer 1 will react with monomer 2 and vice versa.

8. (1500 to 1500) To find:

Degree of Polymerization of a Polymethyl (methacrylate)

Chemical formula of Poly (methyl methacrylate) is $(C_5O_2H_8)_n$

Degree of Polymerization

$$= \frac{\text{Average molecular weight}}{(\text{Mol.wt})_{C_5} + (\text{Mol.wt})_{H_8} + (\text{Mol.wt})_{O_2}}$$

$$= \frac{15000}{12 \times 5 + 1 \times 8 + 16 \times 2} = 1500$$

9. (48.52 to 48.72)

% crystallinity

$$= \frac{\text{(Heat of fusion) polyethylene}}{\text{(Heat of fusion) crystallite polyethylene}}$$

$$= \frac{141}{290} \times 1 = 48.62\%$$

Correct matches are as follows:

10. (d)

P. Butyl rubber	2. Cationic polymerization
Q. Cold SBR	3. Redox polymerization
R. Poly(ethylene terephthalate)	4. Condensation polymerization
S. Polypropylene	1. Metallocene polymerization

Condensation Polymerization: In This type of polymerization, polymers are generated with the help of condensation of two monomer units with the loss of small molecules such as H_2O, HCl, and NH_3 etc. Here the monomer units must have two functional groups in order to condensation reaction took place. Dacron®, nylon 6 and nylon 66 are the few examples for condensation polymers.

Cationic polymerization is a type of chain growth polymerization in which a cationic initiator transfers charge to a monomer which then becomes reactive. This reactive monomer goes on to react similarly with other monomers to form a polymer.

Redox Polymerization: Reduction of hydrogen peroxide or an alkyl hydrogen peroxide by iron. Other reductants such as Cr^{2+}, V^{2+}, Ti^{3+}, Co^{2+}, and Cu^{+} can be employed in place of ferrous ion in many instances.

Metallocene polymerization: The substitution pattern of the "-Cp ligands of metallocene polymerization catalysts is the major factor influencing both propagation rate and type and extent of chain transfer reactions, that in turn determine the molecular weight of the poly(a-olefin) produced.

11. (a)

Polyaramide	Aromatic **polyamide** or aramid fibers known under the trade name Kevlar. Kevlar is a well-known component of personal armor such as combat helmets, ballistic face masks, and ballistic vests.
PTFE	Teflon is a brand name for PTFE, The unique properties of PTFE keep food from sticking to nonstick cookware because it has an amazingly low coefficient of friction.
Polycarbonate	Polycarbonate lenses: Durable, providing extra safety to your eyes and promoting better eye health. 10 times more resistant to impact than plastic eyeglasses, so they don't shatter or break as easily. Boast scratch resistance so they last longer than regular plastic lenses.
Silicone	**Food-grade silicone** is probably the safest, most durable and hygienic material for baby bottle nipples.

12. (b) Flexible PVC tubes are used for watering. If some organic solvents are passed through this tube, it becomes stiff. This is due to the fact that the organic solvents remove plasticizer and raise Tg.

13. (d) P-4; Q-3; R-1; S-2

Applications of :

1. **Injection molding :** wire spools, packaging, bottle caps, automotive dashboards, pocket combs
2. **Extrusion :** Trim parts as used in automobile and construction equipment, railings, window frame members, structural parts etc
3. **Rotational Molding :** storage tanks, furniture, road signs and bollards, planters, pet houses, toys, bins and refuse containers, doll parts, road cones, footballs, helmets, canoes, rowing boats, tornado shelters, kayak hulls and playground slides
4. **Thermoforming :** disposable cups, containers, lids, trays, blisters, clamshells, and other products for the food, medical, and general retail industries

14. (b) 1. Antioxidants are used to prevent thermal degradation and inhibit oxidation (i.e. degradation). Hindered Amine, Hindered Phenol, Thioesters, Phosphites, Hydroxylam-ines, dithiopropionate, phenyl salisylate etc.

2. Flame retardants (FR) are chemical compounds added with an objective to inhibit/retard the ignition/burning of the plastic. Brominated (BFRs), Chlorinated (CFRs), Phosphorous (PFRs), Alumina Trihydrate (ATH), Magnesium Hydroxide (MDH), Antimony Oxide etc.
3. Chemical blowing agents are added to the polymer either prior to or during plasticization. They consist of organic or inorganic compounds that dissociate gas due to a reaction during processing. Chemical blowing agents include isocyanate and water for polyurethane, azodicarbonamide for vinyl, hydrazine and other nitrogen-based materials for thermoplastic and elastomeric foams, and sodium bicarbonate for thermoplastic foams.
4. Addition of light stabilizers / UV absorbers can extend the life and improve the appearance of the plastic. The most commonly used light stabilizers in plastics are hindered amine light stabilizers (HALS); the most common UV absorbers are benzotriazoles, benzophenones and organic nickel compounds.

15. (d) P-2; Q-1; R-4; S-3

1 = Viscoelastic deformation;

2 = Elastic deformation

3 = Viscoelastic recovery;

4 = Elastic recovery

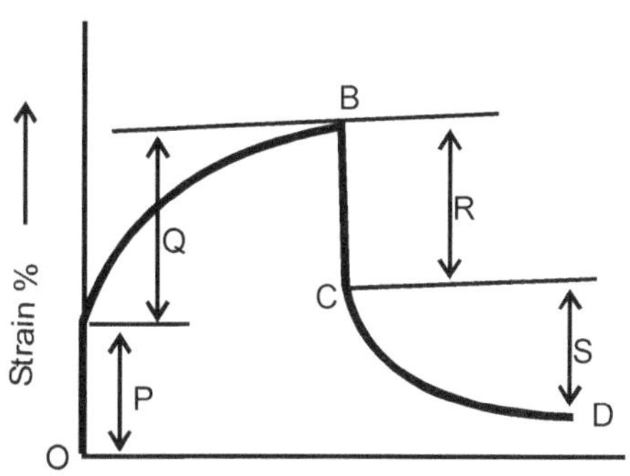

16. (c) P-2; Q-3; R-1

1 = Dilatent fluid;

2 = Newtonian fluid,

3 = Pseudoplastic fluid

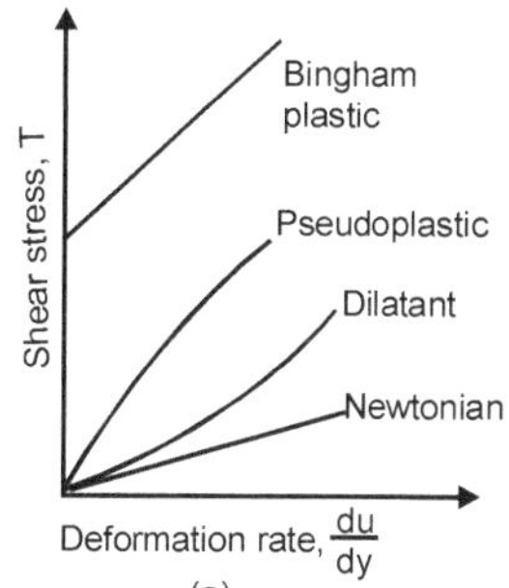

(a)

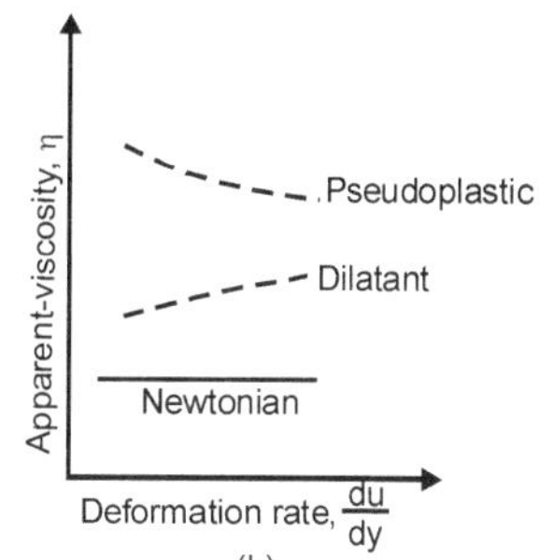

(b)

17. (c) P-2; Q-1; R-4; S-3

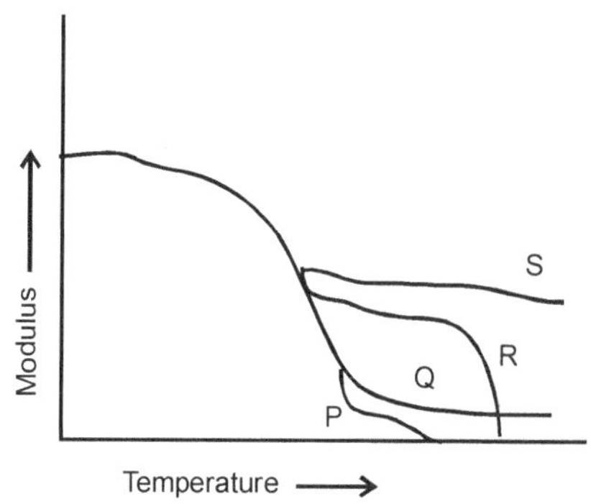

1 = An amorphous polymer of high molecular weight having entanglements

2 = An amorphous polymer of moderate molecular weight

3 = Highly crosslinked polymer

4 = Semi-crystalline polymer

18. (–25.00 to –24.50)

Convert all the temperature into Kelvin scale

$$\frac{1}{T_g} = \frac{W_1}{T_{g1}} = \frac{W_2}{T_{g2}} = \frac{.4}{373} + \frac{.6}{203}$$

$T_g = 248.26$ K

$T_g = -24.74°C$

19. (98.80 to 99.10)

$HO\text{-}(CH_2)_{14}COOH \longrightarrow H\text{-}[O\text{-}(CH_2)_{14}CO]_n\text{-}OH$

Molecular weight of the $HO\text{-}(CH_2)_{14}COOH$

$= 258 - 18 = 240 = M_o$

$$M_n = \frac{M_o}{1-p}$$

$$M_n = 24000 \text{ g/mol}$$

$$24000 = \frac{240}{(1-p)}$$

$$P = 99\%$$

20. (0.90 to 0.93)

$$E_{Total} = 10.5 \times 10^6 \times 0.3 + 0.4 \times 10^6 \times 0.7$$
$$= 3.43 \times 10^6$$

$$\delta_{glass} = \delta_{nylon}$$

$$\frac{P_{glass} l_{glass}}{E_{glass} A_{glass}} = \frac{P_{nylon} \times l_{nylon}}{E_{nylone} \times A_{nylone}}$$

$$\frac{P_{glass}}{P_{nylon}} = \frac{10.5 \times 10^6 \times 0.3}{0.4 \times 10^6 \times 0.7}$$

$$\% \text{ fraction} = \frac{P_{glass}}{P_{total}} = \frac{11.25}{11.25+1} = \frac{11.25}{12.25} = 91.8\%$$

21. (17.91 to 18.00)

$$\{\text{Solubility Parameter of a polymer}\} = \sqrt{\frac{E_{coh}}{V}}$$

$$= \sqrt{\frac{43870}{136}} = 17.96 (J/cm^3)^{1/3}$$

22. (2600 to 2600)

Styrene chemical formulas is $C_6H_5CH = CH_2$

Mass of styrene

$$= \frac{\text{Total heat released} \times \text{Total mol.wt of styrene}}{\text{Heat of Polymerization of styrene}}$$

$$\text{Mass of styrene required} = \frac{5 \times 10^5 \times 104}{20}$$

$$= 2600000 \text{ gms}$$
$$= 2600 \text{ kgs.}$$

SOLVED PAPER - 2017

1. Poly(ethylene terephthalate) is synthesized from

(*a*) Ethylene + dimethyl terephthalate

(*b*) Ethylene + terephthalate

(*c*) Glycerol + terephthalate

(*d*) Ethylene Glycol + terephthalate

2. Poly(vinyl chloride) has a higher T_g than polypropylen due to presence of

(*a*) Bulky side groups

(*b*) Polar interactions

(*c*) Restriction of bond rotation

(*d*) Non-polar interaction

3. The filler which would impart electrical conductivity to a polymer is

(*a*) Carbon Black (*b*) Talc

(*c*) Glass beads (*d*) Calcium carbonate

4. Which one of the following catalysts is used to prepare 'isotactic' polypropylene?

(*a*) Alkyl lithium (*b*) BF_3

(*c*) Ziegler-Natta (*d*) AIBN

5. Novolac and Resole are A–stage low molecualr weight phenolic resin products that are

(*a*) soluble and fusible

(*b*) Insoluble but fusible

(*c*) Insoluble and infusible

(*d*) soluble and infusible

6. Which of the following reagents can act as an initiator at room temperature?

(*a*) AIBN (*b*) dicumyl peroxide

(*c*) Dibenzoyl peroxide (*d*) $Fe^{2+} + H_2O_2$

7. The impact strength of polystyrene can be enhanced by blending/mixing with

(*a*) Carbon black

(*b*) PMMA

(*c*) Polybutadiene

(*d*) Glass fibre

8. The melt processing temperature of a semicrystalline thermoplastic polymer is

(*a*) Between T_g and T_m

(*b*) Equal to T_m

(*c*) Lower then T_m

(*d*) Higher than T_m

9. The unit of viscosity of a polymer is expressed as

(*a*) Pa.s (*b*) Pa/s

(*c*) Pa/s^2 (*d*) Pa/s^3

10. Based on the graph 1-5, which option best described the stress-strain behaviour of materials listed as P, Q, R, S and T?

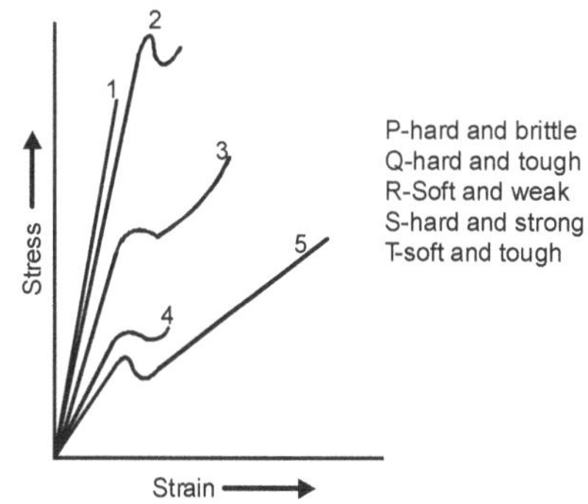

(*a*) P-2; Q-1; R-5; S-4; T-3

(*b*) P-1; Q-3: R-4; S-2; T-5

(*c*) P-1: Q-2; R-5; S-3; T-4

(*d*) P-2; Q-3; R-1; S-4; T-5

11. The two characterization techniques which can be used to determine degree of crystallinity of a polymer are

P. Scanning Electron and Microscopy

Q. Thermogravimetric Analysis

R. Wide Angle X-Ray Diffreaction

S. Differential Scanning Calorimetry.

(*a*) P&R

(*b*) Q&R

(*c*) R&S

(*d*) Q&S

12. The density of polyethylene crystals is 998 kg/m^3 and that of totally amorphous polyethylene is 886 kg/m^3. If the density of a polyethylene sample is 949 kg/m^3, the crystallinity in volume fraction is ___%.

13. The polydispersity index of a polymer sample containing 200 molecules each of molecular weight 10,000g/mol, 300 molecules each of molecular weight 30,000g/mol and 500 molecules each of molecualr weight 50,000 g/mol is_____.

14. Match the following rubber additives to their function:

Additives	Function
P. Dicumyl Peroxide	1.Ultra fast accelerator
Q. Pentachlorothiophenol	2. Activator
R. Zno with stearic acid	3. Curing Agent
S. Zinc diethyldithiocarbamate	4. Peptizer

(*a*) P-3; Q-1; R-2; S-4
(*b*) P-3; Q-1: R-4; S-2
(*c*) P-3: Q-4; R-2; S-1
(*d*) P-3; Q-4; R-1; S-2

15. A composite of polypropylene reinforced with 20% by volume of glass fibre is to be prepared. If the density of glass fiber is 2540 kg/m^3 and polypropylene is 900 kg/m^3, then the mass of glass fiber required perkg of composite is _____g.

16. Match the following terminology to the appropriate polymer processing technique :

Terminology	Process Technique
P. Die Swell	1. Two roll mill mixing
Q. Breathing	2. Thermoforming
R. Plug-assisted	3. Extrusion
S. Mastication	4. compressor moulding

(*a*) P-1; Q-2; R-3; S-4 (*b*) P-3; Q-4: R-2; S-1
(*c*) P-2: Q-3; R-4; S-1 (*d*) P-2; Q-1; R-4; S-3

17. Match the polymer in Column A to its application in Column B:

Column A	Column B
P. Nylon	1.Television cabinet
Q. Polyethylene	2. Tyre
R. Cis-1,4 polyisoprene	3. Mechanical gear
S. Acrylonitrile-butadiene -styrene	4. Packaging

(*a*) P-3; Q-4; R-2; S-1 (*b*) P-4; Q-3: R-2; S-1
(*c*) P-4: Q-2; R-3; S-1 (*d*) P-3; Q-4; R-1; S-2

18. For the polycondensation of equimolar amounts of adipic acid with hexamethylene diamine, if the number average degree of polymerization is 100, then the extent of reaction is___%.

19. The relaxation time for a rubber band at 23°C is 60 days. If it is stressed to 2MPa initially, then the time required before the dtress relaxation to 1 MPa is_____days.

20. Match the processing technique in Column A to the corresponding shear rate(s^{-1}) in Column B

Column A	Column B
P. Injection Moulding	1.1-10
Q. Extrusion	2. 10-100
R. Calendering	3. 100-1000
S. Compression molding	4. 1000-10000

(*a*) P-1; Q-3; R-2; S-4 (*b*) P-4; Q-2: R-3; S-1
(*c*) P-4: Q-3; R-1; S-2 (*d*) P-4; Q-3; R-2; S-1

21. Given T_g of Polymer A is 100°C and that of polymer B is -100°C, then the T_g of a miscible blend of A and B contaning 30wt% of A is______°C.

22. Match plots 1-4 given in the figure below with the the correct flow behavior of polymeric fluid listed as P, Q, R & S

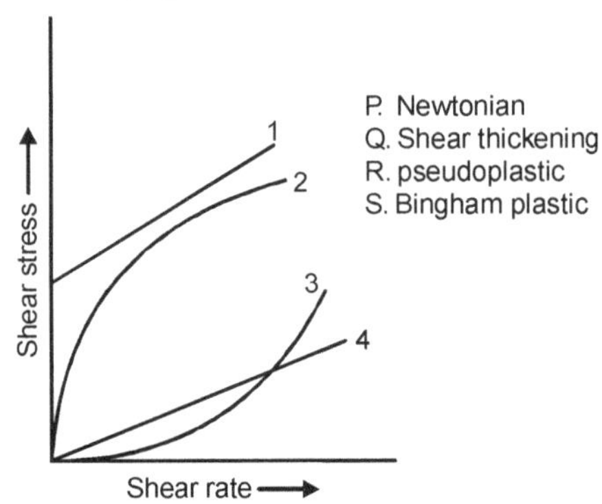

(*a*) P-4; Q-2; R-3; S-1 (*b*) P-4; Q-3: R-2; S-1
(*c*) P-4: Q-3; R-1; S-2 (*d*) P-1; Q-3; R-2; S-4

ANSWERS

1. (*d*)	**2.** (*b*)	**3.** (*a*)	**4.** (*c*)	**5.** (*a*)	**6.** (*d*)	**7.** (*c*)	**8.** (*d*)	**9.** (*a*)	**10.** (*b*)

11. (*c*) **12.** (55.95 to 56.55) **13.** (1.14 to 1.24) **14.** (*c*) **15.** (410 to 418) **16.** (*b*) **17.** (*a*)

18. (98.5 to 99.5) **19.** (41.00 to 42.20) **20.** (*d*) **21.** (– 67.3 to – 66.3) **22.** (*b*)

EXPLANATIONS

1.

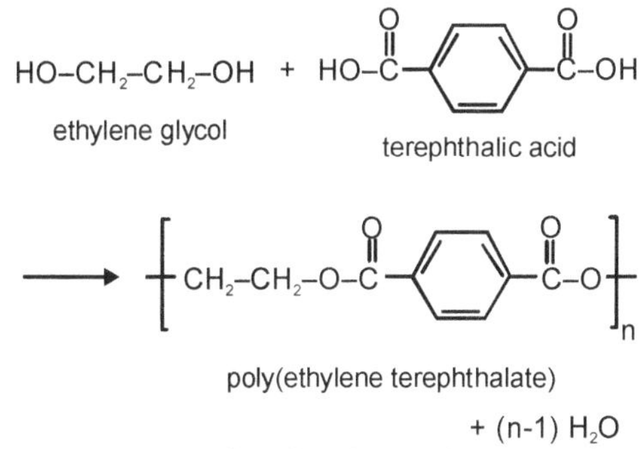

2. Stronger intermolecular forces lead to a higher T_g. PVC has stronger intermolecular forces than polypropylene because of the dipole-dipole forces from the C-Cl bond.

Polypropylene $T_g = -20°C$

Poly(vinyl chloride) = 81°C

3. Carbon black when used to impart electrical conductivity to plastics exhibits a phenomenon known as percolation - where the level of carbon black is sufficient to cause a significant and abrupt increase in electrical conductivity. As the loading of the carbon black in the compound increases, the plastic compound remains initially insulating, as the loading increases the conductivity passes through a sharp and abrupt rise over a very narrow black concentration (loading) range. Further increases in loading part this threshold cause little increase in the conductivity. This narrow range is known as the percolation threshold.

4. Ziegler-Natta catalyst, any of an important class of mixtures of chemical compounds remarkable for their ability to effect the polymerization of olefins (hydrocarbons containing a double carbon-carbon bond) to polymers of high molecular weights and highly ordered (stereoregular) structures.

5.

Resole

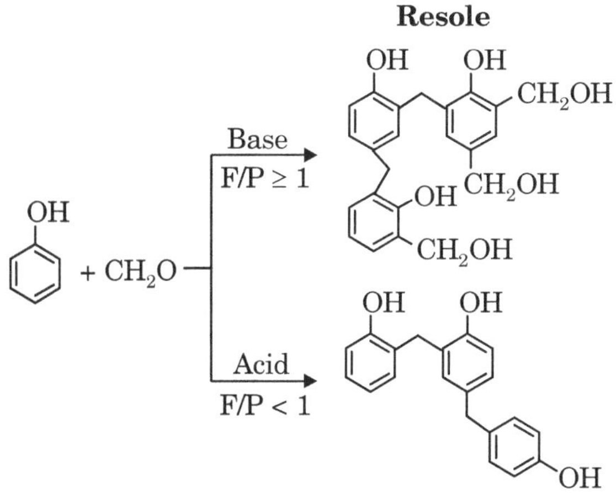

Novolac

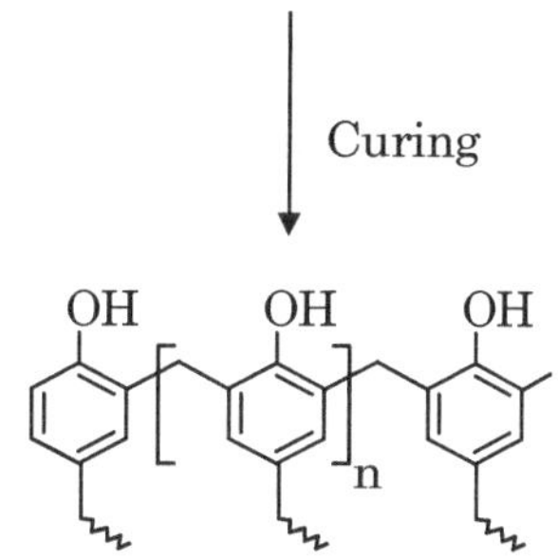

Bakelite

A-stage : soluble and fusible (resol and novolac)

B-stage : may be swollen but not dissolved by a variety of solvents (resitols)

C-stage : rigid, hard, insoluble, infusible (Bakelite)

6.

Initiator	Activation Temperature (°C)
AIBN	65-80
Dicumyl Peroxide	130-140
Dibenzyl Peroxide	100-14
$Fe+H_2O_2$	20-40

7. Polystyrene is toobrittle for many applications. To solve this problem we incorporate some rubber in the matrix of the polystyrene. Butadiene increase the toughness of the polymer and reduce the sofetening point and imparts the impact strength.

8.

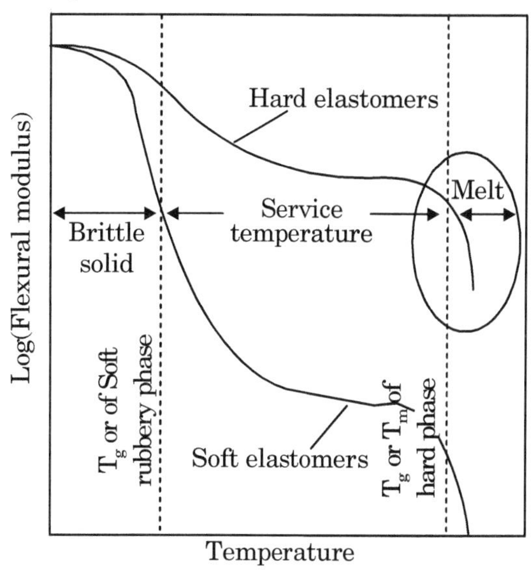

Semi crystalline polymer has higher thickness of spherulites so higher melting temp requires for processing.

9. $$\sigma = \eta \frac{dy}{dt}$$

σ stress (Pa) and dy/dt (shear rate) = sec^{-1}

viscosity = Pa/sec^{-1} = Pa.s

10. Hard means required force is highet to break it. Soft material requires less force to break the material and give higher elongation. Tough means higher the stress strain curve. Brittle materials is similar to glass which requires the higher force to elongate a small percentage.

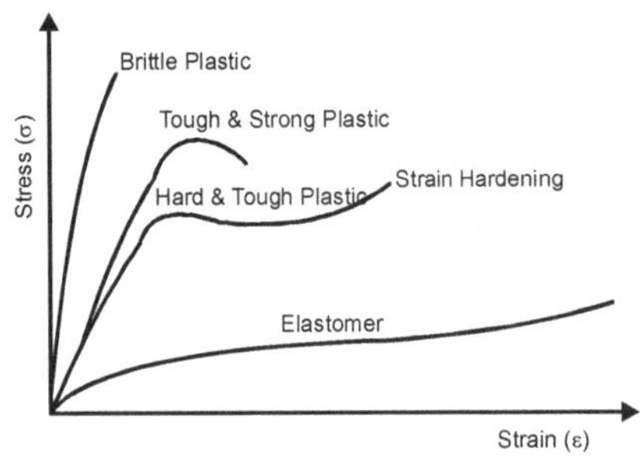

11.

SEM	Morphology of polymer
DSC	Crystallinity, Enthalphy, Tg & Tm
TGA	Ash content, identification of blend ratio and polymer name.
X-ray Diffraction	Crystallinity & Crystal size

12. Degree of crystallinity = X_v

$$= \frac{d_a - d}{d_a - d_c} = \frac{886 - 949}{886 - 998}$$

$$= 0.5625$$

$$X_v = 56.25\%$$

(d_a = density of amorphous part, d_c = density of crystallinity part, d = density of the polymer)

13.

	1	2	3
Molecules	200	300	500
Molecular weight (g/mol)	10,000	30,000	50,000

We know that weight of the sample is

$$W = \sum w_i = \sum N_i M_i$$

Mass in terms of percentage given, we use mass as w_i, and divide w_i by the molecular weight and get the number of chains. Number average molecular weight :

$$M_n = \frac{\Sigma N_i M_i}{\Sigma N_i}$$

$$M_n = \frac{200 * 10^4 + 300 * 3 * 10^4 + 500 * 5 * 10^4}{200 + 300 + 500}$$

$$M_n = 36000$$

Weight average molecular weight :

$$M_w = \frac{\Sigma N_i M_i^2}{\Sigma N_i M_i}$$

$$M_w = \frac{200 * (10^4)^2 + 300 * (3 * 10^4)^2 + 500 * \left(5 * 10^4\right)^2}{200 * 10^4 + 300 * 3 * 10^4 + 500 * 5 * 10^4}$$

$$M_w = 4277$$

$$\text{Poly Dispersity} = \frac{M_w}{M_n}$$

$$\text{Poly Dispersity} = \frac{42777}{36000}$$

$$PD = 1.18$$

14. Phenol generally used as peptizer for Natural rubber in rubber industry. Peroxide used as curing agent. ZnO and stearic acid act as activator in rubber compounding.

15. Mass = volume * density,

Volume fraction of glass fiber is 20% and Volume faction of the polypropylene is 80%.

$$\text{Mass fraction of glass fiber} = \frac{0.2 * 2540}{0.2 * 2540 + 0.8 * 900}$$

$$= 0.4136;\ 41.4\%$$

The mass of glass fiber required per kg of composite is 0.414 * 1000 = 414 g.

16. 1. Die Swell - As the polymer is moved through the screw and pushed through the die, the polymer is compressed. The land, which is the die section with the actual geometry, is usually short. The polymer is squeezed and oriented as it goes through the land. Since it is not in this section very long, the polymer chains do not have enough time to fully realign themselves to this new orientation.

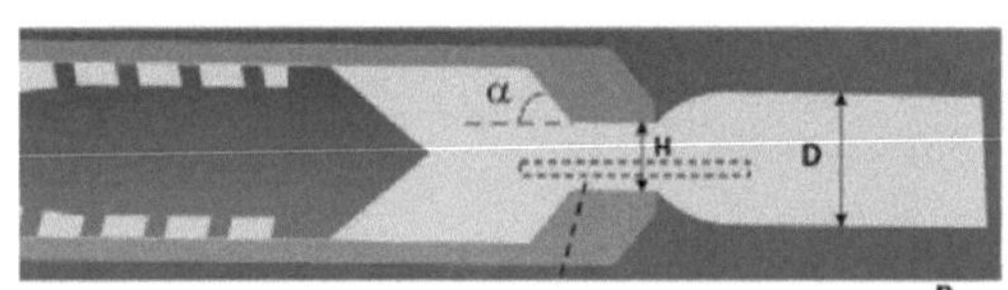

Die swell : $B = \frac{D}{H}$

2. Flashing (Breathing) is necessary to allow the air or gases to escape during the compression moulding.

3. The plug assist **provides additional control of the moulding of heated plastic sheets in conjunction with the vacuum**. These two components (vacuum and plug assist) usually take effect at almost the same time in the cycle of the machine.

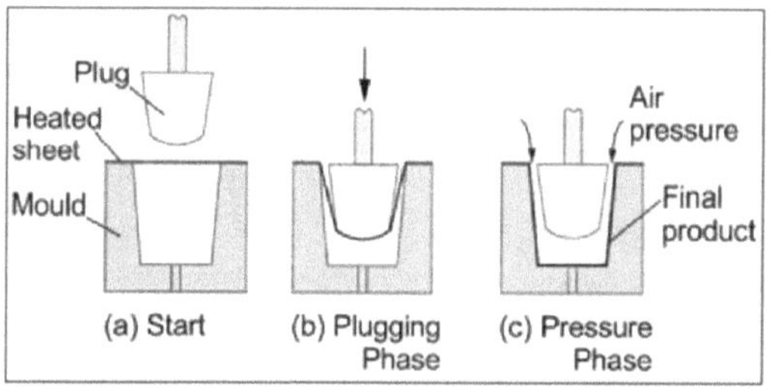

4. A two roll mill consists of two horizontally placed hollow metal rolls rotating towards each other. Two-roll mills have been used for rubber compounding. They were also used for mastication of natural rubber, to break down high-molecular-weight fractions.

17. Polyethylene world wide used in the packaging. C is 1, 4 polyisoprene is the structure of the natural rubber and natural rubber is used in the tire. ABS is used where the hard and durable plastic compound required.

18.
$$X_n = \frac{1+r}{1+r-2Pr}$$

For euimolar $r = 1$

$$X_n = \frac{1}{(1-p)} = 100$$
$$P = 0.99 = 99\%$$

19.
$$\sigma = \sigma_o e^{(-t/\tau)}$$

Where τ **(relaxation time)** = η/E,

σ stress at time t and σ_o initial stress

$$\tau = 60 \text{ days}$$
$$\sigma = 1 \text{ MPa}$$

and $\sigma_o = 2$ MPa

$$1 = 2e^{(-t/60)}$$
$$t = 41.8 \text{ days}$$

20.

Processing	Shear rate (1/s)
Compression molding	1 to 10
Calendering	10 to 100
Extrusion	100 to 1000
Injection molding	10^3 to 10^4
Fiber spinning	$> 10^4$

21. Convert all the temperature in the Kelvin from centrigrade. Total weight fraction is equal to 1.

$$\frac{1}{T_g} = \frac{W_1}{T_{g_1}} + \frac{W_2}{T_{g_2}}$$

$$\frac{1}{T_g} = \frac{0.3}{373} + \frac{0.7}{173}$$
$$T_g = -66.84°C$$

22. The sear stress depends on the strain rate, but not linear like Newtonian fluid.

(*a*) **Bingham Plastic :** A Bingham body represents the case of an ideal plastic material which supports a finite stress before a strain is initiated. Thus, after the material reaches a definite Stress level known as the yield stress, (σ_o), a finite strain rate is generated; the Stress-strain rate relationship is assumed to be linear, as in Newtonian fluids, but only after attainment of the yield stress (σ_o). Shear stress equation for bingham plastic is given by :

$$\sigma = \sigma_o + \eta \frac{dy}{dt}$$

Examples : clay suspensions, drilling mud, toothpaste, mayonnaise, chocolate and mustard.

(*b*) **Pseudoplastic :** The behavior of most real plastics is, however, characterized by non-linear relationships which are concave downward as shown by the pseudoplastic behavior. Most plastic melts, solutions or dispersions exhibit pseudoplastic flow patterns. At rest, long chain molecules of a plastic melt, solution or dispersion are believed to engage each other into stable associations as a consequence of chain entanglements and due to molar cohesion. At low shear rates, the stress required to overcome or undo the effect of chain entanglements is relatively high, but proportionately lower stress is required to allow the melt, solution or dispersion flow at a higher strain rate once the molecules are set in motion with respect to each other. The entanglement effect becomes virtually non-existent and almost Newtonian behavior assumes prominence at high shear rates depending on the exact nature of the fluid materials. If allowed to stand at rest thereafter, the fluid materials set again. Such isothermal reversible sol-gel transformations are known as thixotropy. The equation for Pseudoplastic is given by :

$$\sigma = \eta \frac{dy^n}{dt}$$

$n < 1$ pseudoplastics

Examples : Nail polish, whipped cream, ketchup, molasses, syrups, paper pulp in water, latex paint, ice, blood, some silicone oils, some silicone coatings, sand in water.

(*c*) **Dilatancy :** Concave upward curve in the shear stress vs. shear rate curve represents the behavior of dilatants substance. Such behaviour is exemplified by some highly concentrated suspensions of certain fine powders in appropriate liquids and by some melts in rare cases where crystallization or structure formation occurs at high rate of shearing. Such systems usually resemble a Newtonian fluid at low shear rates, but beyond a specific shear rate, they sharply gain in viscosity which may finally reach a very high value. When set at rest again, they return to the flow behavior of a near-normal viscous liquid. This reversible flow pattern is called *dilatancy.* The equation for Pseudoplastic is given by :

$$\sigma = \eta \frac{dy^n}{dt}$$

$n > 1$ dilatant

Examples : Suspensions of corn starch in water

Pseudoplastic are shear thinning while dilatants are shear thickening.

SOLVED PAPER - 2016

1. The polymer with minimum number of branches is

(*a*) HDPE (*b*) VLDPE

(*c*) LDPE (*d*) LLDPE

2. Nitrile Rubber is a copolymer of

(*a*) isoprene and acrylonitrile

(*b*) butadiene and acrylonitrile

(*c*) cyclopentadiene and acrylonitrile

(*d*) isobutylene and acrylonitrile

3. The functionality of 1,4-divinylbenzene in reactions involving addition across carbon-carbon double bond is

(*a*) 1 (*b*) 2

(*c*) 3 (*d*) 4

4. The comonomer common to Nylon 66 and Nylon 46 is

(*a*) hexamethylene diamine

(*b*) butylene diamine

(*c*) adipic acid

(*d*) octane dicarboxylic acid

5. Polyethylene and polypropylene form an immiscible blend mainly due to

(*a*) entropy factor

(*b*) enthalpy factor

(*c*) crystallinity

(*d*) solubility

6. Rubber modulus is

(*a*) ratio of stress to strain

(*b*) same as Young's modulus

(*c*) stress at specified strain

(*d*) stress at break

7. The solubility parameter is determined by using

(*a*) Bragg's equation

(*b*) Fox equation

(*c*) Hildebrand equation

(*d*) Carother's equation

8. 'Roller die' consists of a combination of

(*a*) a two-roll calender with internal mixer feeding

(*b*) a two-roll calender with open mill feeding

(*c*) a three-roll vertical calender with two-roll mixer feeding

(*d*) a two-roll calender with extruder feeding

9. Resole is an example of

(*a*) thermoplastic polymer

(*b*) thermosetting polymer

(*c*) natural polymer

(*d*) thermoplastic elastomer

10. Match the processing technique to the appropriate product listed below:

Processing Technique	Product
P. Blow molding	1. Bucket
Q. Co-extrusion	2. Blister packaging
R. Injection molding	3. Bottles
S. Thermoforming	4. Multilayered sheets

(*a*) P-3; Q-4; R-2; S-1 (*b*) P-3; Q-1; R-4; S-2

(*c*) P-3; Q-4; R-1; S-2 (*d*) P-3; Q-2; R-1; S-4

11. For a high molecular weight polymer sample with a viscosity of 6×10^{11} Poise and a stress relaxation modulus of 3×10^{6} dyne cm^{-2} at a given temperature, the relaxation time will be _____ hours.

12. Match the following polymer additives to their function :

Additive	Function
P. Azocarbonamide	1. Chemical plasticizer
Q. Antimony trioxide	2. Accelerator
R. Pentachlorothiophenol	3. Flame retardant
S. Mercaptobenzothiazole	4. Blowing agent

(*a*) P-4; Q-1; R-3; S-2

(*b*) P-4; Q-2; R-1; S-3

(*c*) P-4; Q-3; R-2; S-1

(*d*) P-4; Q-3; R-1; S-2

13. Tensile force of 165 N is applied to a piece of vulcanized rubber of dimension 4 mm × 4 mm × 30 mm. If the sample is elongated by 50% of its original length under the same applied force, the true stress will be _______ MPa.

14. The order of glass transition temperature for the given polymers is [NR = natural rubber; PP = polypropylene; PE = polyethylene; PMMA = poly (methyl methacrylate)]

(*a*) NR < PE < PP < PMMA

(*b*) PE < NR < PP < PMMA

(*c*) PE < PP < NR < PMMA

(*d*) NR < PP < PE < PMMA

15. Dynamic mechanical analysis of polystyrene (T_g = 100 °C) measured at a frequency of 1 Hz shows the damping peak at 110°C. If the measurement is made at 10^4 Hz, then the peak temperature (°C) will be

(*a*) 123.2 (*b*) 133.2

(*c*) 143.2 (*d*) 153.2

16. Match the product to the most suitable plastic listed below :

Product	Plastic
P. Baby feeding bottle	1. Polypropylene
Q. Tiffin box	2. Poly(ethylene terephthalate)
R. Water bottle	3. Poly(vinyl chloride)
S. Blood bag	4. Polycarbonate

(*a*) P-1; Q-4; R-2; S-3 (*b*) P-4; Q-1; R-2; S-3

(*c*) P-1; Q-3; R-2; S-4 (*d*) P-4; Q-3; R-2; S-1

17. The number average molecular weight for the polymerization of adipic acid and ethylene glycol (feed ratio 1 : 1) at 99 percent conversion is ________ g mol^{-1}.

18. A composite material contains 30 % by volume of uniaxially aligned glass fibres in a matrix of alkyl resin. The tensile modulus of the glass fibre and alkyl resin are 76 GPa and 3 GPa, respectively. If a tensile stress of 100 MPa is applied parallel to the fibres, the percentage longitudinal strain is _____ .

19. Match the Elastomers listed below to the appropriate curing agent :

Elastomer	Curing Agent
P. Silicone rubber	1. Zinc oxide + ethylene thiourea
Q. Natural rubber	2. Diamine
R. Chloroprene rubber	3. Sulfur
S. Acrylate elastomer	4. Dicumyl peroxide

(*a*) P-4; Q-3; R-1; S-2

(*b*) P-3; Q-4; R-1; S-2

(*c*) P-4; Q-1; R-3; S-2

(*d*) P-2; Q-3; R-4; S-1

20. The weight of graphite fiber (density = 1800 kg m^{-3}) that should be added to 1.00 kg of vinyl ester resin (density = 1250 kg m^{-3}) to produce a composite with a density of 1600 kg m^{-3} is _____kg.

21. If the values of K and *a* in the Mark-Houwink equation are 1.5×10^{-4} dL g^{-1} and 0.60 respectively, the viscosity average molecular weight of a polymer having an intrinsic viscosity of 0.05 dL g^{-1} is ________ kg mol^{-1}

22. A rectangular polymer bar of length 40 mm fits exactly into a steel mold cavity and the entire assembly was heated from 20° to 100 °C. The linear thermal expansion coefficients of the polymer and steel are 80×10^{-6} °C^{-1} and 11×10^{-6} °C^{-1}, respectively. The strain encountered by the polymer sample along the length will be _____ %.

ANSWERS

1. (*a*) **2.** (*b*) **3.** (*d*) **4.** (*c*) **5.** (*a*) **6.** (*c*) **7.** (*c*) **8.** (*d*) **9.** (*b*) **10.** (*c*)

11. (55–56 hr) **12.** (*d*) **13.** (15.42:15.52) **14.** (*b*) **15.** (*) **16.** (*b*) **17.** (8590–8610)

18. (0.35–0.45) **19.** (*a*) **20.** (2.3–2.7) **21.** (14.5–16.5) **22.** (5.4–5.6)

EXPLANATIONS

1. Density α 1/branches

   HDPE : High density polyethylene

   VLDPE : Very Low density polyethylene

   LDPE : Low density polyethylene

   LLDPE : Liner Low density polyethylene

   HDPE has highest density among the 4 polymer. Density is inversely proportionate to the branches in the main Chain. So the right answer is HDPE.

2. Nitrile rubber, also known as Buna-N, Perbunan, acrylonitrile butadiene rubber, and NBR, is a synthetic rubber copolymer of acrylonitrile (ACN) and butadiene.

   BUTADIENE: $CH_2 = CH - CH - CH$

   ACRYLONITRILE: $CH_2 = CH - CN$

   NITRILE RUBBER (NBR)

   $(\text{---}(CH_2 - CH = CH - CH_2) \text{---}(CH_2\text{--}CH) \text{---})_n$ with CN attached to CH

3. The functionality of a molecule is simply its interlinking capacity, or the number of sites available for bonding (presence of reactive functional group like —OH, —COOH, $—NH_2$, — SH, —NCO, etc.) with other molecules under the specific polymerization conditions

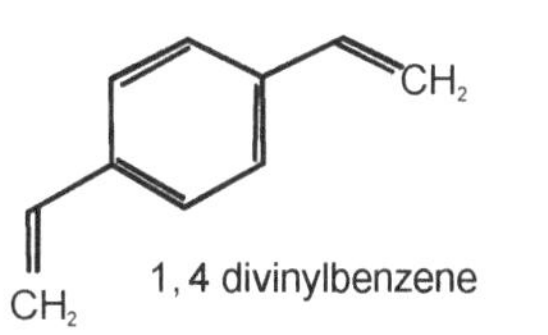

1, 4 divinylbenzene

1, 4 divinylbenzene has 2 nos. of double bond on the chain ends.Each bond gives bifunctionality to the system.The functionality to the system.The functionality of 1, 4-divinylbenzene in reactions involving addition across carbon-carbon double bond is 4 due to presence of the two double bond.

   Some compounds, however, do not contain any reactive functional group but the presence of double bond or triple bonds in the molecule bestows polyfunctionality on them.

   Example :

   (*i*) Ethylene (bifunctional because of the presence of the double bond).

   (*ii*) Acetylene (tetrafunctional because of the presence of the triple bond).

4. Nylon 66

$$nHO-\overset{O}{\overset{\|}{C}}-(CH_2)_4-\overset{O}{\overset{\|}{C}}-OH + nH_2N-(CH_2)_6-NH_2 \longrightarrow$$

Adipic acid   Hexamethylene diamine

$$\left[-\overset{O}{\overset{\|}{C}}-(CH_2)_4-\overset{O}{\overset{\|}{C}}-NH(CH_2)_6-NH-\right]_n + 2\,nH_2O$$

   Nylon 46 : Nylon 46 was synthesized from the salt of l, 4-diaminobutane and adipic acid.

   Common monomer in both nylon is adipic acid.

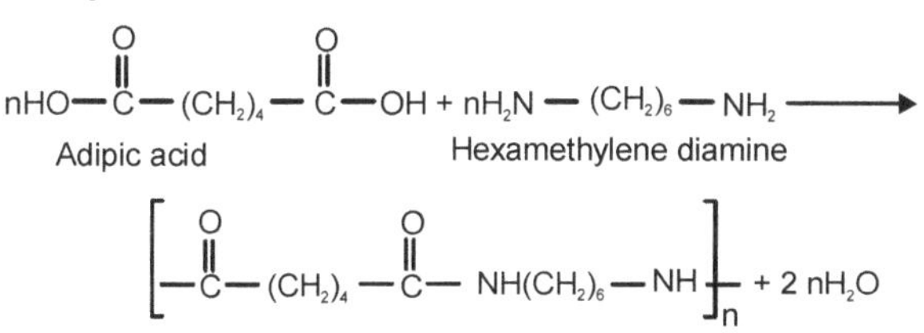

5. Entropy Factor. ***Entropy* is the name we scientists call disorder. Entropy is proportional to the amorphous or disorder in the chains. PE has lower disorder than PP.** Polyethylene and polypropylene form an immiscible blend mainly due to the entropy factor.

6. Young's modulus represents the factor of proportionality in Hooke's law, which relates the stress and the strain. However, Hooke's law is only valid under the assumption of an elastic and linear response. Rubber behavior is not like a linear material when applied the stress on it. Rubber modulus or elastic modulus calculate at different specific strain such as 100%, 200% or 300% due to non-linear behavior of the rubber material when applied stress.

7.

(*a*) Bragg's equation	The Bragg law is useful for measuring wavelengths and for determining the lattice spacing of crystals
(*b*) Fox equation	The Flory-Fox equation is a simple empirical formula that relates molecular weight to the glass transition temperature of a polymer system.
(*c*) Hildebrand equation	The Hildebrand solubility parameter (δ) provides a numerical estimate of the degree of interaction between materials, and can be a good indication of solubility, particularly for nonpolar materials such as many polymers. Materials with similar values of δ are likely to be miscible.
(*d*) Carother's equation	Carothers equation measures the degree of the polymerization

8.

   Combination of extrusion and calendaring that result in better quality product than either extrusion or calendering alone.

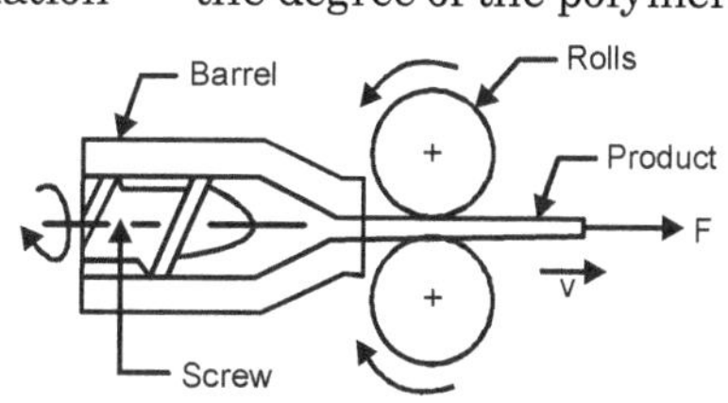

9.

Thermoplastic polymer	Become soft when heat is applied and have a smooth, hard finish when cooled.
Thermosetting polymer	The plastic which when molded once, cannot be softed by heating
Natural polymer	**Natural polymers** occur in nature and can be extracted
Thermoplastic elastomer	Copolymers or a physical mix of polymers (usually a plastic and a rubber) which consist of materials with both **thermoplastic** and **elastomeric** properties.

Resol : Base-catalysed phenol-formaldehyde resins are made with formaldehyde to phenol ratio of greater than one (usually around 1.5). These resins are called resoles. hydroxymethyl phenols will crosslink on heating to around 120 °C to form methylene and methyl ether bridges through the elimination of water molecules. At this point the resin is a 3-dimensional network, which is typical of polymerised phenolic resins. The high crosslinking gives this type of phenolic resin its hardness, good thermal stability, and chemical imperviousness. Presence of the 3-dimesnional network resol comes under the thermosetting polymers.

10.

Blow molding	**Blow molding** is a manufacturing process by which hollow plastic parts are formed
Co-extrusion	**Coextrusion** is the process of pressing two or more materials through the same die to produce a single piece
Injection molding	The plastic is melted in the injection molding machine and then injected into the mold, where it cools and solidifies into the final part
Thermoforming	Thermoforming describes the process of heating a thermoplastic sheet to its softening point, stretching it over or into a single-sided mold, and holding it in place while it cools and solidifies into the desired shape.

11. Use Maxwell model

$$\text{Relaxation time} = \frac{\eta}{E}$$

$$\eta\ (\text{Viscosity}) = 6 \times 10^{11}\ \text{Poise}$$

$$E\ (\text{Modulus}) = 3 \times 10^{6}\ \text{dyne cm}^{-2}$$

$$1\ \text{Poise} = 1\ \text{dyne/cm}^2.\text{S}$$

$$\text{Relaxation time} = \frac{6 \times 10^{11}}{3 \times 10^{6} * 3600} = 55.5\ \text{hours}$$

12.

carbonamide	Blowing agent	Play a role in the formation of air bubbles by breaking down into gas at high temperature.
Antimony trioxide	Flame retardant	reducing the devastating impact of fires
Pentachlorothiophenol	plasticizer	Additives increase plasticity
Thiazole	Accelerator	Accelerators the curing system in rubber curing

13. true stress, S, will actually occer, γ = strain

$$S = \frac{S_o L}{L_o} = S_o(1+\gamma)$$

$$\gamma = \frac{L - L_o}{L_o}$$

$$S_o = \frac{F}{A} = \frac{165}{4 * 10^{-3} * 4 * 10^{-3}} = 10.31 * 10^{6}\ \text{Pa}$$

$$S = 10.31 * 10^{6} * (1 + 0.5) = 15.47\ \text{MPa}$$

14. The glass transition occurs in amorphous (or glassy) and semi-crystalline polymers and is due to a reduction in motion of large segments of molecular chains with decreasing temperature.

PE	-125°C
NR	-70 °C
PP	0-5 °C
PMMA	105°C

15. The viscosity of the polymer at glass transition temperature can be obtained by WLF equation:

$$\ln\frac{t}{t_{Tg}} = \frac{-17.44\times(T-T_g)}{51.6+(T-T_g)}$$

Time is inversely proportional to frequency.

$$\ln\frac{\frac{1}{\omega}}{\frac{1}{\omega_{Tg}}} = \frac{-17.44\times(T-T_g)}{51.6+(T-T_g)}$$

Case 1 : Tg = 100 & T =110; ω at 110°C = 1 hz

$$\ln\frac{\frac{1}{1}}{\frac{1}{\omega_{Tg}}} = \frac{-17.44\times(110-100)}{51.6+(110-100)}$$

$$\omega_{Tg} = 1.475\times10^{-3}$$

Case 2 : Tg = 100 & T = ?; ω at 100°C = 1.475 × 10^{-3}hz

$$\ln\frac{\frac{1}{10^4}}{\frac{1}{1.475\times10^{-3}}} = \frac{-17.44\times(T-100)}{51.6+(T-100)}$$

$$T = 133.2°C$$

16.

Baby Feeding Bottle	Polycarbonate is transparent and better Tensile strength and no harm to body
Tiffin box	Generally made from PE & PP
Water bottle	Bottles are made from PET because Pet is recyclable easily
Blood Bag	PVC is the best material that satisfies the strict criteria in terms of performance, safety and cost for medical applications,

17. Product of the adipic acid and ethylene glycol

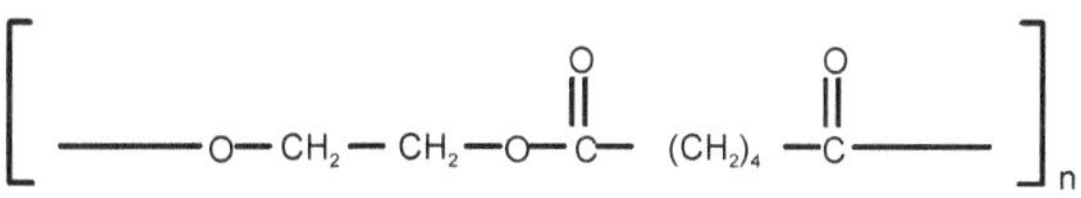

Number average molecular weight :

$$M_n = \frac{M_o}{(1-p)}$$

$$p = 0.99$$

& M_o = molecular weight of the repeated unit/2

$$= \frac{172}{2} = 86$$

$$M_n = \frac{86}{(1-0.99)} = 8600$$

18. Modulus of the composite

$$E_{cl} = E_mV_m + E_fV_f$$

E_m & E_f are the elastic modulus for matrix and fiber.

$$V_m + V_f = 1$$

V_m and V_f are volume fraction for matrix and fiber.

$$V_m = 0.7$$

& $$V_f = 0.3$$

$$E_m = 3GPa$$

$$E_r = 76\ GPa$$

$$E_{cl} = 0.7 * 3 + 0.3 * 76$$

$$= 24.9\ GPa$$

$$\text{Elastic modulus} = \frac{\text{tensile stress}}{\text{strain}}$$

$$\text{Strain}\ (\%) = \frac{\text{Tensile stress}}{\text{Elastic modulus}}$$

$$= \frac{100MPa}{24.9*1000MPa}$$

$$= 0.40\%$$

19.

Sulphur	Natural rubber, Isoprene, SBR, Butyl, Polybutadiene, EPDM, Nitrile,
Organic Peroxide	Urethanes, Silicone, Chlorinated Polyethylene, Crosslinked Polyethylene, PVC/NBR
Metallic Oxide	Polychloroprene, Chlorosulphonated, Polyethylene, Polysulphide
Organic Amines	Acrylic, Fluorocarbon, Epichlorohydrin

20. $$\text{Density} = \frac{\text{mass}}{\text{volume}}$$

	Mass (Kg)	Density (kg m^{-3})	Volume m^3
Fiber	x	1800	x/1800
Resin	1	1250	1/1250
Total	x + 1		x/1800 + 1/1250

$$\text{Composite density} = \frac{\text{total mass}}{\text{total volume}}$$

$$1600 = x + 1/x/1800 + 1/1250$$

$$X = 2.54\ kg;$$

21. Mark-Houwink equation the relationship among the molecular weight and viscosity are given below

$$[\eta] = K\,M^a$$

Where $[\eta]$ is the intrinsic viscosity, 'M' is Molecular weight, 'K' and 'a' are constants for a particular polymer solvent system.

$$K = 1.5 \times 10^{-4}\ \text{dL g}^{-1}$$

$$a = 0.60$$

and $$\eta = 0.05\ \text{dL g}^{-1}$$

$$0.05 = 1.5 \times 10^{-4} * [M]^{0.6}$$

$$M = 16024.995\ \text{g/mol}$$

$$= 16.02\ \text{Kg/mol}$$

22. $$\frac{\Delta L}{L} = \alpha[\Delta T]$$

ΔL = Change in Length

ΔT = Change in Temperature

α = Coefficient of Thermal Expansion (CTE)

Coefficient of thermal expansion

$$= 80 \times 10^{-6} - 11 \times 10^{-6}\ 1/°C = 69 \times 10^{-6}\ 1/°C$$

$$\frac{\Delta L}{L} = 69 \times 10^{-6} \times (100 - 20) = 5520 \times 10^{-6}$$

$$\frac{\Delta L}{L} = 0.552\%$$

SOLVED PAPER - 2015

Q. 1 – 9 carry one mark each.

1. The biodegradable polymer among the following polymers is

(*a*) poly(lactic acid)

(*b*) poly(butyleneterephthalate)

(*c*) polystyrene

(*d*) polypropylene

2. Notched impact strength of a plastic decreases with

(*a*) increase in notch tip radius

(*b*) increase in notch depth

(*c*) increase in temperature

(*d*) decrease in notch depth

3. The compound used as a reactive diluent in unsaturated polyester resins is

(*a*) benzene (*b*) cresol

(*c*) styrene (*d*) adipic acid

4. The diameter of a die of an extruder producing extrudate of diameter 2.4 mm with a die-swell ratio of 2 is __________ mm.

5. The degree of polymerization of Nylon 6 (ignore end-groups) with molar mass of 1,00,000 g mol^{-1} is _________ .

6. The Polymer synthesized by ring opening polymerization is

(*a*) Poly(acrylic acid)

(*b*) Nylon 6

(*c*) Nylon 66

(*d*) Poly (ethylene terephthalate)

7. Which among the following are used as initiators for free radical polymerization?

P. K_2SO_4

Q. $K_2S_2O_8$

R. AIBN

S. t-Butyl hydroperoxide + Fe^{2+}

(*a*) P, Q & R only

(*b*) Q, R & S only

(*c*) P, R & S only

(*d*) P, Q, R & S

8. Weight average molecular weight can be determined by

(*a*) Osmometry (*b*) Ebulliometry

(*c*) End group analysis (*d*) Light scattering

9. Butyl rubber is a copolymer of

(*a*) Isobutylene and butadiene

(*c*) Isobutylene and isoprene

(*b*) Butadiene and 1-butene

(*d*) Isoprene and 1-butene

Q. 10 – 22 carry two marks each.

10. Match the characterization technique with the polymer property it is used to determine

Technique	Property
P. X-ray diffraction	1. Melting temperature
Q. Differential scanning calorimetry	2. Crystallinity & crystal size
R. Thermogravimetric analysis	3. Glass transition temperature
S. Dynamic mechanical analysis	4. Ash content

(*a*) P-3; Q-1; R-4; S-2 (*b*) P-3; Q-4; R-2; S-1

(*c*) P-2; Q-4; R-1; S-3 (*d*) P-2; Q-1; R-4; S-3

11. Match the following plastic additives with their function

Additive	Function
P. Di-isooctyl phthalate	1. Antioxidant
Q. 4-Methyl-2,6-t-butylphenol	2. Plasticizer
R. Dicumyl peroxide	3. Antistatic agent
S. Quaternary ammonium compound	4. Cross-linking agent

(*a*) P-2; Q-4; R-1; S-3 (*b*) P-4; Q-1; R-3; S-2

(*c*) P-2; Q-1; R-4; S-3 (*d*) P-3; Q-1; R-4; S-2

12. The correct statement with respect to electrical property of polymeric materials is

(*a*) For non-polar materials, dielectric constant is independent of frequency & temperature

(*b*) For polar materials, dielectric constant depends on frequency but not on temperature

(*c*) For non polar materials, power losses are high and depend on temperature & frequency

(*d*) For polar materials, power losses are low and independent of frequency

13. The order of melting point for the given polymers is

(*a*) Nylon 66 > PTFE > Nylon 6 > PP

(*b*) Nylon 66 > Nylon 6 > PTFE > PP

(*c*) PTFE > Nylon 66 > Nylon 6 > PP

(*d*) PTFE > Nylon 6 > Nylon 66 > PP

14. Match the processing technique used to manufacture the appropriate product

Processing Technique	Product
P. Calendering	1. Pipes
Q. Extrusion	2. Disposable cups
R. Injection Molding	3. Sheets
S. Thermoforming	4. Nylon gears

(*a*) P-3; Q-2; R-1; S-4 (*b*) P-3; Q-1; R-2; S-4

(*c*) P-3; Q-1; R-4; S-2 (*d*) P-3; Q-2; R-4; S-1

15. Match the thermosetting resins to the raw materials they are synthesized from

Resin	Raw material
P. Epoxy	1. Cresol + furfural
Q. Phenolic	2. Diethylene glycol + diallyl phthalate
R. Unsaturated polyester	3. Bisphenol A + epichlorohydrin
S. Allyl	4. Maleic acid + 1,2-propylene glycol

(*a*) P-4; Q-2; R-3; S-1 (*b*) P-3; Q-1; R-2; S-4

(*c*) P-3; Q-2; R-1; S-4 (*d*) P-3; Q-1; R-4; S-2

16. The damping factor of a solid polymer under sinusoidal loading in single cantilever mode showing 80 percent recovery in modulus is_____.

17. A styrene-butadiene random copolymer with equal weight fraction of polystyrene (T_g = 100 °C) and polybutadiene (T_g = – 100 °C) shows a single glass transition peak. The T_g of the copolymer is ____°C.

18. In a unidirectional carbon fibre reinforced epoxy composite, the ratio of fibre-to-matrix moduli is 30 and the fibres take up 50% of the cross-section. The percentage of applied force taken up by the fibres is __________.

19. The viscoelastic behavior of a plastic is represented by spring and dashpot elements having constants of 2 GN m^{-2} and 90 GN s m^{-2}, respectively. If a constant stress of 12 MN m^{-2} is applied, the strain predicted by Maxwell model after 50 s is ________ %.

20. Match the elastomers given below to their suitable application

Elastomer	Application
P. EPDM	1. Golf balls
Q. Polyurethane	2. Fuel transfer hose
R. Nitrile rubber	3. Cable insulation
S. Polybutadiene	4. Footwear

(*a*) P-3; Q-4; R-2; S-1 (*b*) P-4; Q-3; R-2; S-1

(*c*) P-3; Q-2; R-4; S-1 (*d*) P-1; Q-4; R-2; S-3

21. Match the following reagents to their function in natural rubber latex technology

Reagent	Function
P. Ammonia	1. Prevent storage hardening
Q. Hydroxylamine	2. Delay plugging mechanism
R. Formic acid	3. Stabilizer
S. Ethephone	4. Coagulating agent

(*a*) P-3; Q-1; R-2; S-4 (*b*) P-3; Q-2; R-4; S-1

(*c*) P-3; Q-1; R-4; S-2 (*d*) P-3; Q-4; R-1; S-2

22. 1.0 g of a polybutadiene sample with carboxylic acid groups at both the ends requires 2.5 mL of 0.1 M KOH for complete neutralization. The molecular weight of the polymer in g mol^{-1} is_______.

ANSWERS

1. (*) **2.** (*) **3.** (*) **4.** (*) **5.** (883.7) **6.** (*) **7.** (*) **8.** (*d*) **9.** (*c*) **10.** (*d*)

11. (*c*) **12.** (*a*) **13.** (*c*) **14.** (*c*) **15.** (*d*) **16.** (0.25) **17.** (–37 to –36) **18.** (96.77%)

19. (1.267%) **20.** (*a*) **21.** (*c*) **22.** (8000)

EXPLANATIONS

1. Biodegradable polymers (BPs) disposed in bioactive environments degrade by the enzymatic action of microorganisms such as bacteria, fungi, and algae. Their polymer chains may also be broken down by nonenzymatic processes such as chemical hydrolysis. BPs are often derived from plant processing of atmospheric CO_2. Biodegradation converts them to CO_2, CH_4, water, biomass, humic matter, and other natural substances. These polymers are found both naturally and synthetically made, and largely consist of ester, amide, and ether functional groups. An example of biodegradable polymers are: Poly β-hydroxybutyrate–co-β-hydroxy valerate (PHBV). It is formed by combining 3-hydroxy butanoic acid and 3-hydroxy pentanoic acid. Other examples include polyglycolic acid (PGA), Polyhydroxy butyrate (PHB), Polycaprolactone (pcl), Nylon-2-nylon-6.

2. Notch depth α 1/impact strength

3. Unsaturated polyesters are generally sold to parts manufacturers as a solution of resin in reactive diluent; styrene is the most common diluent and the industry standard.

4. Die swell ratio = D/D_o,

   $D_o = 2.4/2 = 1.2$ mm

   D = extrudate diameter,

   D_o = Die diameter

5. Nylon 6 molecular weight : 113.16

   Molar mass : 10000g/mol

   Degree of polymerization :

$$DP = \frac{\overline{M}_n}{m}$$

$$\frac{100000}{113.16} = 883.7$$

6. Monomer having a ring structure can be opened and polymerised through ring opening polymerization method. Nylon 6 monomer has ring structure only.

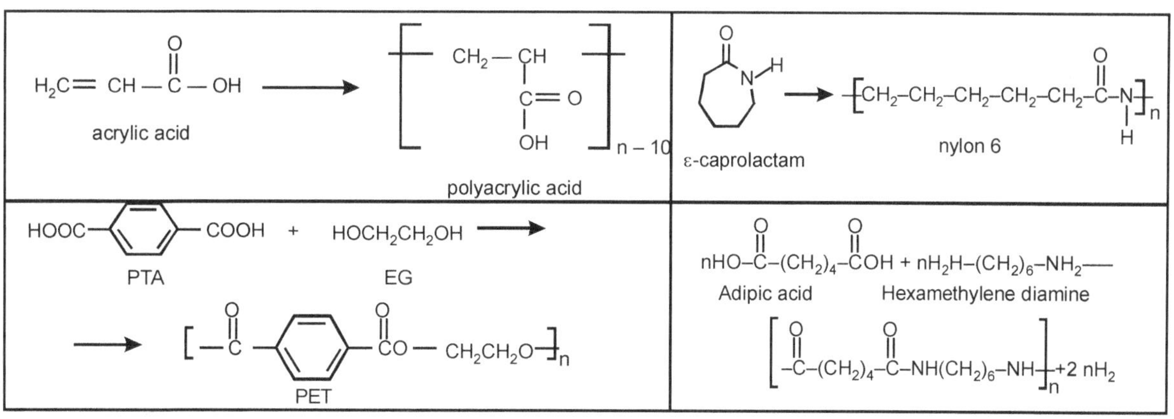

7. Solution: In a free radical addition polymerization, the choice of polymerization initiator depends mainly on two factors: a) its solubility and b) its decomposition temperature. If the polymerization is performed in an organic solvent, then the initiator should be soluble in that solvent and the decomposition temperature of the initiator must be at or below the boiling point of the solvent. Commonly, 2,2'-azo-bis-isobutyrylnitrile (AIBN) and Benzoyl peroxide suit these requirements. Initiator can also induce to decompose into radicals by using suitable catalyst. An electron transfer mechanism resulting in a reduction-oxidation reaction and peroxides and hydroperoxides are more susceptible to this kind of decomposition. Potassium persulfate gives free radical instead of potassium sulfate. Answer is B

8.

Technique	Measures	Range, g/mol
End Group	M_n	Up to 2500
Osmometry	M_n	15000 – 750000
Ebulliometry	M_n	Up to 100000
Light scattering	M_w	20000 to 10^7
Ultra centrifuge	M_w, M_z, MWD	2000 to 10^7
Solution viscosity	M_v, M_w	15000 – 10^6
Vapour-phase osmometry	M_n	Up to 25000
Gel-permiation chromatography	M_n, M_w, M_v, M_z, MWD	Up to 10^6

9.

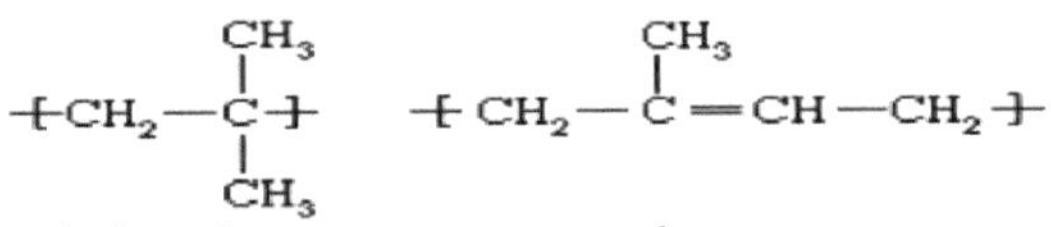

isobutylene isoprene

10.

X-ray Diffraction	Crystallinity & Crystal size
DSC	Crystallinity, Enthalphy, Tg & Tm
TGA	Ash content, identification of blend ratio and polymer name.
DMA	Tm

11. 1. Plasticizer is necessary in rubber formulations for improving the processing of the rubber by lowering the compound's viscosity, and also for aiding in low temperature flexibility of the formulated rubber. The most common plasticisers include esters such as adipates, azelates, citrates, benzoates, ortho-phthalates, terephthalates, sebacates, and trimellitates.
2. Antioxidants are used to prevent thermal degradation and inhibit oxidation (i.e. degradation). Hindered Amine, Hindered Phenol, Thioesters, Phosphites, Hydroxylamines , dithiopropionate etc.
3. An antistatic agent is a compound used for treatment of materials or their surfaces in order to reduce or eliminate buildup of static electricity. Glycerol monostearate (GMS); ethoxylated fatty acid amines; and diethanolamides & quaternary ammonia.
4. The cross-linking or curing agent is the formulation component that causes this reaction to take place. These terms are generally used with all polymeric materials that are capable of forming a thermosetting structure. Example- amines, sulfur, metal oxide and peroxides.

12. Molecules having a center of charge symmetry and zero dipole moment are known as non-polar molecules, while those not having a center of charge symmetry having permanent dipole moment are known as polar molecules. Dielectric constant and dielectric loss factor, as a function of temperature and frequencies is one of the most convenient and sensitive methods of studying the polymer structure. For non-polar plastics the dielectric constant is independent of the alternating current frequency because the electron polarization is effectively instantaneous. Non-polar plastics always have dielectric constants of less than 3. Raising the temperature of a polar plastic allows faster movement of the polymer chains and faster alignment of the dipoles. This is particularly true if the temperature is raised above Tg (see Newsletter on Low Temperature Plastics) because above Tg much more molecular movement is possible. Raising the temperature inevitably raises the dielectric constant of polar plastics. Non-polar plastics, such as the fluoropolymers, are not as affected by the water because they tend not to absorb water and temperature effects are not generally as severe because increased temperature does not affect the electronic polarization.

The dielectric constant is a measure of the influence of a particular dielectric on the capacitance of a condenser. It measures how well a material separates the plates in a capacitor and is defined as the ratio of the capacitance of a set of electrodes with the dielectric material between them to the capacitance of the same electrodes with a vacuum between them. The dielectric constant for a vacuum is 1 and for all other materials it is greater than 1.

13. Polytetrafluoroethylene (PTFE) has a very compact structure and the energy barrier to internal rotation is much higher than other options in the questions. This makes PTFE a very rigid polymer. PTFE melting point is around 327°C. Nylon 66 has strong hydrogen bond compared to the nylon6. The stronger the hydrogen bonds, the more heat or mechanical energy required to break them. Polypropylene has no hydrogen bonding and no compact structure. PP has lower melting point other than available options.

14.

Calendering	Calendering is a finishing process used on cloth, paper, or plastic film. A calender is employed, usually to smooth, coat, or thin a material. With textiles, fabric is passed under rollers at high temperatures and pressures
Extrusion	Extrusion is a process used to create objects of a fixed cross-sectional profile. A material is pushed through a die of the desired cross-section.
Injection molding	The plastic is melted in the injection molding machine and then injected into the mold, where it cools and solidifies into the final part
Thermoforming	Thermoforming describes the process of heating a thermoplastic sheet to its softening point, stretching it over or into a single-sided mold, and holding it in place while it cools and solidifies into the desired shape.

15.

Resin	Raw material
P. Epoxy	3. Bisphenol A + epichlorohydrin
Q. Phenolic	1. Cresol + furfural
R. Unsaturated polyester	4. Maleic acid + 1,2-propylene glycol
S. Allyl	Diethylene glycol + diallyl phthalate

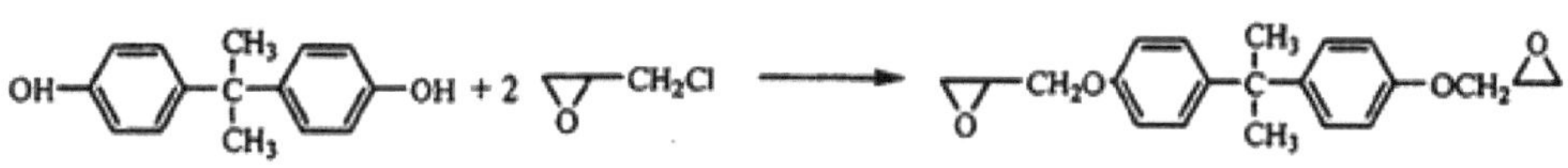

Bisphenol A *Epicholorohydrin* *"Uncured Epoxy Resin"*

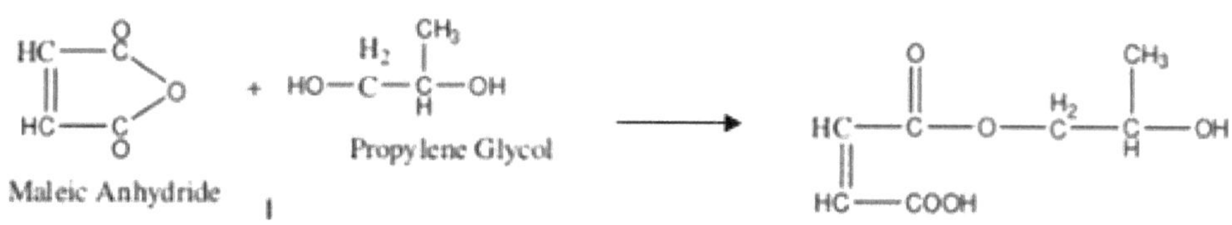

Unsaturated Polyester

16. $$\tan\delta = \frac{\text{loss modulus}}{\text{storage modulus}}$$

Loss modulus = 20% (loss in the recovery)

Storage modulus = 80 (stored in the recovery)

Damping Factor = tanδ

Damping factor = 20/80 = 0.25

17. Convert all the temperature in the Kelvin from centigrade. Total weight fraction is equal to 1.

$$\frac{1}{T_g} = \frac{W_1}{T_{g_1}} + \frac{W_1}{T_{g_2}}$$

$$\frac{1}{T_g} = \frac{0.5}{173} + \frac{0.5}{373}$$

$$T_g = -36.59°C$$

18. $$\frac{P_f}{P_c} = \frac{\sigma_f A_f}{\sigma_f A_f + \sigma_m A_m}$$

P_f = force by fiber & P_m = force by matrix

$P_C = P_f + P_m$

Unidirectional direction applied strain on the composite is equal to fiber and equal to the matrix. So, Stress is equal to the modulus.

Ratio of the fiber and matrix modulus = 30

Ratio of the fiber and matrix area= 0.5/0.5=1

$$\frac{P_f}{P_c} = \frac{1}{1+\frac{\sigma_m A_m}{\sigma_f A_f}}$$

$$\frac{P_f}{P_c} = \frac{1}{1+\frac{1}{30}} = \frac{30}{31}$$

The percentage of applied force taken up by the fibres is 0.9677*100 = 96.77%

19. Maxwell model equation at constant stress is :

$$\gamma_{\text{maxwell}} = \frac{\sigma_0}{E} + \frac{\sigma_0}{\eta}t$$

E = 2 GN/m^2, η = 90 GNs/m^2 , σ_0 = 12 MN/m^2, t = 50s

$$\gamma = \frac{12\times10^3}{2\times10^6} + \frac{12\times10^3}{90\times10^6}\times50$$

$$\gamma = 1.267\%$$

20.

Elastomer	**Application**
P. EPDM	3. Cable insulation
Q. Polyurethane	4. Footwear
R. Nitrile rubber	2. Fuel transfer hose
S. Polybutadiene	1. Golf balls

21.

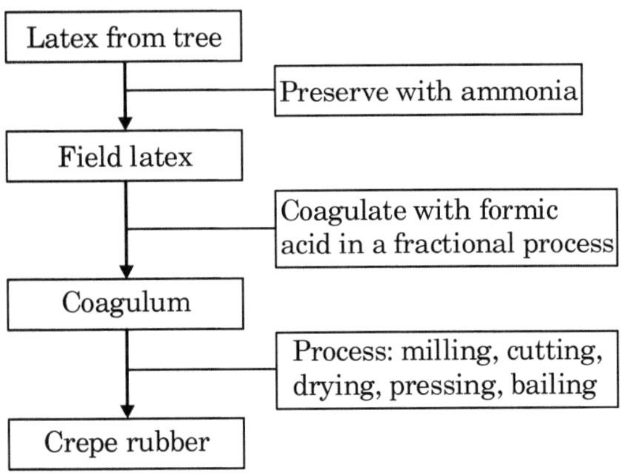

An ethylene generator, 2- chloroethylphosphonic acid (ethephon), applied to the tapping panel, which increases latex yield while reducing tapping frequency to increase land or labour productivity. Ethylene gas or ethylene-generating substances on the tree's tapping cut which increase latex flow time by delaying plugging of latex vessels, (Wenxian et al., 1986) and hence increases production through the activation of metabolism. 2-chloroe- thylphosphonic acid which decomposes in plant tissues to generate ethylene which reacts on the metabo-lism of the plant.

Natural rubber (NR) consists of rubber and non-rubber components, which is mostly *cis*-1, 4-polyisoprene. The main non-rubber components are proteins and phospholipids which are attached at each end of the NR chains. If we store NR for prolong period, the proteins and phospholipids promote formation of a NR network. This causes the gel formation with increasing the Mooney viscosity of NR, and this is called storage hardening. hydroxylamine sulfate is added with the NR to prevent storage hardening of natural rubber.

22. Let the Volume of KOH consumed = 2.5ml

Normality of KOH solution = 0.1

Weight of the sample taken = 1.0g

$$\text{Carboxyl Vlaue} = \frac{VN(56.1)}{W}\text{mg/KOH}$$

Carboxy equivalent/100g

$$= \frac{VN(56.1)}{W\times1000}\times\frac{100}{56.1} = \frac{VN}{10W}$$

Carboxyl equvalent/100g

$$= \frac{2.5\times0.1}{10\times1} = 0.025$$

$$M_n = \frac{\text{functionality}}{\text{functional group equivalent}}$$

$$M_n = \frac{2\times100}{0.025} = 8000$$

SOLVED PAPER - 2014

1. The estimation of the molecular weight of a polymer by gel permeation chromatography (GPC) is based on its

(*a*) polarity

(*b*) size

(*c*) adsorption to stationary phase

(*d*) crystallinity

2. Elastomers are characterized by

(*a*) high modulus and high elongation at break

(*b*) high modulus and low elongation at break

(*c*) low modulus and high elongation at break

(*d*) low modulus and low elongation at break

3. Thermodynamically, two polymers with enthalpy of mixing (ΔH) and entropy of mixing (ΔS) form a miscible blend at temperature T when

(*a*) $\Delta H/\Delta S = 0.5T$ (*b*) $\Delta H/\Delta S = T$

(*c*) $\Delta H/\Delta S = 1.5T$ (*d*) $\Delta H/\Delta S = 2T$

4. The tensile strain of a uniformly extending plastic specimen of initial length L_0 and extended length L is

(*a*) L_0/L (*b*) L / L_0

(*c*) $L_0/(L - L_0)$ (*d*) $(L - L_0) / L_0$

5. In natural rubber compounding, a peptizer is added

(*a*) at the beginning of the compounding cycle

(*b*) after the addition of filler

(*c*) at the end of the compounding cycle

(*d*) after the addition of antioxidant

6. A continuous annular product is produced by

(*a*) compression molding (*b*) extrusion

(*c*) blow molding (*d*) injection molding

7. Relate the three varieties of polyethylene in the left column with their chain structures given in the right column.

P. HDPE	1. long as well as short branches
Q. LDPE	2. only short branches
R. LLDPE	3. no branches

(*a*) P-1, Q-3, R-2 (*b*) P-3, Q-2, R-1

(*c*) P-2, Q-3, R-1 (*d*) P-3, Q-1, R-2

8. Match the following changes observed in the calorimetric analysis of a polymer sample when heat flow (y-axis) is plotted against temperature (x-axis):

P. step increase in heat flow	1. crystallization
Q. exothermic peak	2. melting
R. endothermic peak	3. glass transition

(*a*) P-1, Q-2, R-3 (*b*) P-2, Q-1, R-3

(*c*) P-3, Q-1, R-2 (*d*) P-3, Q-2, R-1

9. A Bingham plastic fluid is flowing under gravity, down a vertical plate, as a film. Find the appropriate match for the fully developed velocity profile of the fluid in the film, from among those shown below.

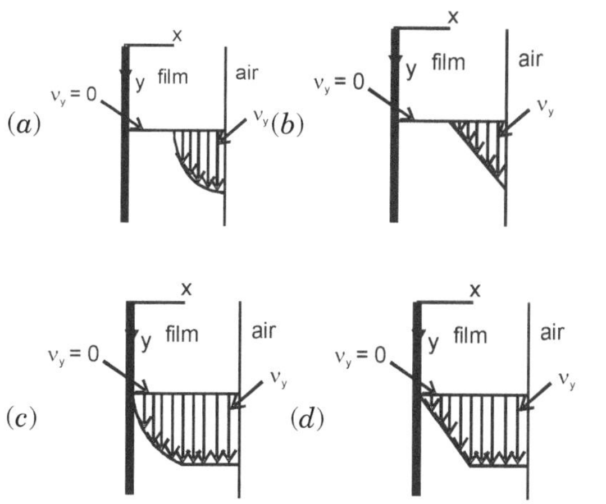

10. Calculate the mass percent of the crystalline phase in a polymer sample of density 975 kg/m^3. The density of amorphous phase is 866 kg/m^3 and that of the crystalline phase is 996 kg/m^3.

11. Find the rate of initiation (mol$L^{-1}s^{-1}$) of a polymerization reaction using a peroxide initiator with a half life of 0.1 s and efficiency of 70%, if the concentration of the initiator is 0.05 molL^{-1}.

12. The constitutive equation of a shear thinning polymeric fluid is given by

$$\sigma = \frac{\mu_0 \gamma}{1 + (\gamma / \gamma_0)}$$

Where σ represents shear stress (Pa), and γ, the corresponding shear rate (s^{-1}). The quantities μ_0 = 20 Pas and γ_0 = 10 s^{-1} are constants. Find the apparent viscosity of the sample (Pas) when the applied shear rate is 40 s^{-1}.

13. Identify the monomer for the polymer shown below prepared by ring opening metathesis polymerization.

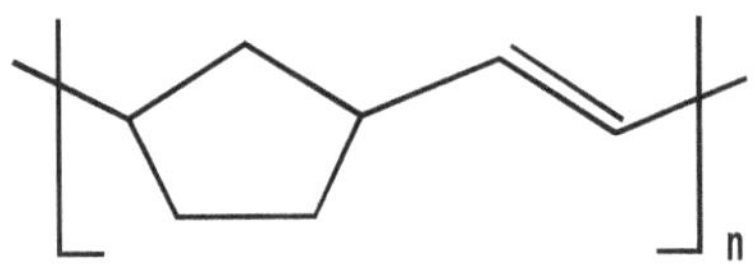

(*a*) 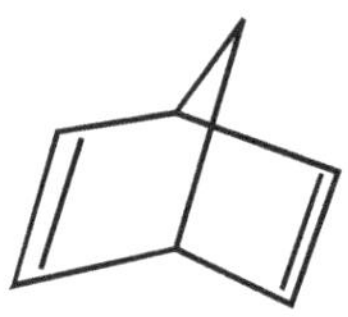 (*b*) 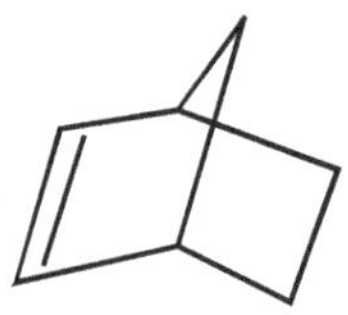

(*c*) 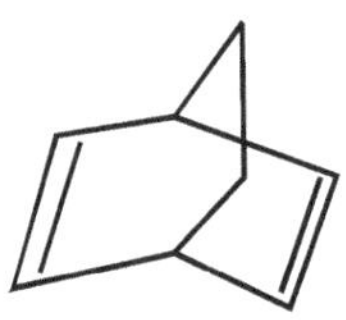 (*d*) 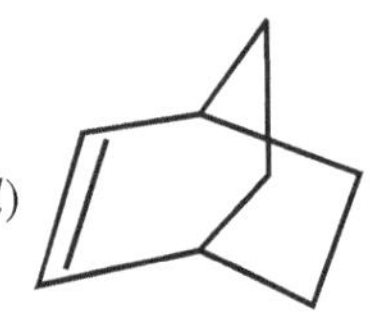

14. The most appropriate order of toughness of nylon based materials is

(*a*) talc filled nylon < dry nylon < wet nylon
(*b*) dry nylon < wet nylon < talc filled nylon
(*c*) wet nylon < dry nylon < talc filled nylon
(*d*) wet nylon < talc filled nylon < dry nylon

15. The shear rates involved in calendaring (ε_{cal}), Compression molding (ε_{comp}), extrusion (ε_{ext}), and injection molding (ε_{inj}) processes follow the order

(*a*) $\varepsilon_{inj} < \varepsilon_{cal} < \varepsilon_{ext} < \varepsilon_{comp}$ (*b*) $\varepsilon_{comp} < \varepsilon_{ext} < \varepsilon_{cal} < \varepsilon_{inj}$
(*c*) $\varepsilon_{comp} < \varepsilon_{inj} < \varepsilon_{ext} < \varepsilon_{cal}$ (*d*) $\varepsilon_{comp} < \varepsilon_{cal} < \varepsilon_{ext} < \varepsilon_{inj}$

16. The dynamic mechanical response of a thermoplastic automotive component has shown a loss angle of 45° and storage modulus of 3500 MPa. Calculate the loss modulus (MPa) of the component.

17. Match the terms in Column A with the appropriate terms in Column B:

Column A	Column B
P. processability	1. Rockwell scale
Q. moisture permeation	2.rubber modification
R. hardness	3. melt flow index
S. fracture toughening	4. Fick's law

(*a*) P-3; Q-4; R-2; S-1 (*b*) P-3; Q-4; R-1; S-2
(*c*) P-4; Q-3; R-1; S-2 (*d*) P-4; Q-3; R-2; S-1

18. Match the following additives for plastics with their respective functions:

Column A	Column B
P. dilaurylthiodipropionate	1. solid layer lubricant
Q. graphite	2. flame retardant
R. antimony trioxide	3. reinforcement
S. carbon fibre	4. antioxidant

(*a*) P-4; Q-1; R-2; S-3 (*b*) P-1; Q-4; R-2; S-3
(*c*) P-4; Q-1; R-3; S-2 (*d*) P-1; Q-4; R-3; S-2

19. Match the following catalyst/initiator with the type of polymerization reaction:

Catalyst/initiator	Polymerization reaction
P. butyl lithium	1. Ziegler-Natta
Q. $TiCl_4 + Et_3Al$	2. cationic
R. CuBr	3. anionic
S. H_2SO_4	4. atom transfer radical polymerization

(*a*) P-2; Q-1; R-4; S-3 (*b*) P-2; Q-4; R-1; S-3
(*c*) P-3; Q-1; R-4; S-2 (*d*) P-3; Q-4; R-1; S-2;

20. For AIBN (mol. wt. = 164 gmol-1) initiated free radical polymerization of methyl methacrylate (mol. wt. = 100 gmol-1), where the termination is only by radical coupling, the M_n of PMMA is found to be 4636 gmol-1. Calculate the degree of polymerization.

21. Polymer solution is made by dissolving 5 g of polymer in 1000 ml of solvent. The flow time of the solvent and that of the polymer solution between two appropriate marks in a viscometer are 40 s and 60 s, respectively. The reduced viscosity (in dLg-1) of the polymer solution is:

(*a*) 0.25 (*b*) 0.50
(*c*) 1.0 (*d*) 1.5

22. The volume resistivity of a polymeric material is 107 Ωm. Find the resistance (in MΩ) of a cube of the material of side 1 cm. The direction of current flow is as shown in the figure below.

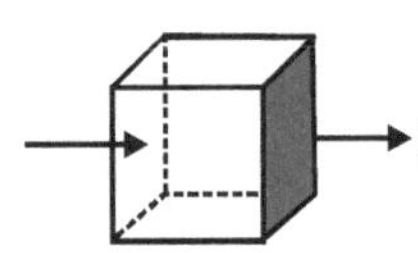

ANSWERS

1. (*b*) **2.** (*c*) **3.** (*a*) **4.** (*d*) **5.** (*a*) **6.** (*b*) **7.** (*d*) **8.** (*c*) **9.** (*c*) **10.** (85.15 to 86.15)
11. (0.48 to 0.50) **12.** (4) **13.** (*b*) **14.** (*a*) **15.** (*d*) **16.** (3500 Mpa) **17.** (*b*) **18.** (*a*) **19.** (*c*) **20.** (45)
21. (*c*) **22.** (1000)

EXPLANATIONS

1. Gel permeation chromatography (GPC) is a type of size exclusion chromatography (SEC) that separates analytes on the basis of size. The technique is often used for the analysis of polymers.

2. **Elastomer**, any rubbery material composed of long chainlike molecules, or polymers, that are capable of recovering their original shape after being stretched to great extents—hence the name *elastomer*, from "elastic polymer." Under normal conditions the long molecules making up an elastomeric material are irregularly coiled. With the application of force, however, the molecules straighten out in the direction in which they are being pulled. Upon release, the molecules spontaneously return to their normal compact, random arrangement. A small force on the elastomer gives the 400-500% strain to it.

3. Generally, polymer blends can be completely miscible, partially miscible or immiscible, depending on the value of ΔGm. The free energy of mixing is given by

$\Delta G_m = \Delta H_m - T.\ \Delta S_m$

For miscibility (binary blend), the following two conditions must be satisfied: the first condition ΔGm < 0; and the second condition

$$\left(\frac{\partial(\Delta Gm}{\partial\phi_i^2}\right)_{T.p} > 0$$

$\Delta Gm < 0$

$\Delta H_m - T.\ \Delta S_m < 0$

$\Delta H/\Delta S < T$

Now we have to wisely choose the condition amongst the options. Option a is only satisfied the condition of miscibility.

4. Elongation: final length –initial length

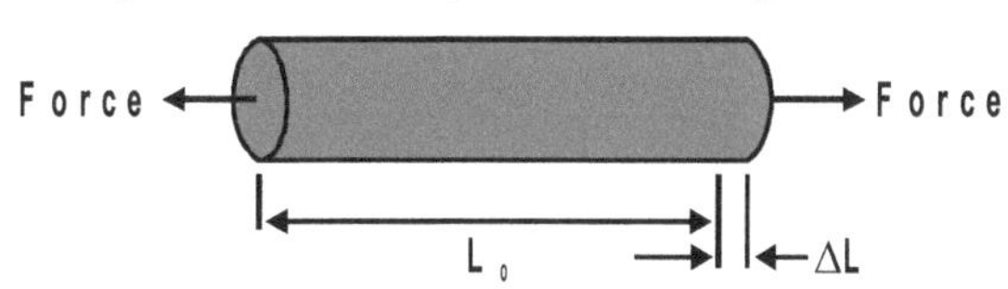

$$\text{Strain} = \frac{\text{Elongation}}{\text{Orininal Length}} = \frac{\Delta L}{L_0}$$

5. Peptizer: Mastication and peptization are processing stages, on the open mill or in the internal mixer, in which the viscosity of the rubber is reduced to a level facilitating further processing or even making processing feasible. Natural molecular weight is very high; Processing of the NR rubber is very difficult due to high molecular weight. Peptizer add at the beginning of the compounding cycle to lower the molecular weight and viscosity and rubber become easy processable.

6. Compression molding, blow molding and injection molding are the batch process. Extrusion is the continuous process. Continuous annular product(Pipes) is produced by only extrusion process.

7. Density α1/branches

Density order: HDPE > LDPE

LDPE (Low Density Polyethylene) has the most excessive branching. This causes the low density to have a less compact molecular structure which is what makes it less dense. It has a density of 0.910 – 0.925 g/cm^3.

HDPE (High Density Polyethylene) has minimal branching of its' polymer chains. Because it is denser it is more rigid and less permeable then the LDPE. It has a density of 0.941 – 0.965 g/cm^3.

LLDPE (Linear Low Density Polyethylene) has a significant number of short branches. Because it has shorter and more branches its chains are able slide against each other upon elongation without becoming entangled like LPDE which has long branching chains that would get caught on each other. This gives LLDPE higher tensile strength and higher impact and puncture resistance than the LDPE. It has a density of 0.91 – 0.94 g/cm^3.

8.

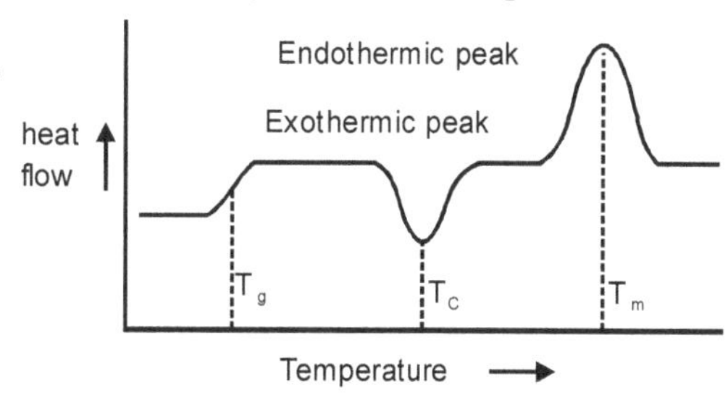

The entire DSC plot, right before your very eyes!

9. Bingham Plastics

Bingham plastics exhibit Newtonian behavior after the shear stress exceeds τ_0. For flow in circular conduits Bingham plastics behave in an interesting fashion.

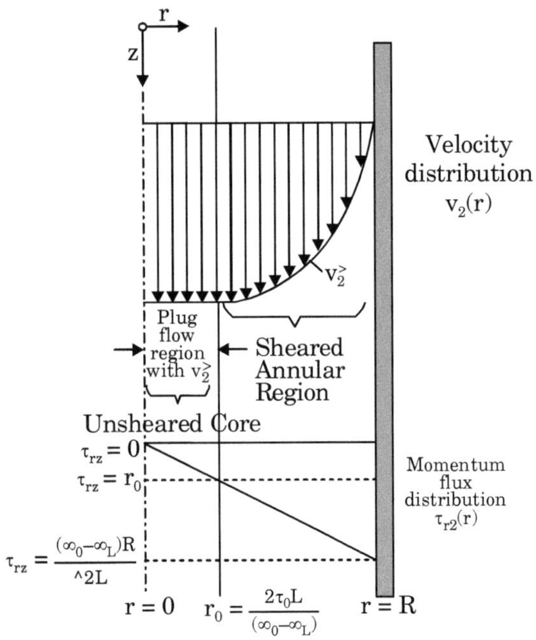

10. Mass fraction of the crystallinity

$$= X_c = \frac{\frac{1}{d_a}-\frac{1}{d}}{\frac{1}{d_a}-\frac{1}{d_c}} = \frac{\frac{1}{866}-\frac{1}{975}}{\frac{1}{866}-\frac{1}{996}} = 0.8565$$

X_c = 85.65% (da= density of amorphous part, dc = density of crystallinity part, d = density of the polymer)

11. The rate expression for initiation may be written as:

$$Ri = \frac{d[M]}{dt} = 2fkd[1]$$

Where [I] represents the initiator concentration and f is the efficiency of the initiator.

Free radical polymerization is the first order reaction;

$$K_d = \frac{0.693}{half\ life \frac{t_1}{2}} = \frac{0.963}{0.1} = 6.93$$

$$Ri = 2 * 0.7 * 0.05 * 6.93 = 0.4851\ \frac{mol}{L.s}$$

12. μ_0 = 20 Pas, $\gamma_0 = 10s^{-1}$ & $\gamma = 40\ s^{-1}$ Put all the values in the above equation

$$\sigma = \frac{40 \times 20}{1+\frac{40}{10}} = 160$$

$\sigma = \eta\gamma$ where η = viscosity

η = 160/40 = 4Pas

13. Ring-opening metathesis polymerization (ROMP) is a type of olefin metathesis chain-growth polymerization. The driving force of the reaction is relief of ring strain in cyclic olefins (e.g. norbornene or cyclopentene). Example: Norborne

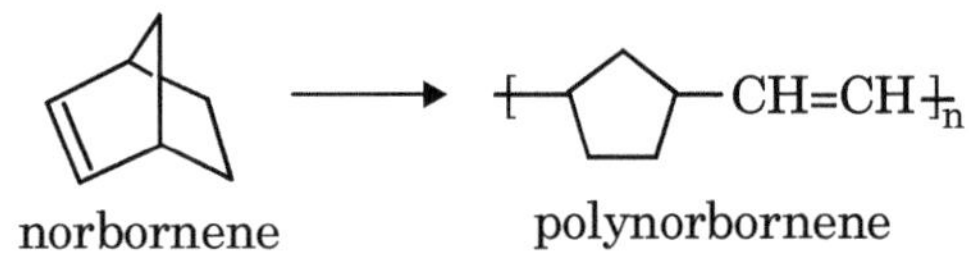

Ring-opening polymerization is a reaction in which one polymer chain has a reactive center on its terminal end that reacts with another cyclic monomer, hence opening its ring system to form a longer polymer chain. The reactive center on the terminal end of the polymer chain can be ionic, cationic, or radical.

14. Toughness is really a measure of the energy a sample can absorb before it breaks.

15.

Processing	**Shear rate (1/s)**
Compression molding	1 to 10
Calendering	10 to 100
Extrusion	100 to 1000
Injection molding	10^3 to 10^4
Fiber spining	$> 10^4$

16. $\tan\delta = \frac{\text{loss modulus}}{\text{storage modulus}}$

Loss modulus = ?

Storage modulus = 3500MPa

δ = 45

Loss modulus = tan45* 3500 = 3500MPa

17.
1. **Fick's law :** It states that 'the rate of diffusion is proportional to both the surface area and concentration difference and is inversely proportional to the thickness of the membrane'. Fick's law can be written as: **Rate of diffusion α surface area × concentration difference thickness of membrane**.
2. **Melt flow index :** It gives the tentative idea about the polymer processability. Higher value of melt flow index indicates good processability.
3. **Hardness :** Rockwell, Shore A & Shore B is the measurement method of Hardness.
4. **Fracture Toughening :** Rubber modification.

18. 1. Generally fillers incorporated in rubber composites can be divided into two categories, reinforcing and non-reinforcing fillers. The reinforcing fillers play a significant role in increasing or at least maintaining the strength of rubber composites, while the non-reinforcing fillers are added to reduce cost. **Carbon black (CB) and silica** have been used as the main reinforcing fillers that increase the usefulness of rubbers.

2. Flame retardants (FR)are chemical compounds added with an objective to inhibit/retard the ignition/burning of the plastic. Brominated (BFRs), Chlorinated (CFRs), Phosphorous (PFRs), Alumina Trihydrate (ATH), Magnesium Hydroxide (MDH), Antimony Oxide etc.

3. Dry lubricants or solid lubricants are materials that, despite being in the solid phase, are able to reduce friction between two surfaces sliding against each other without the need for a liquid oil medium. Graphite and molybdenum disulfide (MoS2) are the predominant materials used as solid lubricant.

4. Antioxidants are used to prevent thermal degradation and inhibit oxidation (i.e. degradation). Hindered Amine, Hindered Phenol, Thioesters, Phosphites, Hydroxylamines , dithiopropionate etc.

19. 1. Ziegler-Natta catalyst: These are complex catalyst systems derived from a transition metal compound from groups IVB to VIIIB of the periodic table and an organometallic compound usually from a group IA or IIIA metal. Aluminium alkyls (AlEt or $AlEt_2Cl$) acts as electron acceptor in combination with the electron donor titanium chloride ($TiCl_3$ & $TiCl_4$) are used most commonly.

2. Cationic catalyst: Strong Lewis acid like boron trifluoride (BF_3) or Friedel–Crafts catalysts such as $AlCl_3$, H_2SO_4, $SnCl_4$ and $TiCl_4$

3. Anionic catalyst: Strong base Butyl lithium, triphenylmethyl potassium, ethyl sodium, alkali metal amides, alcoxides and hyderoxides

20. Decomposition of the AIBN catalyst is

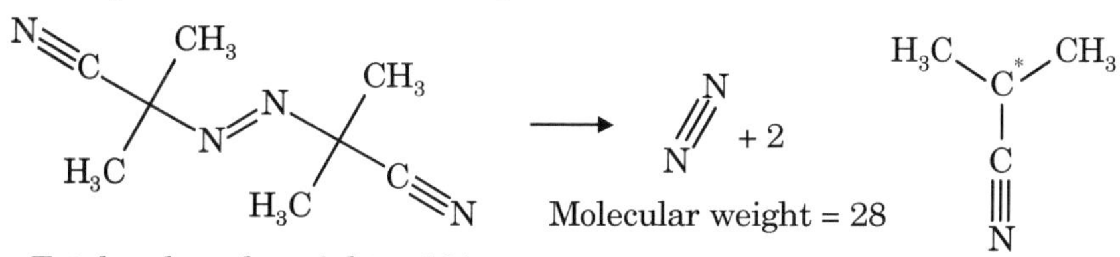

Total molecualr weight = 164   Molecular weight = 28   Molecular weight = 136

(i) Radical formation : $I \xrightarrow{\text{UV Energy}} 2I+$

(ii) Initiatior $I^* + C = C \longrightarrow I - C - C^*$

(iii)Propagation: $I - C - C - + C = C \longrightarrow I - C - C - C - C^*$

(iv) Termination : $I - C - C^* + = C - C - I \longrightarrow I - C - C - C - C - I$

Termination by coupling; free radical active center are present at the both end of the polymer chain length.

AIBN Total molecular weight is = 164; Part of AIBN present in the polymer which molecular weight is = 136

Polymer weight = 4636 – 136 = 4500

Degree of polymerization

= Polymer weight/monomer weight

$= \dfrac{4500}{100} = 45$

MMA monomer weight = 100

21. The time of flow of liquid depends on the viscosity and composition. If η and η_o are the absolute viscosities of a solution and the pure solvent, respectively, and t and to are their corresponding ratio of flow times.

$\frac{t}{t_0} = \frac{\eta}{\eta_o} = \eta_r$ $\frac{60}{40} = \frac{\eta}{\eta_o} = 1.5$

concentration C = 5/1000 = 0.5 dl/gm [1dl = 100ml]

Reduced viscosity $\frac{\eta_{sp}}{C} = \eta_{red}, dl/g$ Specific viscosity $\eta_{sp} = \eta_r - 1 = 1.5 - 1 = 0.5$

Reduced viscosity = 0.5/0.5 = 1 dl/g.

22. R = ρ L /A where L = length, A = are of cross section and ρ = volume resistivity

L = 1cm and Area = 1*1 cm^2

Resistance R = 10^{7*} 10^{-2} / 10^{-4} = 109Ω

R = 1000 MΩ

SOLVED PAPER - 2013

1. In free radical polymerization, one of the following techniques permits simultaneous increase in rate of polymerization and polymer molecular weight.

(a) Solution polymerization.

(b) Suspension polymerization.

(c) Bulk polymerization.

(d) Emulsion polymerization.

2. The shear modulus, G, of plastic is related to the elastic modulus, E, and the Poisson ratio, as

(a) $E = 2(1 - \upsilon)\ G$ (b) $G = 2(1 + \upsilon)\ E$

(c) $E = 2(1 + \upsilon)\ G$ (d) $E = (1 + \upsilon)\ G$

3. LLDPE is obtained by

(a) Ziegler-Natta polymerization of ethylene.

(b) free-Radical polymerization of ethylene.

(c) free-Radical polymerization of ethylene and alpha-olefins.

(d) Ziegler-Natta copolymerization of ethylene and alpha-olefins.

4. A hindered phenol is added to a polyolefin

(a) to increase ozone resistance

(b) to increase foamability

(c) to increase oxidation resistance

(d) to increase crosslinkability

5. Stretching of rubber leads to

(a) decrease in alignment of polymer chains

(b) increase in alignment of polymer chains

(c) no change in alignment of polymer chains

(d) decrease in strength of rubber

6. In a cone and plate viscometer, the rate of strain is related to the speed of rotation of the cone, ? (radian/second), and the angle between the cone and the plate, ? (radian), by the following relation

(a) $\omega\alpha$ (b) $\omega\ \cos\omega\alpha$

(c) α/ω (d) ω/α

7. The tensile breaking strength of polycarbonate (I), low density polyethylene (II), polystyrene (III) and polypropylene (IV) can be arranged as

(a) IV > II > I > III (b) I > II > IV > III

(c) I > III > IV > II (d) III > I > II > IV

8. High molecular weight polymers could be obtained even at low monomer conversion in case of

(a) Step growth polymerization

(b) Living polymerization

(c) Chain growth polymerization

(d) Solid state polymerization

9. A reinforced polymer composite is made by the incorporation of

(a) elastomers into the polymer.

(b) fibers into the polymer.

(c) plasticizers into the polymer.

(d) gaseous additives into the polymer.

10. Match the following for free-radical copolymerization of two monomers with reactivity ratios, r1 and r2.

Reactivity Ratios	**Copolymer Nature**
P. r1 = r2 = 0	1. Random copolymer
Q. r1 = r2 = 1	2. Alternate copolymer
R. r1 >1, r2 > 1	3. Block copolymer
S. 0 < r1r2 < 1	4. Random-Block copolymer

(a) P-2; Q-1; R-3; S-4 (b) P-3; Q-1; R-2; S-4

(c) P-2; Q-4; R-3; S-1 (d) P-2; Q-3; R-1; S-4

11. The relative viscosity of a 1% solution (weight/volume) of a given polymer was found to be 1.1. The inherent viscosity of this polymer will be

(a) 0.065 dl/g (b) 0.075 dl/g

(c) 0.085 dl/g (d) 0.095 dl/g

12. Match the following in case of step-growth polymerization, where A reacts only with B, and reacts only with A (Note: A – A is expressed as A_2, and A

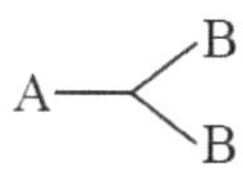

is expressed as AB_2).

Monomers	Polymer
P. $A_2 + AB_3$	1. Hyperbranched Polymer
Q. AB_2	2. Crosslinked Polymer
R. $AB + B_3$	3. Star Polymer
S. $A_2 + B_2$	4. Linear Polymer

(a) P–2: Q–3; R–1; S–4 (b) P–2: Q–1; R–3; S–4
(c) P–1: Q–2; R–3; S–4 (d) P–2: Q–4; R–1; S–3

13. Match each of the following additives for plastics with its function

Additive	Function
P. α-Cellulose	1. Flame retarder
Q. Zinc chromate	2. Plasticizer extender
R. Alumina trihydrate	3. Organic fibrous filler
S. Chlorinated paraffin wax	4. Colorant

(a) P-1; Q-2; R-3; S-4 (b) P-2; Q-3; R-4; S-1
(c) P-3; Q-4; R-1; S-2 (d) P-4; Q-1; R-2; S-3

14. The length of a glass fiber reinforced polymer increased by 0.03mm, from its initial length of 100mm, when the temperature was changed from -30°C to +30°C. The coefficient of linear thermal expansion is

(a) 1.03×10^{-5} °C^{-1} (b) 9.82×10^{-6} °C^{-1}
(c) 5.00×10^{-6} °C^{-1} (d) 14.4×10^{-5} °C^{-1}

15. A 40mm × 40mm square polymer composite sample with 5mm thickness (heat transfer distance) exhibited a heat flow rate of 60W, when the temperatures of the warm and cold surfaces were 90 °C and 25 °C respectively. The thermal conductivity of the sample in W.m^{-1}.K^{-1}

(a) 5.67 (b) 15.3
(c) 2.88 (d) 0.667

16. An extruder is supplied with 40 kW of power. The mass flow rate of a polymer through the extruder is 240 kg h^{-1} and the specific heat capacity of the polymer is 4 kJ kg^{-1} K^{-1}. The maximum possible temperature rise in the polymer is

(a) 150 K (b) 100 K
(c) 600 K (d) Zero

Common Data Questions

Common Data for Questions 17 and 18:

For a given free-radical polymerization, the only mode of termination is the bimolecular termination and there is no chain transfer. The final polymer produced was analyzed to contain an average of 1.60 initiator fragments per polymer chain.

17. Percentage of final polymer chains containing one initiator fragment per chain is

(a) 40 % (b) 50 %
(c) 60 % (d) 70 %

18. Percentage of polymer radicals terminated by coupling is

(a) 65 % (b) 75 %
(c) 85 % (d) 95 %

Common Data for Questions 19 and 20:

For the synthesis of polyester, 1.5 mole of pentaerythritol (tetra-ol) was reacted with 1.0 mole of a tricarboxylic acid.

19. The extent of reaction when the number average degree of polymerization of the reaction mixture approaches infinity is

(a) 80.33% (b) 83.33%
(c) 84.33% (d) 86.33%

20. The number average degree of polymerization of the reaction mixture when the polymerization was stopped at 80% conversion, is

(a) 1000 (b) 100
(c) 50 (d) 25

Linked Answer Questions

Statement for Linked Answer Questions 21 and 22:

A viscoelastic fluid is modeled as a spring and two dashpots, all connected in series. The spring has elastic modulus G and the fluids in two dashpots have viscosities η_1 and η_2.

21. The constitutive equation (relation between stress α and γ in which overdot represents the time derivative) for the fluid is:

(a) $\sigma = G\gamma + (\eta_1 + \eta_2)\dot{\gamma}$ (b) $\sigma = G\gamma + (\eta_1 - \eta_2)\dot{\gamma}$

(c) $\dot{\gamma} = \frac{\dot{\sigma}}{G} + \left(\frac{1}{\eta_1} + \frac{1}{\eta_2}\right)\sigma$ (d) $\dot{\gamma} = \frac{\dot{\sigma}}{G} + \frac{\sigma}{\eta_1 + \eta_2}$

22. For a periodic stress $_0e^{i\ \ t}$ the strain is given by

(a) $\gamma = \sigma_0\left[\frac{1}{G} + \frac{i}{\omega}\left(\frac{1}{\eta_1} + \frac{1}{\eta_2}\right)\right]e^{i\omega t}$

(b) $\gamma = \sigma_0\left[\frac{1}{G} - \frac{i}{\omega}\left(\frac{1}{\eta_1} + \frac{1}{\eta_2}\right)\right]e^{i\omega t}$

(c) $\gamma = \left[\sigma_0 + (\eta_1 + \eta_2)\omega i\right]\frac{e^{i\omega t}}{G}$

(d) $\gamma = \left[\sigma_0 - (\eta_1 + \eta_2)\omega i\right]\frac{e^{i\omega t}}{G}$

ANSWERS

1. (*d*)	**2.** (*c*)	**3.** (*d*)	**4.** (*c*)	**5.** (*b*)	**6.** (*d*)	**7.** (*c*)	**8.** (*c*)	**9.** (*b*)	**10.** (*a*)
11. (*d*)	**12.** (*)	**13.** (*c*)	**14.** (*c*)	**15.** (*c*)	**16.** (*a*)	**17.** (*a*)	**18.** (b)	**19.** (*b*)	**20.** (*d*)
21. (*c*)	**22.** (*b*)								

EXPLANATIONS

1. Emulsion polymerization
2. E = 2G(1 + V)
3.

(A) Ziegler-Natta polymerization of ethylene.	HDPE
(B) free-Radical polymerization of ethylene.	LDPE
(C) free-Radical polymerization of ethylene and alpha-olefins.	------
(D) Ziegler-Natta copolymerization of ethylene and alpha-olefins.	LLDPE

4. Phenols (ArOH) are known to reduce the rates of oxidation of organic matter by transferring a H atom (from their OH groups) to the chain-carrying ROO* radicals, a mechanism that most likely involves a concerted transfer of the hydrogen as a proton and of one electron between the two oxygen atoms, O-H---O* (proton-coupled electron transfer mechanism). The antioxidant capabilities of phenols are strongly reduced by hydrogen-bond accepting solvents since the hydrogen-bonded molecules ArOH---S are virtually unreactive toward ROO* radicals.
5. Rubber is composed of long hydrocarbon chains that are interlinked to one another at very distant intervals along the polymer backbone. These chains tend to form random coils -- you might think of them as very long chains of spaghetti. When you pull on the rubber band, the chains tend to uncoil and partially align with one another. However, because the chains are linked together by these bridging bonds, there is a limit to how much the coils can be stretched out. When that point is reached it gets harder to stretch the rubber band any further.

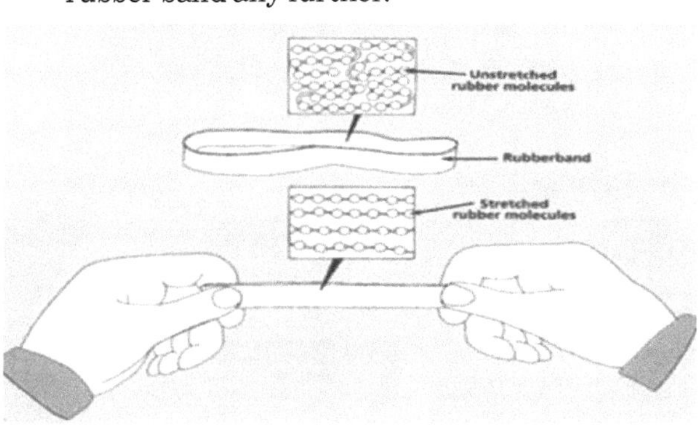

6. Rate of strian G(1/sec) =

Speed of rotation (radian/sec)/the angle between the cone and the plate (radian)

$G = \omega/\alpha$

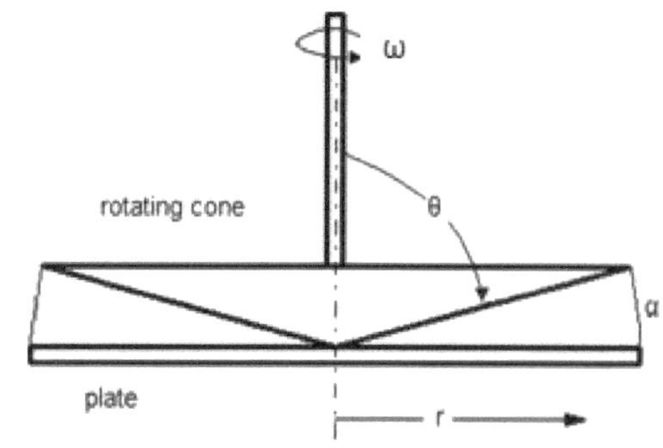

7. Crystallinity makes a material strong, but it also makes it brittle. A completely crystalline polymer would be too brittle to be used as plastic. The amorphous regions give polymer toughness, that is, the ability to bend without breaking. Higher the crystallinity in the polymer region required more force to break it. In other words, Lower the glass transition temp lower the tensile strength.

Polymer	Glass Transition temp
PC	147°C
PS	100°C
PE	-125°C
PP	5-15°C

8. Chain-growth polymerization or chain polymerization is a polymerization technique where unsaturated monomer molecules add onto the active site of a growing polymer chain one at a time. Growth of the polymer occurs only at one (or possibly more) ends. Addition of each monomer unit regenerates the active site. This type of polymerization results in high molecular weight polymer being formed at low conversion. This final weight is determined by the rate of propagation compared to the rate of individual chain termination, which includes both chain transfer and chain termination steps. Above a certain ceiling temperature, no polymerization occurs.

9. Polymer Matrix Composites combine a resin system and reinforcing fibres, the properties of the resulting composite material will combine something of the properties of the resin on its own with that of the fibres on their own.

10. 1. An alternating copolymer consists of two different repeat units that alternate in sequence in the polymer chain. A regularity in repetition of structural units is only possible if the two monomers M_1 or M_2 are unable to hompolymerize or have a strong preference to react with each other (quasi alternating copolymer). This is only the case if the reactivity ratios defined by

$$r_1 = \frac{k_{11}}{k_{12}}$$

$$r_2 = \frac{k_{22}}{k_{21}}$$

approach zero,

$$r_1 = r_2 \text{ H} \approx 0,$$

It means K_{11} & $K_{22} = 0$; Monomer 1 will react with monomer 2 and vice versa.

2. Random Copolymer

$$r_1 = r_2 = 1,$$

$$K_{11} = K_{12} \;\&\; K_{22} = K_{21}$$

Monomer 1 react with monomer 2 or as well as monomer 1; similarly Monomer 2 react with monomer 2 or as well as monomer 1. No preference to monomer. In the Resulting copolymer arrangement of monomers are random.

3. Block copolymer

$$r_1 > 1 \;\&\; r_2 > 1$$

$$K_{11} > K_{12} \;\&\; K_{22} > K_{21}$$

Monomer 1 give preference to monomer 1 & monomer 2 give to the preference to monomer 2. So, block type arrangement of monomers present in the copolymer

4. Random-block copolymer

$$0 < r_1 r_2 < 1$$

May be $r_1 > 1$ or $r_2 < 1$ or $r_2 > 1$ or $r_1 < 1$

In both the condition one monomer prefer the block copolymer and second will prefer random copolymer.

11. Inherent Viscosity dL/g

$$\eta_{in\,h} = \frac{(\ln \eta_r)}{C}$$

Inherent Viscosity $\eta_{in\,h}$

$$= \frac{\ln \eta_r}{C} = \frac{\ln 1.1}{1} = 0.095$$

12. [Question has some technical error.][Marks to all]

13.

Additive	Function
P. α-Cellulose	3. Organic fibrous filler
Q. Zinc chromate	4. Colorant
R. Alumina trihydrate	1. Flame retarder
S. Chlorinated paraffin wax	2. Plasticizer extender

Wax is used as plasticizer in the rubber or plastic industries to reduce the viscosity and friction.

14. $$\frac{\Delta L}{L} = \alpha[\Delta T]$$

ΔL = change in Length

ΔT = Change in Temperature

α = Coefficient of Thermal Expansion (CTE)

$\Delta L = 0.03$ mm; $L = 100$ mm; $\Delta T = 30 - (-)\,30 = 60°C$

$$\frac{0.03}{100} = \alpha.60$$

$$\alpha = 5.00 \times 10^{-6} °C^{-1}$$

15.

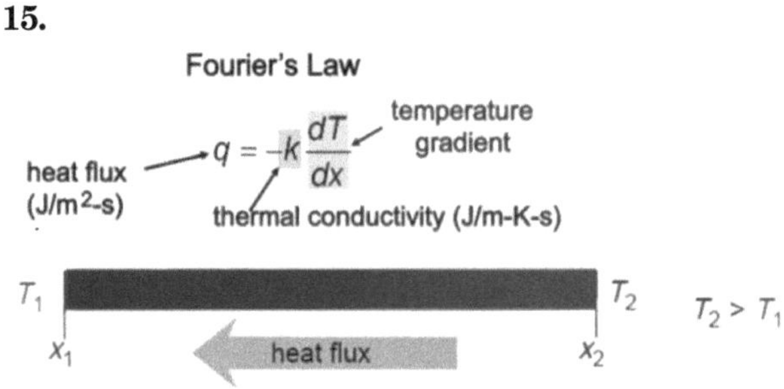

Thermal conductivity can be calculated from a number of measured quantities, but normally is defined as: the quantity of Heat Q, transmitted through a thickness L, in a direction normal to a surface with area A, due to a temperature difference, under steady state condition and when the heat transfer is dependent only on the temperature gradient.

$$k = \frac{Q \times L}{A \times \Delta T}$$

Q = 60W, L =5mm, $\Delta T = 90 - 25 = 65$ °C,

Area(A) = 40mm*40mm = 1600mm^2

$k = 60 \times 5*10^{-3} / (1600*10^{-6} \times 65)$

k = 2.88

16. Power = energy/time Energy = $mc_p\,\Delta T$

$P = mc_p\,\Delta T/T$

$\Delta T = P \times T/(m\,C_p)$, m/T = 240 kg/h

$\Delta T = 40*10^3 \times 3600/(240*4*103)$

ΔT= 150K

19. $\overline{X}_n = \dfrac{1+r}{1+r-2rp_A}$

$r = N_A/N_B = 1.5/1 = 1.5$

When the number average degree of polymerization of the reaction mixture approaches infinity it means [1 + r – 2rp] goes to zero.

1+ 1.2 - 2*1.5*P = 0

P = 0.8333

P = 83.33%

20. $\overline{X}_n = \dfrac{1+r}{1+r-2rp_A}$

r =1.5 & p=0.8

X_n= [1+1.5]/ [1+1.5-2*1.5*0.8]

X_n = 25

21. In the series stress is constant.

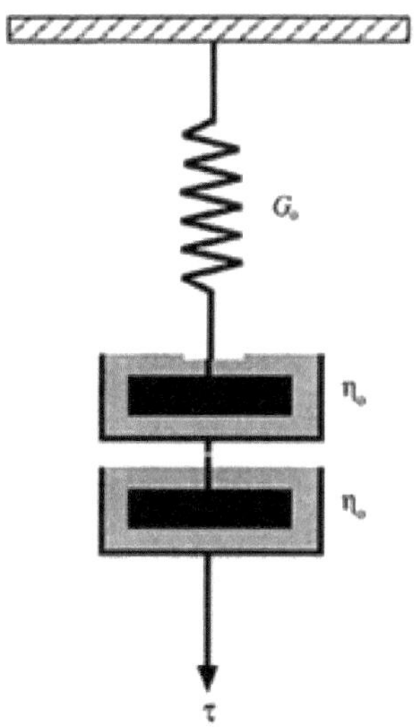

For spring strain = $\varepsilon_1 = \dfrac{\sigma}{G}$

Total strain = $\varepsilon_1 + \varepsilon_2 + \varepsilon_3$

For dashpot 1 & 2 strain rate $\dfrac{d\varepsilon}{dt} = \dfrac{\sigma}{\eta}$

Take differentiation both sides:

$$\frac{d\varepsilon_t}{dt} = \frac{d\varepsilon_1}{dt} + \frac{d\varepsilon_2}{dt} + \frac{d\varepsilon_3}{dt}$$

$$= \frac{d\sigma}{dt} + \frac{\sigma_1}{\eta_1} + \sigma_2$$

$$= \frac{d\sigma}{dt} + \sigma\left(\frac{1}{\eta_1} + \frac{1}{\eta_2}\right)$$

22. Total strain = $\varepsilon_1 + \varepsilon_2 + \varepsilon_3$

$\varepsilon_1 = \dfrac{\sigma_0 e^{i\omega t}}{G}$ (for spring),

For Dashpots

$\sigma = \eta\dfrac{d\varepsilon}{dt}, \sigma_0 e^{i\omega t} = \eta\dfrac{d\varepsilon}{dt}$

take both sides integrations

$\varepsilon = \dfrac{\sigma_0 e^{i\omega t}}{\eta . i\omega}$ put all the values in the total strain

$$\varepsilon = \sigma_0\left[\frac{1}{G} - \frac{i}{\omega}\left(\frac{1}{\eta_1} + \frac{1}{\eta_2}\right)\right]$$

SOLVED PAPER - 2012

1. The diamine used for the synthesis of nylon 6,4 is

(*a*) tetramethylene diamine

(*b*) hexamethylene diamine

(*c*) phenylene diamine

(*d*) cyclohexane-1,4-diamine

2. A small amount of hydroquinone is added to methyl methacrylate monomer in order to

(*a*) improve its thermal stability

(*b*) improve its hydrolytic stability

(*c*) inhibit polymerization

(*d*) regulate molecular

3. Which of the following compounds is used in Zeigler-Natta catalyst?

(*a*) $TiCl_3$ (*b*) $CaCl_2$

(*c*) $ZnCl_2$ (*d*) NaCl

4. The z-average molecular weight, Mz can be estimated using

(*a*) End group analysis

(*b*) Osmometry

(*c*) Viscometry

(*d*) Ultracentrifugation

5. The unit of intrinsic viscosity is

(*a*) dl/g (*b*) g/dl

(*c*) poise (*d*) g/mol

6. Heat dissipation is most inefficient in

(*a*) Emulsion polymerization

(*b*) Solution polymerization

(*c*) Bulk polymerization

(*d*) Suspension polymerization

7. The crystalline melting temperature of the polymers high density polyethylene (HDPE), isotactic polypropylene (iPP), nylon 6 (PA6) and poly(ethylene terephthalate) (PET) can be arranged as

(*a*) THDPE > TPET > TiPP > TPA6

(*b*) TPET > TPA6 > TiPP > THDPE

(*c*) TPA6 > THDPE > TPET > TiPP

(*d*) TiPP > TPA6 > TPET > THDPE

8. Which of the following polymers is sensitive to moisture absorption?

(*a*) Polyethylene

(*b*) Polystyrene

(*c*) Polyamide 6

(*d*) Polybutadiene

9. Most engineering polymers have heat distortion temperature (HDT) in excess of

(*a*) –80°C (*b*) 0°C

(*c*) 20°C (*d*) 80°C

10. Two miscible polymers A and B are blended in weight ratio of 30:70. If the glass transition temperature, T_g of polymer A is –50°C and that of polymer B is 100°C, then the T_g of the blend is

(*a*) –10.5°C (*b*) 25.0°C

(*c*) 37.5°C (*d*) 74.8°C

11. If the flow curves of two viscous fluids are represented by

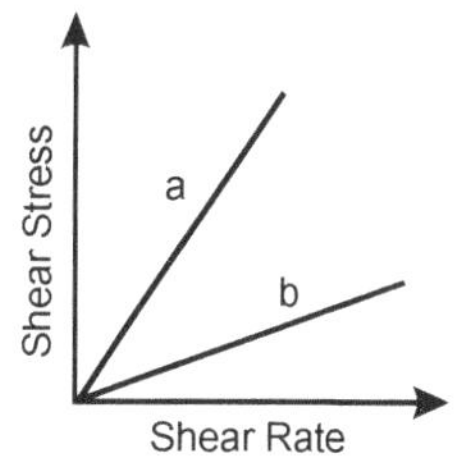

then, the viscosity plots of the fluids will be

(*a*) 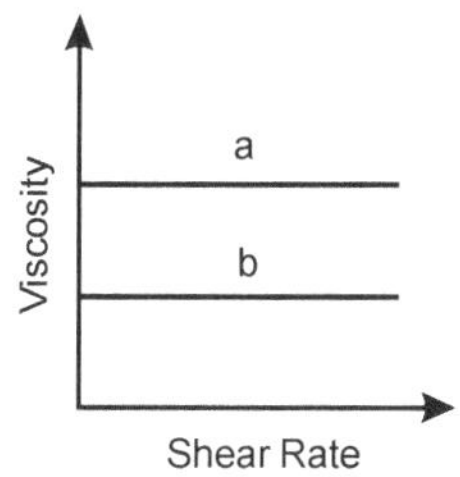

(*b*) 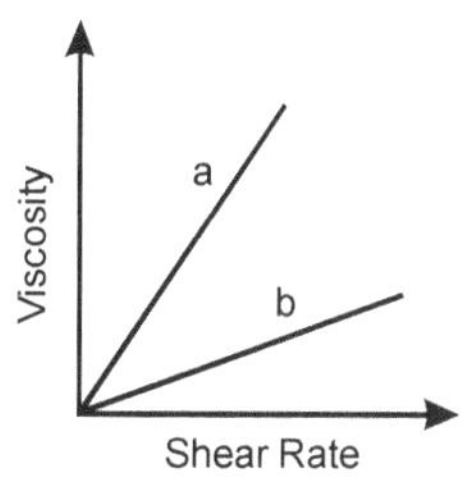

(*c*) 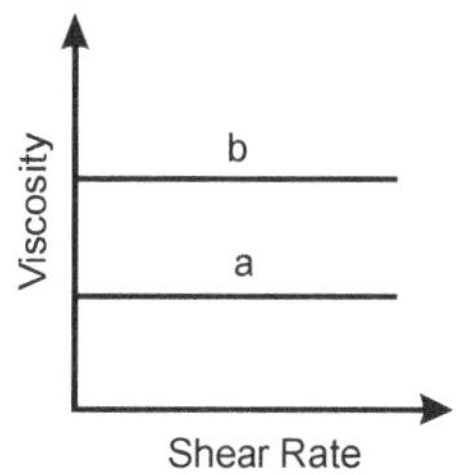

(*d*) 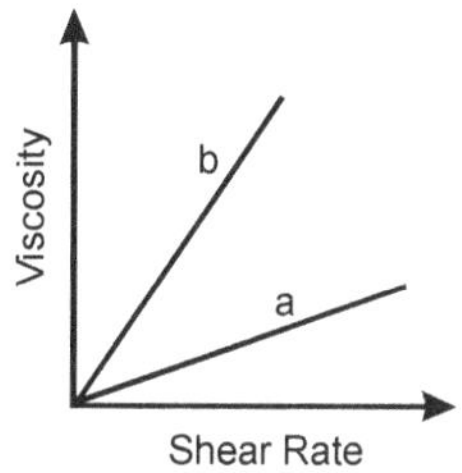

12. Match the following **compounding ingredients** in plastic technology with their respective **functions**:

Compounding ingredients	**Functions**
P. Tricresyl phosphate	1. Filler
Q. Calcium carbonate	2. UV stabilizer
R. Azodicarbonamide	3. Plasticizer
S. *o*-Hydroxybenzophenone	4. Blowing agent

(*a*) P-3, Q-1, R-4, S-2 (*b*) P-1, Q-4, R-3, S-2
(*c*) P-4, Q-1, R-2, S-3 (*d*) P-3, Q-4, R-1, S-2

13. In a three-point bending mode for flexural test of a polymer sample with the following data:

load applied in the mid-span = 80 kg
width of the specimen = 3 cm
depth of the specimen = 2 cm
length of the specimen = 30 cm

the flexural strength will be
(*a*) 17.5 MPa (*b*) 29.4 MPa
(*c*) 35.7 MPa (*d*) 41.3 MPa

14. How many stereo isomers are possible in total on polymerization of butadiene?
(*a*) 2 (*b*) 3
(*c*) 4 (*d*) 5

15. Match the following **processing operations** with their respective **tools:**

Processing operations	**Tools**
P. Injection molding	1. Parison mold
Q. Twin screw extrusion	2. Sprue-runner system
R. Blow molding	3. Mixing head
S. Reaction injection molding	4. Kneading blocks

(*a*) P-1, Q-2, R-3, S-4 (*b*) P-2, Q-4, R-1, S-3
(*c*) P-2, Q-1, R-4, S-3 (*d*) P-4, Q-1, R-2, S-3

16. If a solid elastomer ball of weight 100 g is allowed to free fall from a height of 10 m and it rebounds back to a height of 8 m, the hysteresis loss is
(*a*) 19.60 J (*b*) 9.80 J
(*c*) 1.96 J (*d*) 0.98 J

Common Data for Questions 17 and 18:

A polymer mixture contains three monodisperse polystyrene samples A, B and C of molecular weights 10000, 20000 and 30000 g mol^{-1}, respectively.

17. If the mixture contains equal number of molecules of A, B and C, the weight average molecular weight, *Mw* will be
(*a*) 1.93×10^4 g mol^{-1}
(*b*) 2.13×10^4 g mol^{-1}
(*c*) 2.33×10^4 g mol^{-1}
(*d*) 2.53×10^4 g mol^{-1}

18. If the mixture contains equal masses of A, B and C, then the number average molecular weight, *Mn* will be
(*a*) 1.64 * 10^4 g mol^{-1}
(*b*) 1.74 * 10^4 g mol^{-1}
(*c*) 1.84 *10^4 g mol^{-1}
(*d*) 1.94 * 10^4 g mol^{-1}

Common Data for Questions 19 and 20:

The stress relaxation equation for polymers is given by, $\sigma = \sigma_0\, e^{-t/\tau}$,where σ is the stress at any time instant t, σ_0 is the initial stress and τ is the relaxation time. The relaxation process is temperature dependent and follows the Arrhenius law. For a rubber sample, the relaxation time is 60 days at 25°C.

19. If the above sample is stressed to 2 MPa initially, then the time required to relax the stress to 1 MPa will be
(*a*) 31.6 days (*b*) 41.6 days
(*c*) 51.6 days (*d*) 61.6 days

20. If the activation energy for relaxation is 30 KJ/mol, the relaxation time at 35°C will be
(*a*) 30.5 days (*b*) 35.5 days
(*c*) 40.5 days (*d*) 45.5 days

Statement for Linked Answer Questions 21 and 22:

In tensile testing of carbon fiber reinforced epoxy composite samples, the following data were recorded:
gauge length = 4 cm
cross-section = 0.8 cm × 0.3 cm
increase in gauge length at the break point = 0.03 cm
breaking load = 50 kg

21. Considering the stress-strain curve to be linear up to the break point, the tensile strength is
(*a*) 191.2 kg/cm^2 (*b*) 208.3 kg/cm^2
(*c*) 312.1 kg/cm^2 (*d*) 535.5 kg/cm^2

22. The Young's modulus of the composite is
(*a*) 1.77×10^4 kg/cm^2 (*b*) 1.99×10^4 kg/cm^2
(*c*) 2.34×10^4 kg/cm^2 (*d*) 2.77×10^4 kg/cm^2

ANSWERS

1. (*b*)	**2.** (*c*)	**3.** (*a*)	**4.** (*d*)	**5.** (*a*)	**6.** (*c*)	**7.** (*b*)	**8.** (*c*)	**9.** (*d*)	**10.** (*c*)
11. (*a*)	**12.** (*a*)	**13.** (*b*)	**14.** (*d*)	**15.** (*b*)	**16.** (*c*)	**17.** (*c*)	**18.** (*a*)	**19.** (*b*)	**20.** (*c*)
21. (*b*)	**22.** (*d*)								

EXPLANATIONS

1.

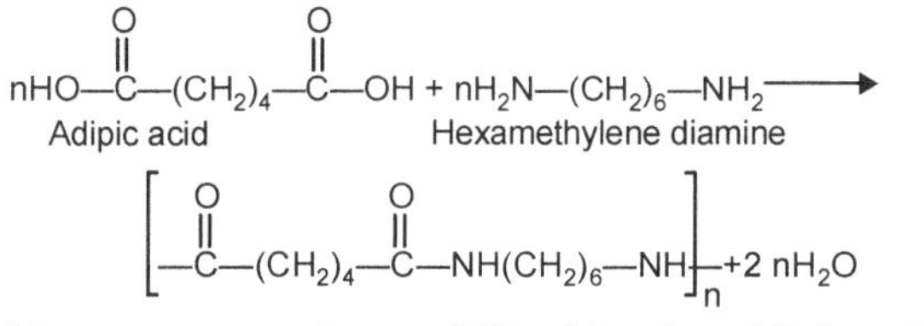

2. Monomers are often stabilized by the addition of inhibitors to prevent polymerization initiation by light, heat and air. For example, stable radical compounds which can trap free radicals are used to inhibit radical polymerization.

3. Zeigler-Natta complex catalyst systems derived from a transition metal compound from groups IVB to VIIIB of the periodic table and an organometallic compound usually from a group IA or IIIA metal. Aluminium alkyls(AlEt or $AlEt_2Cl$) acts as electron acceptor in combination with the electron donor titanium chloride ($TiCl_3$& $TiCl_4$) are used most commonly. The complex formed is insoluble in the solvent and is, hence, heterogeneous in nature.

4.

Technique	Measures	Range, g/mol
End Group	M_n	up to 2500
Osmometry	M_n	15000 – 750000
Ebulliometry	M_n	up to 100000
Light scattering	M_w	20000 to 10^7
Ultra centrifuge	M_w,M_z,MWD	2000 to 10^7
Solution viscosity	M_v, M_w	15000 – 10^6
Vapour-phase osmometry	M_n	up to 25000
Gel-permiation chromatography	M_n, M_w, M_v, M_z, MWD	up to 10^6

5. Intrinsic Viscosity dL/g [h]

$$[\eta] = \left(\frac{\eta_{sp}}{C}\right) | C \to 0$$

6. Bulk polymerization of pure liquid monomer is the simplest process and carried out by using initiator in the absence of diluent or solvent. For this process reaction rate is high due to high monomer concentration and result in high yield per volume of reactor. Another advantage is that the relatively pure product is produced. However, control of the bulk polymerization, exothermic in nature, is difficult. The viscosity of the reaction system increases rapidly even at relatively low conversion. The heat removal is difficult due to high viscosity and low thermal conductivity of the polymer melt. Consequently local hot spots may occur resulting in degradation and discoloration of the polymer product. Bulk polymerization requires careful temperature control and strong elaborate stirring equipment. Though, bulk polymerization is commercially less used, polymerization of ethylene, styrene and methyl methcrylate are carried out by this method. The heat dissipation and viscosity problem are reduced by carrying out polymerization at low conversion. Bulk polymerization can be carried out in conventional stirred tank reactor, long tubular reactor with high surface to volume ratio and screw extruder reactors.

7.

HDPE	iPP	PA6	PET
134°C	165°C	220°C	260°C

Presence of aromatic group in the PET increases the melting point. Nylon 6, polar group increases the chain attraction between the chains hence increases the melting point compared to PP. PP has –CH3 side group in the structure increase the melting point compared to HDPE.

8. Polyamide is more sensitive to moisture absorption due to presence of the functional group $-NH_2$.

9. Heat deflection temperature is a **measure of polymer's resistance to distortion under a given load at elevated temperature**. HDT value for commodity polymer is below 80°C whereas engineering plastic its value is higher than the 80°C.

10. Convert all the temperature in the Kelvin from centigrade. Total weight fraction is equal to 1.

$$\frac{1}{T_g} = \frac{W_1}{T_{g_1}} + \frac{W_2}{T_{g_2}}$$

$$\frac{1}{T_g} = \frac{0.3}{223} + \frac{0.7}{373}$$

$$T_g = 37.36°C$$

11. Shear stress α strain rate

$$\sigma = \eta \, d\varepsilon/dt$$

Viscosity is constant

From the question if strain rate is same for the both the situation and stress is different than viscosity is higher in the case where stress is higher.

12.

carbonamide	Blowing agent	Play a role in the formation of air bubbles by breaking down into gas at high temperature.
Calcium carbonate	Filler	Used as fillers in rubber industry
Tricresyl phosphate	plasticizer	Additives increase plasticity
o-Hydroxyben-zophenone	UV stabilizer	The primary function is to protect the substance from the long term UV degradation effects from ultraviolet radition.

13. Flexural strength $\sigma_f = \frac{3FL}{2bd^2}$

where, **F** is the force at midspan, **L** is the support span, **h** the specimen thickness, b the width and **s** is the selection of the tensile surface of the specimen at midpoint

Force = mg = 80*9.8

$$\text{Flexural strength } \sigma_f = \frac{3 \times 80 \times 9.8 \times 0.3}{2 \times 0.03 \times 0.02^2}$$

$$= 29.4 \text{ MPa}$$

14. Stereoisomerism in which two substances have the same molecular formula and the same constitution but differ in the arrangement of their atoms in space

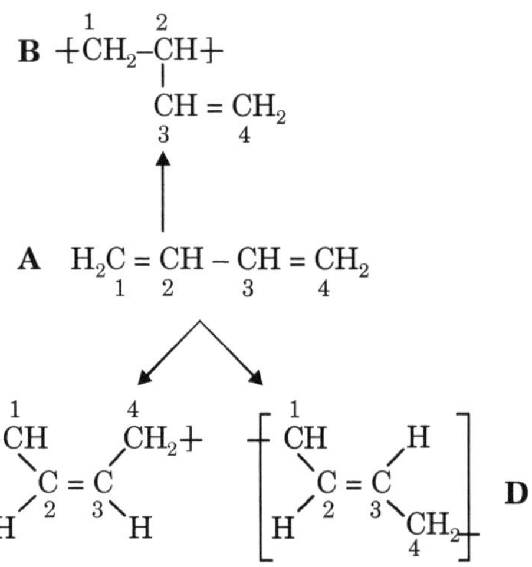

1,2-atactic-polybutadiene

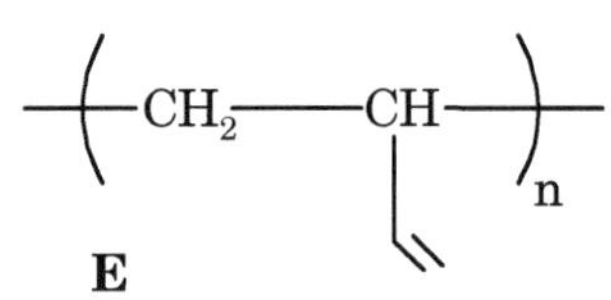

15.

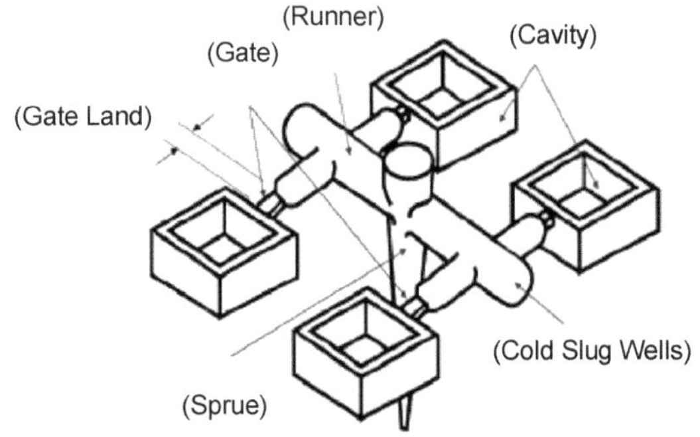

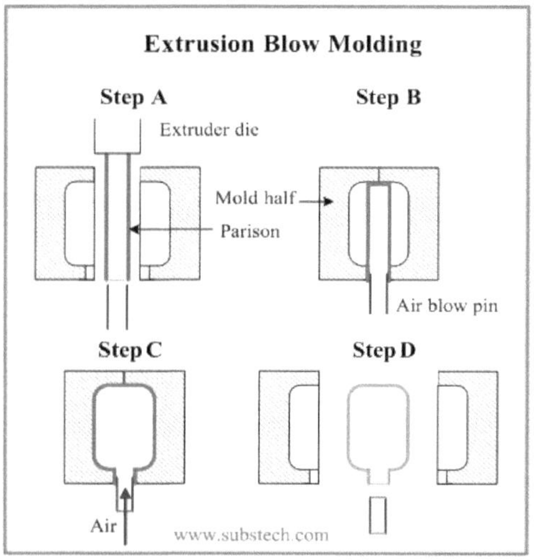

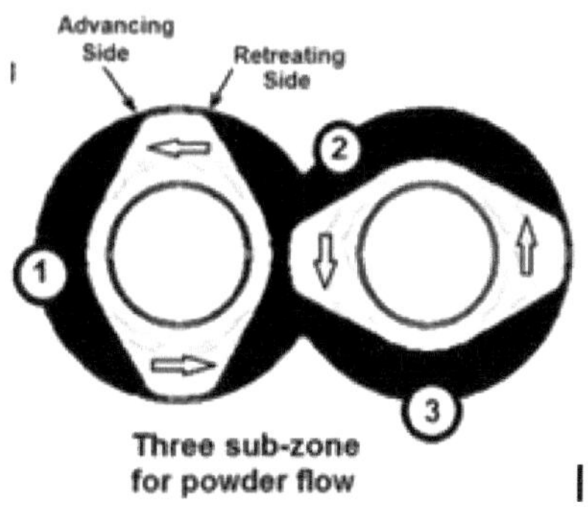

Kneading block

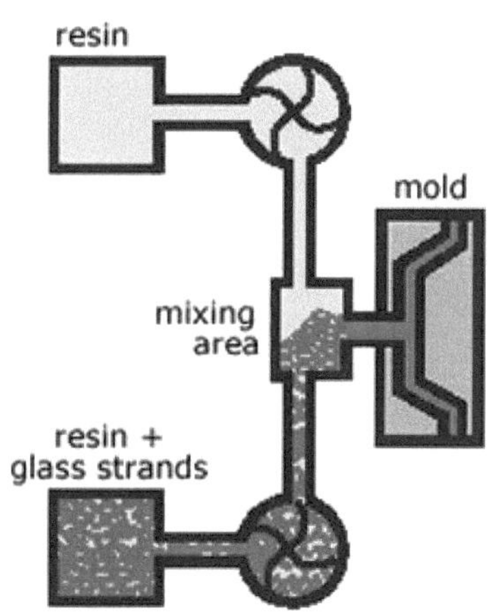

16. Hysteresis loss = $Mg(H_2-H_1)$, H_1= initial height, H_2 = height after rebound,

loss = 0.1* 9.8*(10-8) = 1.96 J

17. We know that weight of the sample is

$$W = \sum w_i = \sum N_i M_i$$

Mass in terms of percentage given, we use mass as w_i, and divide w_i by the molecular weight and get the number of chains. Weight average molecular weight:

$$M_w = \frac{\sum N_i M_i^2}{\sum N_i M_i}$$

N_i = x for all samples given condition

$$M_w = \frac{X \times 10000^2 + X \times 20000^2 + X \times 30000^2}{X + X + X}$$

weight average molecular weight, M_w will be $= 2.33 \times 10^4$ g/mol

18.

$$M_n = \frac{\Sigma N_i M_i}{\Sigma N_i M_i}$$

$$W = \sum w_i = \sum N_i M_i$$

w_i is equal for all sample given condition = x

$$M_n = \frac{X + X + X}{\frac{X}{10000} + \frac{X}{20000} + \frac{X}{30000}}$$

The number average molecular weight, Mn will be $= 1.64 \times 10^4$ g/mol

19.

$$\sigma = \sigma_o e^{(-t/60)}$$

Where τ **(relaxation time)**=η/E, σ stress at time t and σ_o initial stress

τ = 60 days σ = 1 MPa and σ_o = 2MPa

$$1 = 2e^{(-t/60)}$$

$$t = 41.8 \text{ days.}$$

20. In $\frac{\tau_2}{\tau_1} = \frac{E_a}{R}\left(\frac{1}{T_1} - \frac{1}{T_2}\right)$, T_1 = 273 + 25 = 298, T_2 = 273 + 35 = 308, τ_1 = 60 days

$$\text{In}\frac{\tau_2}{90} = \frac{30000}{8.317}\left(\frac{1}{298} - \frac{1}{318}\right), \ \tau_2 = 40.5 \text{ days}$$

21. Tensile strength = force/ Area = 50/0.8*0.3 = 208.3 kg/cm^2

22. Young modulus = tensile stress/ strain = 208.3/(0.03/4) $= 2.77 \times 10^4$ kg/cm^2

Strain = increase in length / original length

SOLVED PAPER - 2011

1. Monomers that undergo free radical polymerization have

(*a*) one hydroxyl and one carboxylic group

(*b*) double bonds

(*c*) one amine group and one carboxylic group

(*d*) two amine groups

2. In the polymerization of phthalic anhydride (3 moles) and glycerols (3 moles), the average functionality of the reacting system is

(*a*) 1.2 (*b*) 4.2

(*c*) 3.8 (*d*) 2.5

3. A mixture consists of 10 moles of dimer, 15 moles of trimer, 20 moles of tetramer and 5 moles of pentamer. The average chain length of the mixture is

(*a*) 3.4 (*b*) 8.5

(*c*) 6.8 (*d*) 1.7

4. Polyurethane is formed by

(*a*) self condensation of polyols

(*b*) self condensation of diisocyane

(*c*) reaction of polyol and diisocyanate

(*d*) reaction of polyol with adipic acid

5. The glass transition temperature (T g) is governed by

(*a*) translational motion of entire molecule

(*b*) long cooperative wriggling motion of 40 to 50 C-C bonds

(*c*) short cooperative motion of 5 to 6 bonds of the molecules

(*d*) vibration of carbon atoms of the polymer molecules

6. The miscibility in binary polymer blends of poly vinyl fluoride and poly acrylate is governed by which one of the following interactions?

(*a*) dipole-dipole (*b*) acid-base type

(*c*) hydrogen bonding (*d*) ion-dipole

7. The melting temperature of poly tetrafluoroethylene is higher than its degradation temperature due to

(*a*) hydrogen bonding

(*b*) n-hydrogen bonding

(*c*) van der Waal's interaction

(*d*) dipole moment interaction

8. As the molecular weight (M) increases beyond the critical molecular weight (Mc), the zero shear viscosity of a polymer melt becomes proportional to

(*a*) $M^{0.5}$ (*b*) $M^{3.4}$

(*c*) $M^{1.0}$ (*d*) M^{0}

9. In the step-growth polymerization of phenol with formaldehyde the functionality of phenol is

(*a*) 2 (*b*) 5

(*c*) 4 (*d*) 3

10. During the processing of polymers, degradation occurs. Pair each item in Column-I with the appropriate one in Column-II.

Column-I	Column-II
P. Poly vinyl chloride	1. Elimination of low molecular weight compound
Q. Poly acrylonitrile	2. Unzipping
R. Poly methyl methacrylate	3. Cyclization
S. Polyethylene	4. Random scission

(*a*) P-1, Q-3, R-2, S-4 (*b*) P-1, Q-2, R-3, S-4

(*c*) P-2, Q-1, R-3, S-4 (*d*) P-4, Q-2, R-3, S-1

11. The solubility parameter of polystyrene is 9.1 $(cal/cm^3)^{1/2}$, the solubility parameter of n-hexane is 7.3 $(cal/cm^3)^{1/2}$ and that of benzene is 9.2 $(cal/cm^3)^{1/2}$. Then polystyrene will

(*a*) dissolve inn-hexane

(*b*) not dissolve in 80:20 mixture ofn-hexane and benzene

(*c*) not dissolve in benzene

(*d*) dissolve in benzene

12. Fiber glass composites are prepared by coating unidirectional fiber glass with epoxy prepolymer. If slippage **DOES NOT** occur at the interface in the loading in the direction of fiber, then

(*a*) force sheared by fiber glass (Pr) and matrix (P m) should be equal

(*b*) strain as well force in fiber (Er and Pr) are both equal to strain and the force in matrix (Er and Pm)

(*c*) strain at the interface between fiber glass (Er) and matrix (Em) should be equal

(*d*) None of the above is true

13. The power factor (PF) and dissipative factor (DF) of polymeric materials are related by

(*a*) PF = DF/ $(1\text{-}DF^2)^{1/2}$ (*b*) DF = PF/ $(1\text{-}PF^2)^{1/2}$

(*c*) DF = 1/ $(1\text{-}PF^2)^{1/2}$ (*d*) PF = 1 / $(1\text{-}DF^2)^{1/2}$

14. Poly methyl methacrylate (PMMA) and silicone can be used respectively in

(*a*) medical syringe and hip joint

(*b*) soft tissue replacement and contact lenses

(*c*) hip joint and medical syringe

(*d*) contact lenses and soft tissue replacement

15. In the log (viscosity) versus log (shear rate) behaviour of polymer melts, the upper (μ_{upper}) and lower (μ_{lower}) Newtonian viscosities are related as

(*a*) μ_{upper} and μ_{lower} versus shear rate are connected by discontinuous curve

(*b*) $\mu_{upper} > \mu_{lower}$

(*c*) $\mu_{upper} < \mu_{lower}$

(*d*) $\mu_{upper} = \mu_{lower}$

16. Match the following **additives** for plastic with their respective **functions.**

Additives	**Functions**
P. Cetyl Palmitate	1. Fire retardant
Q. Asbestos	2. Heat stabilizer
R. $BaSO_4$	3. Lubricant
S. SbO_2	4. Filler

(*a*) P-1, Q-2, R-3, S-4 (*b*) P-3, Q-4, R-2, S-1

(*c*) P-3, Q-2, R-1, S-4 (*d*) P-4, Q-3, R-2, S-1

Common Data for Questions 17 and 18:

In a single-screw extruder the dimensions of the channel are Diameter (D)= 5.03 cm, Width (W) = 1.1 cm, Height (H)= 0.36 cm, Screw Angle (8) = 6.3° and Speed of Rotation= 10 revolution per second (rps)

17. Assume a flat plate model in the melt zone of a single-screw extruder $\partial P/\partial z = \eta\partial^2 v_z/\partial y^2$; $v_z = 0$ at y = 0 and $v_z = V_{bz}$ at y = H

For fully developed flow in the z direction v_z is found to be

(*a*) $v_z = V_{bz}(y/H) - [y(H-y)\,\partial P/\partial z]/(2\eta)$

(*b*) $v_z = (y/H) + [y(H-y)\,\partial P/\partial z]/(2\eta)$

(*c*) $v_z = (y^2/H) + [y(H-y)\,\partial P/\partial z]/(2\eta)$

(*d*) $v_z = (y^2/H) - [y(H-y)\,\partial P/\partial z]/(2\eta)$

18. In the absence of a die in a single screw extruder $\Delta P = 0$ and Q is equal to

(*a*) 0.31 cm^3/sec

(*b*) 3.11 cm^3/sec

(*c*) 311 cm^3/sec

(*d*) 31.1 cm^3/sec

Common Data for Questions 19 and 20:

In the polymerization of styrene at 60°C, it is assumed that all steps are irreversible and

propagation rate constant (kp) = 145 lit/mol-sec

mutual termination rate constant (k1) = 0.13×10^7 lit/mol-sec

initiator rate constant (ki) = 4.38×10^{-6} sec–1

initiator concentration ([I2])= 1.65×10^{-2} mol/lit

monomer concentration([M])= 7.69 mol/lit

19. Assuming the rate constant for combination of initiator radical with monomer, $k_1 = 10k_p$ in the polymerization of styrene, the primary radical concentration ([I·]) can be calculated as

(*a*) [I·] = 0.364 X 10^{-8} mol/lit

(*b*) [I·] = 1.65 X 10^{-10} mol/lit

(*c*) [I·] = 6.48 X 10^{-12} mol/lit

(*d*) [I·] = 2.74 X 10^{-4} mol/lit

20. The total molar concentration of the growing polymer radicals (λp) in the polymerization of styrene is given by

(*a*) $\lambda_p = 4.72 \times 10^{-8}$ mol/lit

(*b*) $\lambda_p = 2.36 \times 10^{-7}$ mol/lit

(*c*) $\lambda_p = 7.08 \times 10^{-6}$ mol/lit

(*d*) $\lambda_p = 9.44 \times 10^{-5}$ mol/lit

Statement for Linked Answer Questions 21 and 22:

For semi-crystalline polymeric materials, free of voids and impurities, we define the following:

d = average density of a semi-crystalline polymer

dc = density of the crystalline phase

da = density of the amorphous phase

21. The relation between the average density and the densities of crystalline and amorphous phases can be related to mass fraction of the crystalline phase (X) as

The degree of crystallinity of the sample can be calculated by given equation:

Degree of crystallinity by mass = $X_c = \dfrac{1/d_a - 1/d}{1/d_a - 1/d_c}$

$1/d = (X_C/d_c) + \{(1 - X_C)/d_a$

22. When a fiber is made of PET, it has crystalline as well as amorphous phases and experiments have revealed that the average density of the overall material is 1.375 g/cm^3 .It is known that the density of the crystalline phase is 1.455 g/cm^3 and that of amorphous phase is 1.335 g/cm^3. The mass fraction crystallinity (X) in % is given by

(*a*) 35.3% (*b*) 50.5%

(*c*) 80.1% (*d*) 5.1%

ANSWERS

1. (*b*)	**2.** (*d*)	**3.** (*a*)	**4.** (*c*)	**5.** (*b*)	**6.** (*a*)	**7.** (*c*)	**8.** (*b*)	**9.** (*d*)	**10.** (*a*)
11. (*d*)	**12.** (*c*)	**13.** (*b*)	**14.** (*d*)	**15.** (*c*)	**16.** (*b*)	**17.** (*a*)	**18.** (*d*)	**19.** (*c*)	**20.** (*b*)
21. (*d*)	**22.** (*a*)								

EXPLANATIONS

1. Monomer has double bond will undergo free radical polymerization. Monomer has functional group will undergo step growth polymerization.
2. The functionality of a molecule is simply its interlinking capacity, or the number of sites available for bonding(presence of reactive functional group like %OH, %COOH,% NH_2, % SH, % NCO, etc.) with other molecules under the specific polymerization conditions

Average functionality

$$= \frac{\text{Functionality of compound 1*no.of mole} + \text{Functionality of compound 2*no.of mole}}{\text{Total mole}}$$

Figure. Structure of Glycerol

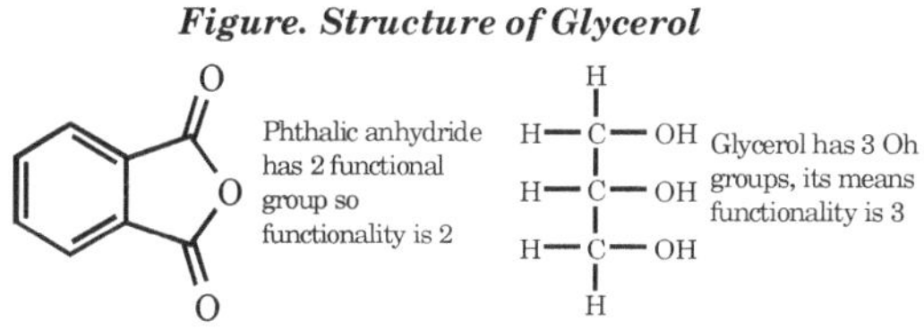

Average functionality = 2*3+ 3*3 / (3+3) = 2.5

3. Average chain length

$$= \frac{10\times 2 + 15\times 3 + 20\times 4 + 5\times 5}{(10 + 15 + 20 + 5)} = 3.4$$

4. 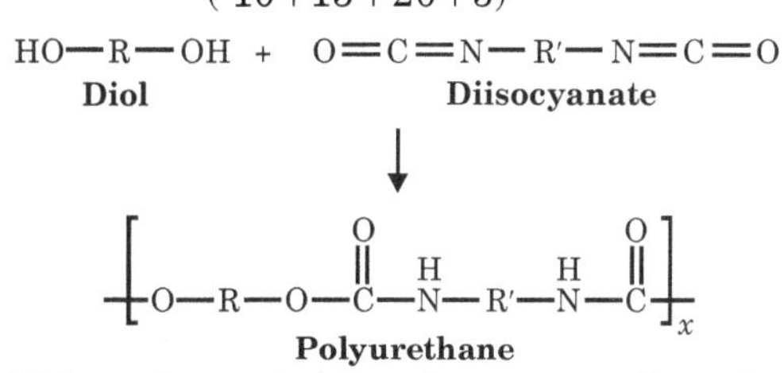

5. If the polymer is heated it eventually will reach its **glass transition temperature**. At this temperature portions of the molecules can start to wriggle around as is illustrated by the red molecule in the diagram. The polymer now is in its **rubbery state**. The rubbery state lends softness and flexibility to a polymer.

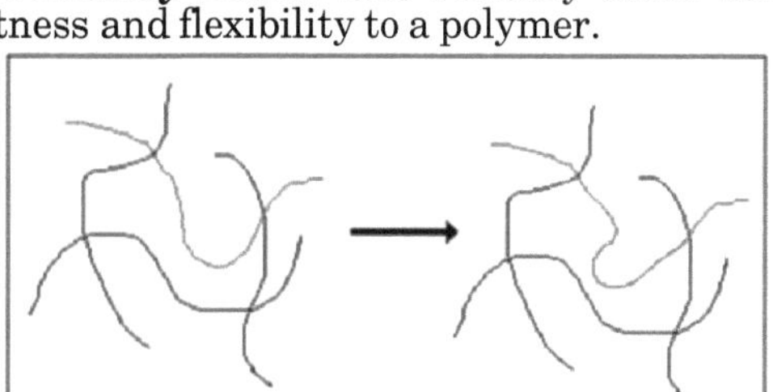

6.

Interaction	Contributing	Groups of polymer pairs
acid-base	$-SO_3^- \; ^+N<$	Anionic polymer with Cationic polymer
	$>C=O\cdots H-O-$	Polyester of carbonyl polymer with Phenoxy or Polyvinyl phenol
	$>C=O\cdots H-C-Cl$	Aliphatic Polyester with PVC
	$>O\cdots H-O-$	PEO, PVHE with Phenoxy
	$>O\cdots H-O-C(=O)-$	PEO, PVME with PAA, PMAA [PVME = POLY VINYL METHYL ETHER]
dipole-dipole	$>C=O\cdots CF_2<$	PVF_2 with Variuos Poly Acrylates, PVAc
ion-dipole	$-SO_3Li\cdots O=C(-NH-)-$	Styrene Sulphuric acid (metal salts) containing Polymers with PA
π-hydrogen bonding	$-C_6H_4-H_3C-C_6H_3(CH_3)-O-$	PS with PPO
n-π complex	$C_6H_4\cdots O=C<$	PC with PMMA. PC with Polyester
π-π complex	$-C_6H_4-\cdots C_6H_4$	PS with TMPC

7. PTFE is very crystalline in the sense that there are large areas where the molecules are lying in a very regular arrangement. Remember that PTFE molecules can be thought of as long thin rods. These rods will pack very closely together. Due to weak van der waal's interaction its degrade before to melt.
8. At low molar mass values

$$\eta_0 = K_L M^{1.0}$$

melt viscosity is directly proportional to molar mass. For M values larger than a critical molar mass, M_c, there is a sharp increase in melt viscosity since

$$\eta_0 = K_H M^{3.4}$$

K_L and K_H in the equations reported above represent constants that are temperature dependent.

9. 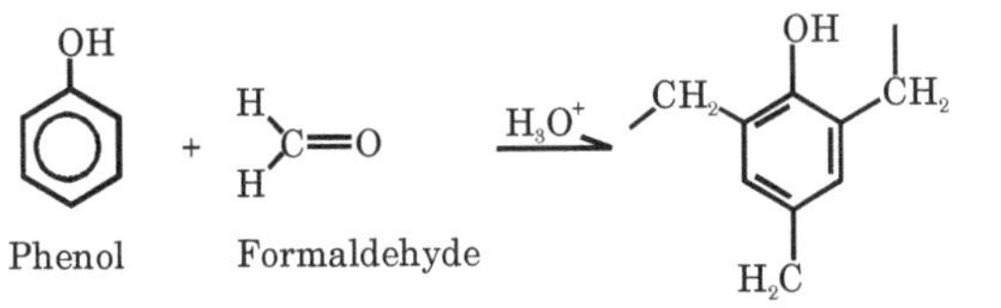

Formaldehyde attach on the 3 position on the phenol. At every place accommodate the formaldehyde. So functionality o phenol is 3.

10. 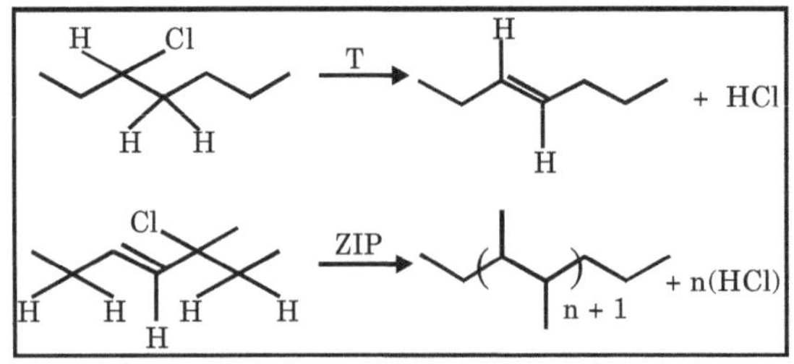

Scheme-1 - dehydrochlorination reactions in PVC macromolecules (Veronelli et al., 19999)

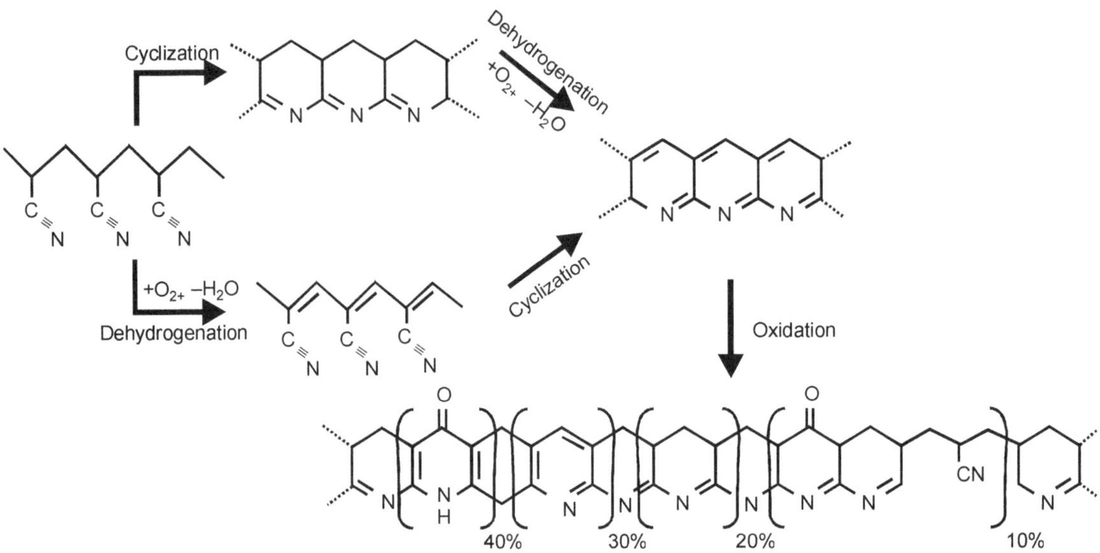

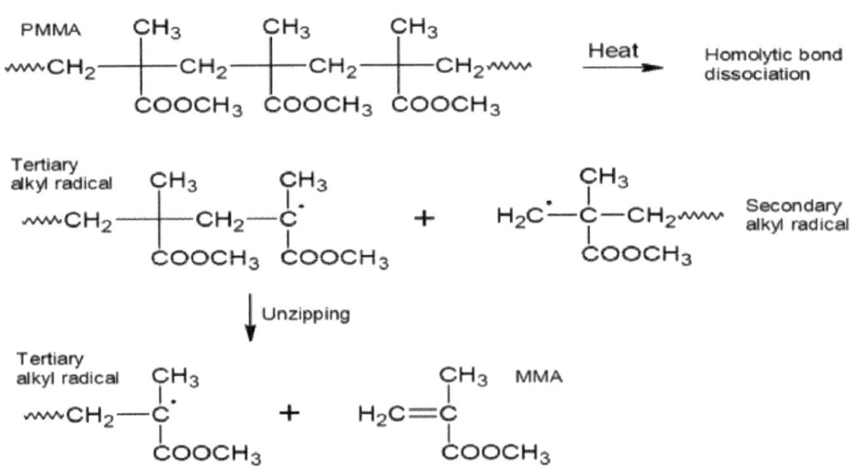

11. The above equation may be rewritten;

$$\frac{\Delta H_m}{V} = \phi_1\phi_2\left[\delta_1 - \delta_2\right]^2$$

This equation is validi only when ΔH_m is zero or greater. It is invalid for exothermic mixing, that is, when ΔHm is negative.

The square of the difference between the solubility parameters of two liquids decides the magnitude of the heat of mixing. Hence, for the positive heat of mixing to be at a minimum value so as to let mixing occur, the difference between the solubility parameters (δ_1-δ_2) of the two liquids must be as low as possible.

Difference of the solubility in the polystyrene and benzene are low compare to the hexane, so polystyrene will dissolve in benzenes.

12. Strain should be equal on the interface of fibre and polymer to avoid slippage. Unidirectional direction applied strain on the composite is equal to fiber and equal to the matrix. So, Stress is equal to the modulus.

13. The power factor is a measure of the energy absorbed by the material as the alternating current constantly changes direction and the dipoles try to align themselves with the field.

The dissipation factor (D) is the ratio of the current of the current of the resistive component (I_r) to the current of the capacitive component (I_c) and is also equal to the tangent to the dielectric loss angle δ, i.e.

$$D = \frac{I_r}{I_c} = \tan\delta$$

Typical values of the dissipation factor vary from 01 to less than 0.0005.

The power factor (PF) is the ratio of power dissipated to the product of the effective power output (volts × amps) and is a measure of the dielectric loss in the insulating plastic (which is effectively acting as capacitor). The power factor and dissipation factor are related by the equation:

$$DF = \frac{PF}{\sqrt{\left[1-(PF)^2\right]}}$$

Power factors for most of the plastics are fairly low, so the PF^2 terms in the equation can be ignored, making the power factor approximately equal to the dissipation factor.

14. 1. Polymethyl methacrylate (PMMA), also known as acrylic or acrylic glass, is a transparent and rigid thermoplastic material widely used as a shatterproof replacement for glass. PMMA has many technical advantages over other transparent polymer (PC, polystyrene etc.), few of them include:

- High resistance to UV light and weathering,
- Excellent light transmission
- Unlimited coloring options
- Scratch resistance

Advantage over other transparent polymer, is using in lens.

2. Silicone is the ideal material for prosthetic appliances. It is light, incredibly flexible and is translucent – all of which add realism to the finished product.

15. In rheology, **shear thinning** is the non-Newtonian behavior of fluids whose viscosity decreases under shear strain. Polymer melt shows the behavior of shear thinning. Increasing shear rate decreasing in the viscosity of melt.

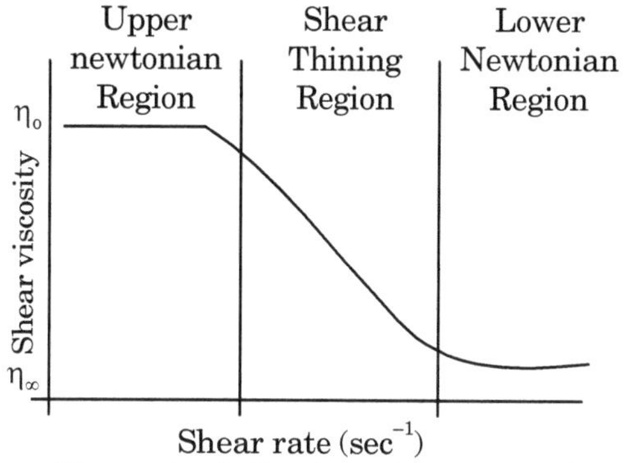

Characteristic viscosity curve of thermoplasties (log-log plot)

16. 1. Fire retardants (FR) are chemical compounds added with an objective to inhibit/retard the ignition/burning of the plastic. Brominated (BFRs), Chlorinated (CFRs), Phosphorous (PFRs), Alumina Trihydrate (ATH), Magnesium Hydroxide (MDH), Antimony Oxide [SbO_2] etc.

2. Heat stabilizers are used to prevent degradation of plastics by heat, especially during processing, but also in applications. Barium-zinc additives are very effective heat stabilizers for PVC but are restricted for medical applications in some countries. Alternatives like calcium-zinc formulations are often used to stabilize medical-grade PVC against heat. Heat stabilizers trap the hydrogen chloride that is generated when PVC decomposes at high temperatures and prevent discoloration and degradation.

3. Lubricants as additives for polymers assist the movement of one object passing another object. Their primary role is to reduce friction, minimize wear and prevent overheating of parts. While wear and heat cannot be completely eliminated, reducing them to negligible or acceptable levels is must to maintain performance in your application. Internal lubricants used for PVC are amine

waxes, montan wax ester derivatives, glyceryl esters such as glyceryl monostearate and long chain esters such as cetyl palmitate.

4. Fillers are added to a polymer formulation **to reduce the costs and improve the properties**. Carbon black, calcium carbonates and silicates, clay (hard or soft), talc (platy talc is uniquely pure), thermal carbon, wollastonite (very white and abrasive), zinc oxide, silica, Asbestos etc.

17. Take a flat model for fully developed flow

$$\frac{\partial^2 V_z}{\partial y^2} = \frac{1}{\eta}\frac{dp}{dz}$$

Given conditions Vz 0 at y = 0 & Vz = V_{bz} at y = H to solve the above equation

$$V_z = \frac{1}{\eta}\frac{dp}{dz}\frac{y^2}{2} + C_1 y + C_2$$

Finally solve the equation we will get option A.

18. $$Q_D = \frac{\pi}{2} W H D N \cos\theta$$

Put the all the value in the equation form the question

Q = 3.14*1.1*0.36*5.03*10*cos(6.3)/2

= 31.08 cm^3/sec

19. $[I_2] = 1.65 \times 10^{-2}$; $[I] = 1.65/2 \times 10^{-2}$

$K_1 = 10\ Kp = 10 \times 145$; Kp = 145

[M] = 7.69;

f = 1

ki = 4.38×10^{-6}

Rate of initiation of thermo decomposition of initiator = rate of initiation of primary radicals

$$R_i = K_1 [M][I\cdot] = 2 K_i f[I]$$

$$[I\cdot] = \frac{2K_i f[I]}{K_1[M]}$$

$$= \frac{4.38\times10^{-6}\times1.65/2\times10^{-2}\times1}{10\times145\times7.69}$$

$= 6.48 \times 10^{-12}$

20. At steady state;

Rate of initiation = Rate of termination

$$K_1[M][I\cdot] = K_t[M\cdot]^2$$

K1 = 10 Kp

Kt = 0.13×10^7

$$[M\cdot]^2 = \frac{10K_p[M][I\cdot]}{K_t}$$

$$\frac{10\times145\times[7.69]\times6.48\times10^{-12}}{0.13\times10^7} = [M\cdot]^2$$

$[M\cdot] = 2.3558 \text{ X } 10^{-7}$mol/lit

21. Degree of crystallinity by mass

$$= \Omega = \frac{\frac{1}{d} - \frac{1}{d_a}}{\frac{1}{d_c} - \frac{1}{d_a}}$$

d = density of the polymer

d_a = density of amorphous part,

d_c = density of crystallinity part

$$\frac{\Omega}{d_c} - \frac{\Omega}{d_a} = \frac{1}{d} - \frac{1}{d_a}$$

$$\frac{1}{d} = \frac{\Omega}{d_c} - \frac{1-\Omega}{d_a}$$

22. $$X_c = \frac{1/1.335 - 1/1.375}{1/1.335 - 1/1.455}$$

= 35.27%

SOLVED PAPER - 2010

1. Which one of the following molecules undergoes ring opening polymerization?

(a) 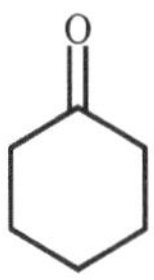

(b) 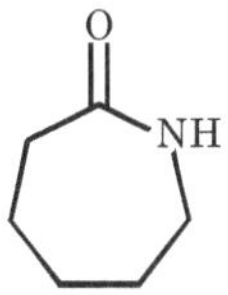

(c) 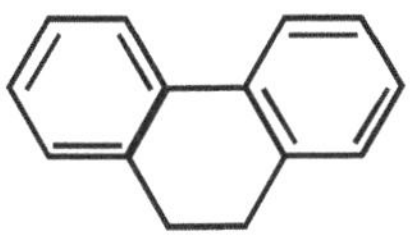

(d) 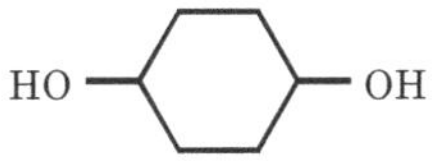

2. Out of the following polymers, which one shows the highest melting temperature?

(a) Poly (ethylene terephthalate)

(b) Poly(propylene terephthalate)

(c) Poly (butylene terephthalate)

(d) Poly (hexylene terephthalate)

3. Which one of the following reagents is used to prevent coagulation of natural rubber latex?

(a) Ammonia

(b) Acetic acid

(c) Tolyl mercaptan

(d) Sodium chloride

4. From the following four groups of polymers, identify the group in which all four polymer are semi crystalline

(a) HDPE, PP, PS, UF

(b) PET, PVC, PF, ABS

(c) Nylon 6. EPDM, PMMA. SBR

(d) Nylon 66, PP, HDPE. PET

5. If η represents viscosity of polymer solution and η_o represents viscosity of pure solvent, then the specific viscosity (η_{sp})of the polymer solution is expressed as

(a) η/η_o (b) $\eta/\eta_o - 1$

(c) $\eta_o/\eta - 1$ (d) η_o/η

6. A polymer blend is developed by mixing

(a) A polymer and a monomer

(b) A polymer and a stabilizer

(c) A polymer with another polymer

(d) A polymer and a filler

7. In shear deformation of a polymer melt, the unit of shear rate is

(a) $m^3\ sec^{-1}$ (b) $m^2\ sec^{-1}$

(c) $m\ sec^{-1}$ (d) sec^{-1}

8. A rubber compound is made by mixing functional additives with the rubber using

(a) Two-roll mill

(b) Compression molding machine

(c) Three-roll calender

(d) Thermoforming machine

9. The group of polymer consisting of LDPE. PP, PS and PVC is best categorized as

(a) Engineering polymers

(b) Biodegradable polymers

(c) Commodity polymers

(d) Natural polymers

10. A small molecule is eliminated as a byproduct during the synthesis of

(a) Polycaprolactone

(b) Poly (ethylene terephthalate)

(c) Styrene butadiene copolymer

(d) Polytetrafluoroethylene

11. For free radical copolymerization of monomers M_1 and M_2, if the reactivity ratios r_1 and r_2 are both found to be zero, then the resulting copolymer is

(a) Random

(b) Branched

(c) Block

(d) Alternating

12. Pair each item in Column I with the appropriate one in Column II

Column I	Column II
P. Shampoo bottles	1. Injection molding
Q. Overhead tank	2. Extrusion
R. Helmet	3. Blow molding
S. Insulation for cables	4. Rotomolding

(a) P-1; Q-2; R-4; S-3 (b) P-2; Q-1: R-3; S-4

(c) P-3: Q-4; R-1; S-2 (d) P-4; Q-3; R-2; S-1

13. Toughness of a plastic material can be judged from the area under the stress-strain curve obtained from tensile test. The plastic having the highest toughness exhibits

(*a*) High tensile strength and low elongation

(*b*) Low tensile strength and high elongation

(*c*) High tensile strength and high elongation

(*d*) Low tensile strength and low elongation

14. Match the following additives for plastics with their respective functions

Additives	*Functions*
P. Iron oxide	1. Blowing agent
Q. Azodicarbonamide	2. Coloring ageut
R. Phenyl salicylate	3. Filler
S. Calcium carbonate	4. UV stabilizer

(*a*) P-1; Q-2; R-3; S-4

(*b*) P-2; Q-1; R-4; S-3

(*c*) P-3; Q-4; R-1; S-2

(*d*) P-4; Q-3; R-2; S-1

15. The volume fraction of epoxy resin in a glass fibre/ epoxy composite is 0.48. The densities of glass fibre and composite are 2540 kg/m^3 and 1950 kg/m^3, respectively. The weight fraction of the fibre in the composite is:

(*a*) 0.68 (*b*) 0.52

(*c*) 0.48 (*d*) 0.32

16. The change of shear stress with shear rate of a polymer melt as shown in the figure below indicates

(*a*) Viscosity increase with increase in shear rate

(*b*) Viscosity decrease with increase in shear rate

(*c*) Viscosity remaining independent of shear rate

(*d*) Viscosity oscillation with increase in shear rare

Common Data for Questions 17 and 18 :

For polyesterification of $HO\text{-}(CH_2)_{14}COOH$, the number average degree of polymerization, X_n, is related to the stoichiometric imbalance *r* between the functional group and the extent of polymerization *p* by the equation

$$X_n = \frac{1+r}{1+r-2Pr}$$

17. For 100% polyesterification, the X_n will be

(*a*) 100 (*b*) 1000

(*c*) 10000 (*d*) infinity

18. The percentage Conversion of functional groups required to obtain the polyester with a molecular weight of 24000 g/mol will

(*a*) 99 (*b*) 96

(*c*) 93 (*d*) 90

Common Data for Questions 19 and 20 :

The glass transition temperatures of PVC, plasticized PVC and nitrile rubber are 81°C, –3°C and –50°C respectively. For making a plastic raincoat, 40 mass percent of polymeric plasticizer is added to PVC

19. The glass transition temperature of the polymeric plasticizer will be

(*a*) –84°C (*b*) –74°C

(*c*) 74 °C (*d*) 84°C

20. If the polymeric plasticizer is replaced by nitrile rubber to make the same raincoat, the mass percent of rubber to be blended with PVC is

(*a*) 40 (*b*) 47

(*c*) 53 (*d*) 60

Question no.19 and 20 marks to all due to technical error in the questions.

Linked Answer Questions

Statement for Linked Answer Questions 21 and 22:

A polydisperse polymer consists of the following three different fractions

	Fraction 1	Fraction 2	Fraction 3
Mass of Polymer (%)	30	20	50
Molecular weight (g/mol)	30,000	80,000	150,000

21. The number average molecular weight, M_n(g/mol) of the polymer is

(*a*) 1.02×10^5

(*b*) 0.99×10^5

(*c*) 0.63×10^5

(*d*) 0.55×10^5

22. The polydispersity index of the polymer is

(*a*) 2.59 (*b*) 1.87

(*c*) 1.72 (*d*) 1.59

ANSWERS

1. (*b*)	**2.** (*a*)	**3.** (*a*)	**4.** (*d*)	**5.** (*b*)	**6.** (*c*)	**7.** (*d*)	**8.** (*a*)	**9.** (*c*)	**10.** (*)
11. (*d*)	**12.** (*c*)	**13.** (*c*)	**14.** (*b*)	**15.** (*a*)	**16.** (*c*)	**17.** (*d*)	**18.** (*a*)	**19.** (*)	**20.** (*)
21. (*c*)	**22.** (*d*)								

EXPLANATIONS

1. Structure in Option B is caprolactum. Nylon 6 is polymerization by caprolactum by ring opening polymerization.

2. Presence of the more (–CH2–) groups in the chain increases the flexibility of polymer chain. Flexibility in the polymer chain reduces the melting point.

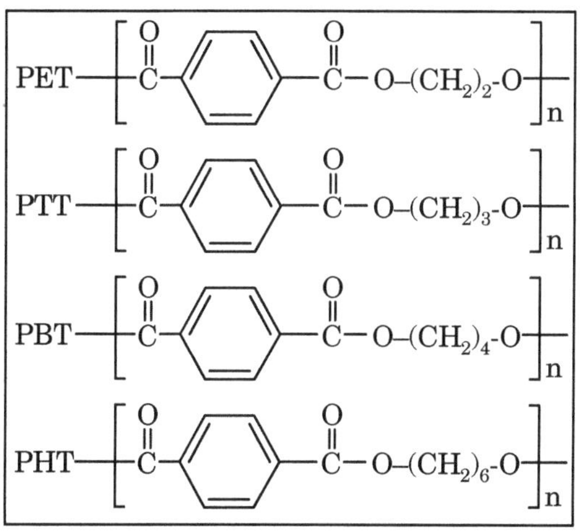

PET	PBT	PPT(PTT)	PHT
265°C	228°C	225°C	200°C

3.
- The rubber polymers start to coagulate by combining together to form large lumps of rubber polymers which then precipitate out of the latex solution.
- Latex can still coagulate if acids are not added. Normally, the latex will coagulate if left overnight.
- Bacteria from the air slowly attack the protein on the membrane to produce lactic acid. Ionisation of the lactic acid produces hydrogen ions. The hydrogen ions neutralise the negative charges to form neutral rubber particles, allowing coagulation to occur.
- Alkalis such as ammonia solution are added to latex to prevent coagulation.

4. Materials such as polystyrene (PS), polycarbonate (PC), acrylics (PMMA), acrylonitrile-butadiene styrene (ABS) and polyvinyl chloride (PVC) are said to be amorphous thermoplastics. This signifies that in the solid state their molecular structure is random and disordered the long chain molecules being all entangled rather like solidified spaghetti.

Materials such as most of the nylons (PA), polyacetal (POM), polypropylene (PP), polyethylene (PE) and the thermoplastic polyesters (PET) have a much more ordered structure in the solid state, a considerable proportion of the long chain molecules being closely packed in regular alignment. These materials are known as semi crystalline thermoplastics.

5. $$\frac{t - t_0}{t_0} = \frac{\eta - \eta_o}{\eta_o} = \eta_r - 1 = \eta_{sp}$$

6. Polymer blends are physical mixtures of two or more polymers with/without any chemical bonding between them.

7. $\sigma = \eta \frac{d\gamma}{dt}$

σ stress (Pa) and η viscosity (Pa-s)

$$\frac{d\gamma}{dt} = \frac{pa}{(pa\text{-}s)} = 1/\text{sec}$$

8. Two roll is used for the mixing purpose. Option B, C & D is used to shape the product.

9.

Engineering polymers	ABS, Nylon, PA, PBT, PEEK, PET etc.
Biodegradable polymers	Poly(α-esters), Polylactide
Commodity polymers	PE, PP, PS, PVC
Natural polymers	Silk, wool, DNA, cellulose and NR

10.

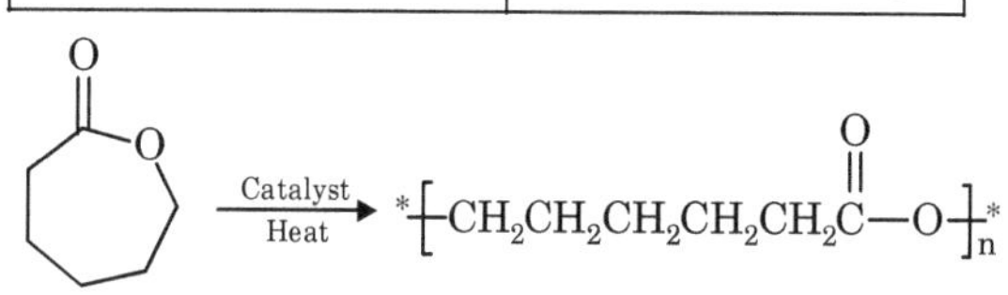

Caprolactone **PCL**

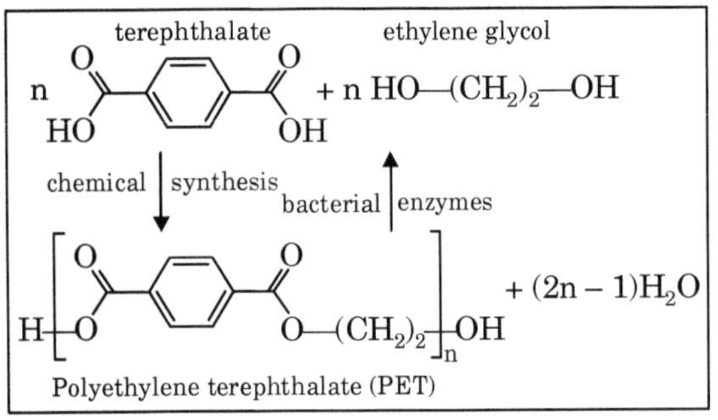

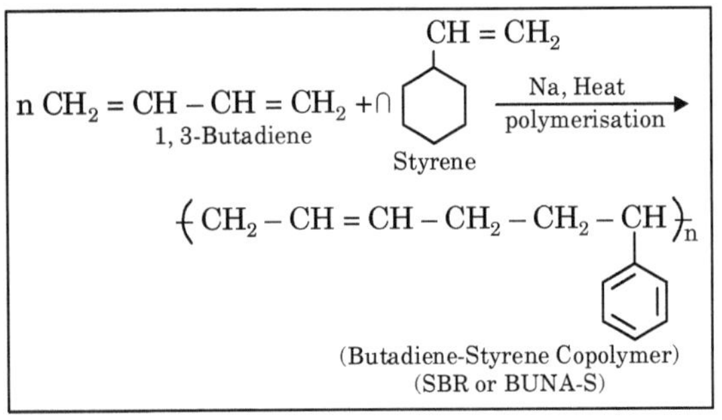

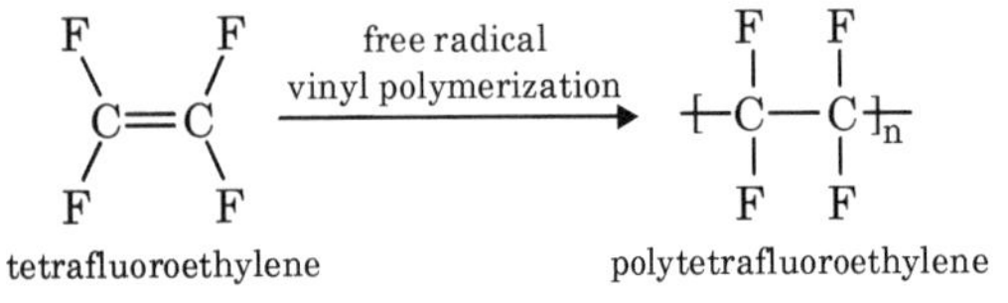

11. $r_1 = r_2 = 0$

a. Monomer 1 reacts exclusively with monomer 2 and vice versa

b. Alternating copolymer

c. Example: styrene: maleic anhydride $r_1 = 0.041$: $r_2 = 0.01$

12.
- Injection moulding is used to create many things such as wire spools, packaging, bottle caps, automotive parts and components, toys, pocket combs, some musical instruments (and parts of them), one-piece chairs and small tables, storage containers, mechanical parts (including gears), and most other plastic products available today. Injection moulding is the most common modern method of manufacturing plastic parts; it is ideal for producing high volumes of the same object
- Plastics extrusion is a high-volume manufacturing process in which raw plastic is melted and formed into a continuous profile. Extrusion produces items such as pipe/tubing, weatherstripping, fencing, deck railings, window frames, plastic films and sheeting, thermoplastic coatings, and wire insulation.
- Blow molding is a manufacturing process for forming and joining together hollow plastic parts. Application -Bottles, jars and fuel container and other containers
- Rotational molding, also known as rotomolding, is a thermoplastic molding process best suited for large, one-piece hollow parts and double-walled open containers such as tanks, kayaks, and coolers.

13.

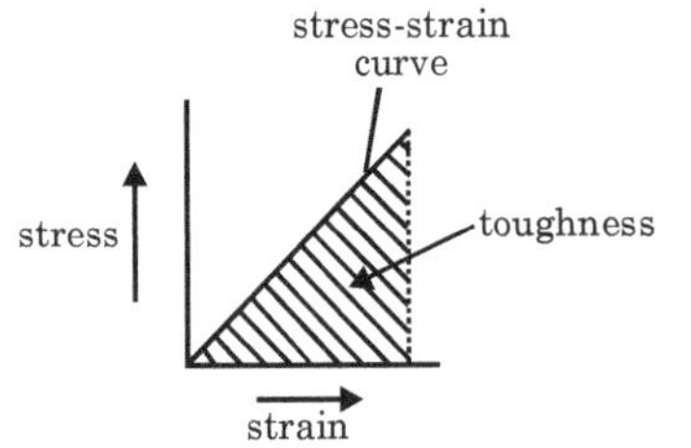

Toughness = /12*stress * strain

High tensile and high elongation both will give high value of the ear under the curve by stress and strain.

14.

carbonamide	Blowing agent	Play a role in the formation of air bubbles by breaking down into gas at high temperature.
Calcium carbonate	Filler	Used as fillers in rubber industry
lron oxide	Coloring agent	Using as pigment
Phenyl salicylate	UV stabilizer	The primary function is to protect the substance from the long term UV degradation effects from ultraviolet radition.

15. Mass fraction of the fiber in the composite

= mass of fiber / total composite mass

Assume total composite volume is 1

$$V_c = V_m + V_f$$

$$V_f = 1 - 0.48 = 0.52$$

Mass of fiber = density * volume

$$\text{weight fraction of the fiber} = \frac{(2540*0.52)}{(1950*1)} = 0.6777$$

16. Stress is proportional to the strain rate. According to Newton's law, the response of a fluid to a shearing stress σ is viscous flow, given by

$$\sigma \, \alpha \, \frac{d\gamma}{dt}$$

$$\sigma = \eta \frac{d\gamma}{dt}$$

Where η is viscosity and $d\gamma/dt$ is strain rate.

Viscosity constant with the shear rate and stress.

17. $$P = 100\%$$

$$X_n = \frac{1+r}{1+r-2Pr}$$

At 100% of the extent reaction number average degree of polymerization equal to infinity

18. Molecular weight of the

$HO\text{–}(CH_2)_{14}COOH = 258 = M_o$

$$M_n = \frac{M_o}{1-p}$$

$$M_n = 24000 \text{ g/mol}$$

$$24000 = \frac{258}{(1-p)}$$

$$P = 99\%$$

19. $$\frac{1}{T_g} = \frac{W_1}{T_{g_1}} + \frac{W_2}{T_{g_2}}$$

1 – PVC & 2 – Plasticizer

Plasticizer amount = 40% = 0.4

$T_{g1} = 81 + 273 = 354$ K, $W_1 = 1 - 0.4 = 0.6$

$T_{g2} = ?$, & $W_2 = 0.4$

Tg of plasticized PVC = – 3 + 273 = 270 K

$$\frac{1}{270} = \frac{0.6}{354} + \frac{0.4}{T_{g2}}$$

$$Tg_2 = 199 \text{ K}$$

$$T_{g2} = 199 - 273 = -74°C$$

20. $$\frac{1}{T_g} = \frac{W_1}{T_{g_1}} + \frac{W_2}{T_{g_2}}$$

1 – PVC & 2 – Nitrile rubber

$W_1 = X$ is the weight fraction of PVC & $W_2 = 1 - X$ is the weight fraction of nitrile rubber

$$T_{g1} = 81 + 273 = 354 \text{ K},$$

$$T_{g2} = -50 + 273 = 223 \text{ K},$$

Tg of plasticized PVC = – 3 + 273 = 270 K

$$\frac{1}{270} = \frac{X}{354} + \frac{1-X}{223}$$

$$X = 0.47$$

Weight fraction of nitrile rubber

$$= 1 - X = 1 - 47 = 0.53$$

Weight percentage of nitrile rubber in composition = 53%

21. We know that weight of the sample is

$$W = \sum w_i = \sum N_i M_i$$

Mass in terms of percentage given, we use mass as w_i, and divide w_i by the molecular weight and get the number of chains. Number average molecular weight:

$$M_n = \frac{\sum N_i M_i}{\sum N_i}$$

$$M_n = \frac{30+20+50}{\frac{30}{3000} + \frac{20}{80000} + \frac{50}{150000}}$$

$$M_n = 0.633 \times 10^5$$

22. Weight average molecualr weight:

$$M_w = \frac{\sum N_i M_i^2}{\sum N_i M_i}$$

$$M_w = \frac{(30 \times 30000 + 20 \times 80000 + 50 \times 150000)}{30 + 20 + 50}$$

$$M_w = 10^5$$

$$\text{Poly Dispersity} = \frac{M_w}{M_n}$$

$$\text{Poly Dispersity} = \frac{10^5}{0.633 \times 10^5}$$

$$PD = 1.59$$

SOLVED PAPER - 2009

1. Which of the following trends is the most appropriate for a thixotropic fluid?

(*a*) Viscosity increases with increase in the rate of shear.

(*b*) Viscosity increases with increase in the time of application of shear.

(*c*) Viscosity decreases with increase in the time of application of shear.

(*d*) Viscosity increases with decrease in the rate of shear.

2. The temperature at which thermoforming is best carried out is

(*a*) Softening temperature

(*b*) melting temperature

(*c*) Glass transition temperature

(*d*) 10 % above melting temperature

3. Which of the following blends is immiscible?

(*a*) SAN/ PMMA (*b*) PE/ PP

(*c*) PC / PS (*d*) PET /PBT

4. A flexible garden hose pipe made of PVC was observed to get hardened after a length of time. The observation is most likely due to

(*a*) Chain scission

(*b*) loss of plasticizer

(*c*) Loss of UV stabilizer

(*d*) loss of thermal stabilizer

5. A doped polymer that conducts electricity is

(*a*) poly(vinyl chloride) (*b*) polyethylene

(*c*) polypropylene (*d*) polypyrrole

6. During chain growth polymerization, the molecular weight of the polymer

(*a*) increases with conversion

(*b*) decreases with conversion

(*c*) does not change with conversion

(*d*) first increases and then decreases with conversion

7. Based on the solubility parameter (δ) the best solvent for polyethylene ($\delta = 16.2\ MPa^{1/2}$) is

(*a*) tetrahydrofuran ($\delta = 20.3\ MPa^{1/2}$)

(*b*) toluene ($\delta = 18.3\ MPa^{1/2}$)

(*c*) acetone ($\delta = 19.9\ MPa^{1/2}$)

(*d*) methanol ($\delta = 29.7\ MPa^{1/2}$)

8. For any polymer, the number average molecular weight (Mn). weight average molecular weight (Mw) and viscosity average molecular weight (Mv). in general, obey the following relationship :

(*a*) Mn > Mw > Mv

(*b*) Mv > Mn > Mw

(*c*) Mw > Mv > Mn

(*d*) Mv > Mw > Mn

9. Pair the items in the Column I with those in the Column II.

Processing step	***Item***
P. rotational molding	1. polyurethane
Q. extrusion	2. use of a gas
R. reaction injection molding	3. centrifugal force
S. blow molding	4. twin screw

(*a*) P-3, Q-1, R-2, S-4 (*b*) P-2, Q-4, R-3, S-1

(*c*) P-4, Q-2, R-1, S-3 (*d*) P-3, Q-4, R-1, S-2

10. Strain γ, in a polymer melt varies with time on application of stress *s* by the following relation :

$$\eta\frac{d\gamma}{dt} + G\gamma = s$$

If a steady shear stress, s_o, is applied, the strain at the steady state, γ_o is given by

(*a*) s_o/G (*b*) s_o/η

(*c*) s_oG (*d*) $s_o\eta$

11. Match the polymerization initiator with the respective process.

Initiator	***Process***
P. benzyl lithium	1. coordination polymerization
Q. tropylium chloride	2. anionic polymerization
R. AIBN	3. cationic polymerization
S. $TiCl_4/Al(Et)_3$	4. radical polymerization

(*a*) P-2, Q-3, R-4, S-1

(*b*) P-2, Q-3, R-1, S-4

(*c*) P-3, Q-1, R-2, S-4

(*d*) P-4, Q-2, R-1, S-3

12. Arrange the following polyamides (PA) in decreasing order of their melting points:

I. PA66

II. PA6

III. PA10

IV. PA12

(*a*) IV > I > II > III

(*b*) I > II > III > IV

(*c*) III > II > IV > I

(*d*) II > IV > III > I

13. Match the characterization technique with the most appropriate property

Characterization technique	***Property***
P. infrared spectroscopy	1. melting point
Q. thermo-gravimetric analysis	2. functional group
R. transmission electron microscopy	3. degradation temperature
S. differential scanning calorimetry	4. morphology

(*a*) P-3, Q-2, R-4, S-1

(*b*) P-3, Q-4, R-2, S-1

(*c*) P-2, Q-1, R-4, S-3

(*d*) P-2, Q-3, R-4, S-1

14. Match the rubber ingredients with their appropriate function.

Rubber ingredient	***Function***
P. ZnO	1. tackifier
Q. salicylic acid	2. extender
R. ester gum	3. accelerator
S. paraffin oil	4. retarder

(*a*) P-3. Q-4, R-1, S-2

(*b*) P-3, Q-4, R-2, S-1

(*c*) P-4. Q-3, R-2, S-1

(*d*) P-4, Q-3, R-1, S-2

15. At the start of a step growth polymerization there are N_0 moles of monomer A (molecular weight M_A) and N_0 moles of monomer B (molecular weight M_B). At the end of the polymerization there are N moles of polymer chains. Assuming no condensation product, the number of average molecular weight is

(*a*) $2\ N_0\ (M_A + M_B)/\ N$

(*b*) $N_0\ (M_A + M_B)/\ N$

(*c*) $N_0\ (M_A + M_B)/2\ N$

(*d*) $N_0^2\ (M_A + M_B)/\ N^2$

16. The ratio of the complex dynamic modulus to the storage modulus of a polymer system with a phase angle of 45° is

(*a*) 0 (*b*) 1 – i

(*c*) $1 + i$ (*d*) $1 \pm i$

17. Match the additive to its most common function.

Additive	***Function***
P. talc	1. plasticizer
Q. carbon fibre	2. flame retardant
R. dioctyl phthalate	3. filler
S. antimony trioxide	4. reinforcement

(*a*) P-3, Q-4, R-2, S-1

(*b*) P-4, Q-3, R-1, S-2

(*c*) P-4, Q-3, R-2, S-1

(*d*) P-3, Q-4, R-1, S-2

18. Match the polymer mechanical property with the appropriate testing method.

Mechanical property	***Testing method***
P. flexural strength	1. notched Izod
Q. impact strength	2. Shore-D
R. hardness	3. ASTM D 638
S. tensile strength	4. three-point bending

(*a*) P-4, Q-1, R-2, S-3

(*b*) P-3, Q-2, R-1, S-4

(*c*) P-3, Q-1, R-2, S-4

(*d*) P-4, Q-1, R-3, S-2

Common Data for Questions 19 and 20:

An aligned short carbon fibre reinforced polyester composite has a fibre content of 40% by volume. The elastic moduli of carbon fibre and polyester resin are 250 GPa and 35 GPa respectively. The fibre diameter is 5µm and the ultimate tensile strength of the fibre is 1240 MPa.

19. The modulus of the composite is

(*a*) 121 GPa (*b*) 215 GPa

(*c*) 285 GPa (*d*) 142.5 GPa

20. The fibre-matrix bond strength, assuming a critical fibre length of 12 mm, is

(*a*) 258 MPa (*b*) 2.58 MPa

(*c*) 25.8 MPa (*d*) 0.258 MPa

Common Data for Questions 21 and 22:

A plasticating screw of an injection molding unit injects 0.1 L/s of polymer through a mold, which is a cylindrical tube having a diameter of 20 mm and a length of 100 mm. The pressure drop across the mold is 100 MPa.

21. The shear stress exerted by the polymer on the wall of the mold is

(*a*) 2.5 MPa (*b*) 10 MPa

(*c*) 5 MPa (*d*) 1 MPa

22. The power consumed by the plasticizing screw is

(*a*) 5 kW (*b*) 1 kW

(*c*) 2.5 kW (*d*) 10 kW

Statement for Linked Answer Questions 23 and 24:

The density of a poly (ethylene terephthalate) (PET) sample is 1.407 g/cm^3, and the heat of fusion of the sample obtained from differential scanning calorimetry (DSC) is 54.6 J/g. The density of the PET crystalline phase is 1.515 g/cm^3 and of the PET amorphous phase is 1.335 g/cm^3

23. The fractional crystallinity of the sample is

(*a*) 0.23 (*b*) 0.36

(*c*) 0.40 (*d*) 0.43

24. The heat of fusion of the PET crystalline phase is

(*a*) 21.8 J/g (*b*) 136.5 J/g

(*c*) 68.2 J/g (*d*) 158.3 J/g

ANSWERS

1. (*c*) **2.** (*b*) **3.** (*b*) **4.** (*c*) **5.** (*d*) **6.** (*a*) **7.** (*b*) **8.** (*c*) **9.** (*d*) **10.** (*a*)

11. (*a*) **12.** (*b*) **13.** (*d*) **14.** (*a*) **15.** (*c*) **16.** (*c*) **17.** (*d*) **18.** (*a*) **19.** (*a*) **20.** (*d*)

21. (*c*) **22.** (*d*) **23.** (*d*)

24. Marks to all (*heat of fusion of the PET amorphous phase is not given)

EXPLANATIONS

1. 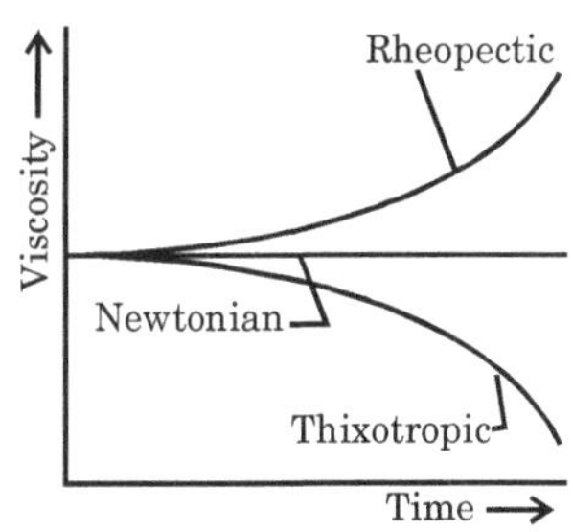

Thixotropic Fluids are fluids that show a shear thinning property. .. In more technical language: some non-Newtonian pseudoplastic fluids show time-dependent change in viscosity; the longer the fluid undergoes shear stress, the lower its **viscosity**.

2. Thermoforming is a process of heating a thermoplastic sheet to its softening point. The sheet is stretched across a single-sided mold and then manipulated. Then, it cools into the desired shape. The most common methods to get the sheet to conform to its final shape are vacuum-forming, pressure-forming, and mechanical forming.

3. Immiscible Blend- PC-PS, PET-PBT, PE-PP & PP-PS

Miscible blend- SAN/PMMA, PS-PPO

4. Exposure to ultraviolet (UV) radiation may cause the significant degradation of many materials. UV radiation causes photooxidative degradation which results in breaking of the polymer chains, produces free radical and reduces the molecular weight, causing deterioration of mechanical properties and leading to useless materials, after an unpredictable time.

5. 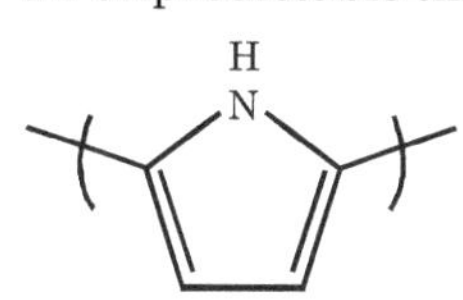

polypyrrole (PPy)

Conducting Polymers are organic polymers that conduct electricity. Conductive polymers are generally not thermoplastics, i.e., they are not thermoformable. But, like insulating polymers, they are organic materials. They can offer high electrical conductivity but do not show similar mechanical properties to other commercially available polymers. The electrical properties can be fine-tuned using the methods of organic synthesis and by advanced dispersion techniques. All conducting polymer system is alternating single bond and double bond along the backbone.

6. Chain-growth polymerization is a process in which the high molecular weight polymer is formed early in the polymerization process and the polymer yield (the percentage conversion of the monomer into the polymer) gradually increases with time.

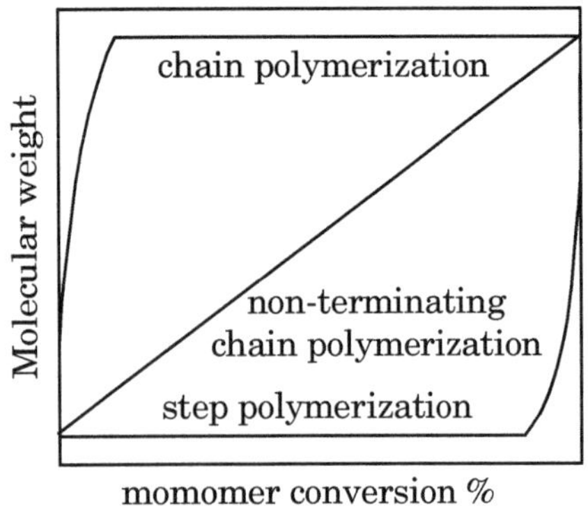

7. The above equation may be rewritten;

$$\frac{\Delta H_m}{V} = \phi, \phi_2[\delta_1 - \delta_2]^2$$

This equation is valid only when ΔHm is zero or greater. It is invalid for exothermic mixing, that is, when ΔHm is negative.

The square of the difference between the solubility parameters of two liquids decides the magnitude of the heat of mixing. Hence, for the positive heat of mixing to be at a minimum value so as to let mixing occur, the difference between the solubility parameters $(\delta_1 - \delta_2)$ of the two liquids must be as low as possible.

Difference of the solubility parameters is low between toluene and polyethylene. So best solvent is toluene for polyethylene.

8.

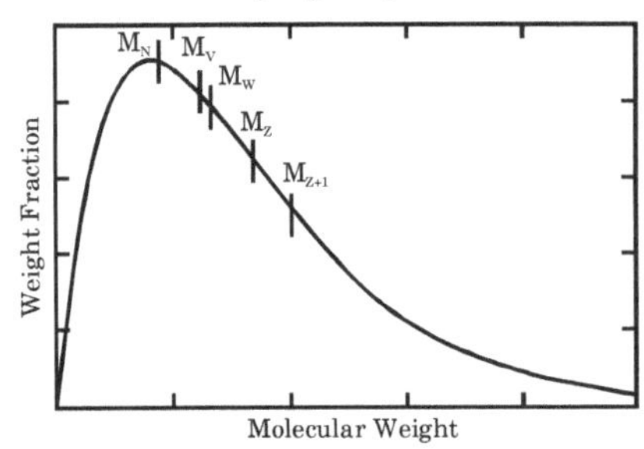

9. P. **Rotational Moulding**

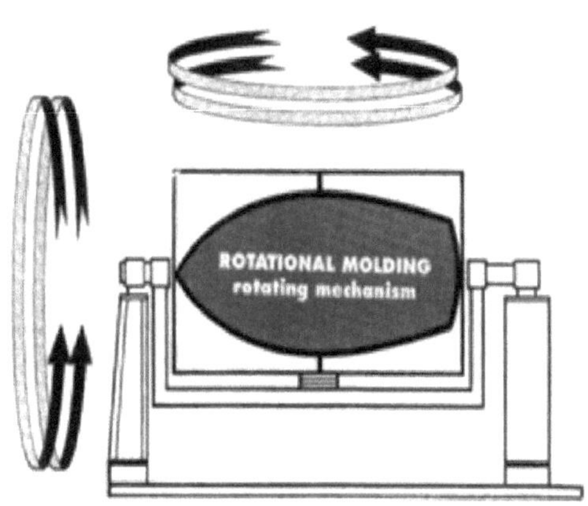

Q. **Extrusion**

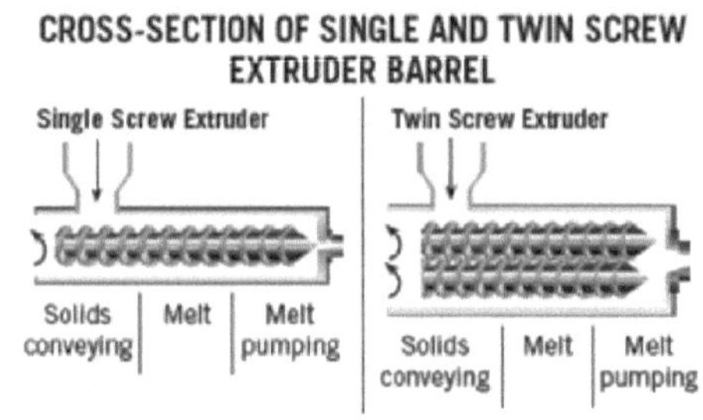

R. **Reaction Injection Molding**

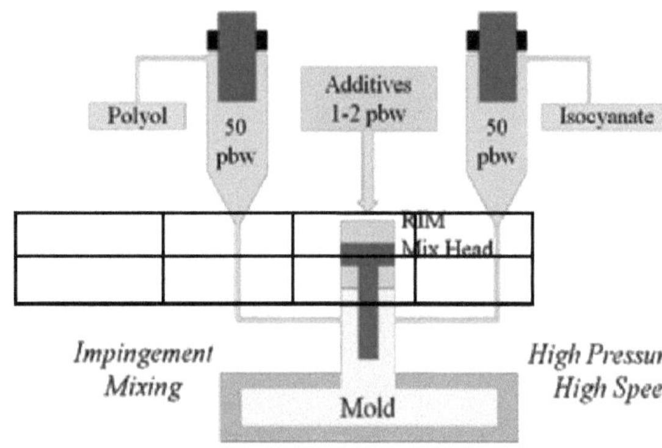

S. **Blow moulding**

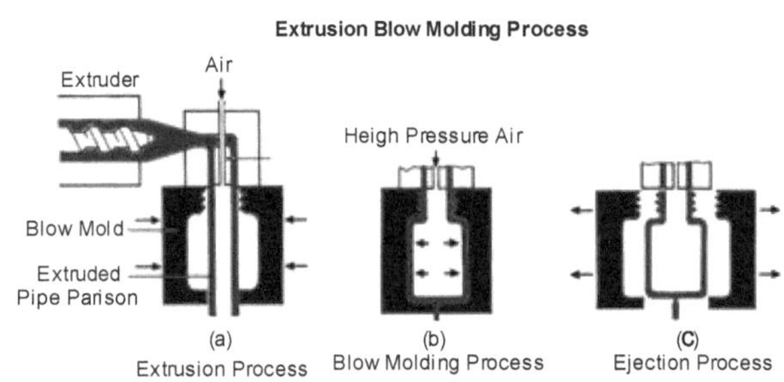

1. **Rotational Molding :** Two centrifugal motions at right angles to each other are required to process the material.
2. **Extrusion :** Twin screw extruder used in the additive industry for homogeneous mixing.
3. **Reaction Injection moulding :** The RIM process typically involves the high-pressure impingement mixing of two liquid components which are then injected into a preformed mold. The components chemically react to form a polyurethane which takes the shape of the mold.
4. **Blow Moulding :** Blow molding is a manufacturing process for forming and joining together hollow plastic parts. A pressurized gas, normally air, is introduced into the parison blowing the heated parison out against the cavity walls to form the product.

10. At steady state condition means process unchanged with the time.

$$\eta\frac{d\gamma_o}{dt}+G\gamma_0 = s_o$$

at steady state $\frac{d\gamma_o}{dt}$ = 0 hence

$$\gamma_o = s_o/G$$

11. **1.** Ziegler-Natta catalyst: These are complex catalyst systems derived from a transition metal compound from groups IVB to VIIIB of the periodic table and an organometallic compound usually from a group IA or IIIA metal. Aluminium alkyls (AlEt or $AlEt_2Cl$) acts as electron acceptor in combination with the electron donor titanium chloride ($TiCl_3$& $TiCl_4$) are used most commonly.

2. Cationic catalyst: Strong Lewis acid like boron trifluoride (BF_3) or Friedel-Crafts catalysts such as $AlCl_3$, H_2SO_4, $SnCl_4$ and $TiCl_4$

3. Anionic catalyst: Strong base Butyl lithium, triphenylmethyl potassium, ethyl sodium, alkali metal amides, alcoxides and hyderoxides.

4. Radical catalyst: AIBN, Benzoyl Peroxides,

12.

PA 66	PA 6	PA10	PA 12
268°C	220°C	185°C	181°C

Polyamide (nylon)	**Repeating unit**
Nylon 6	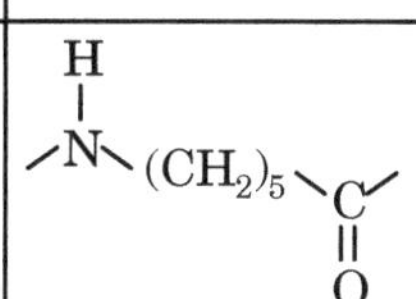
Nylon 6,6	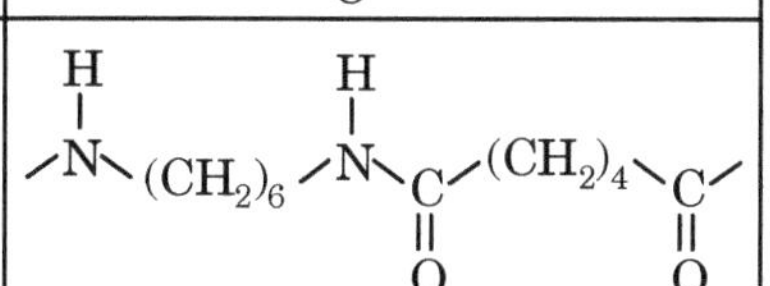
Nylon 10	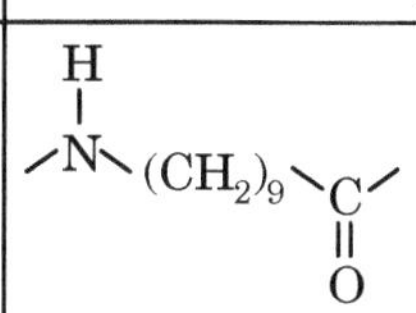
Nylon 12	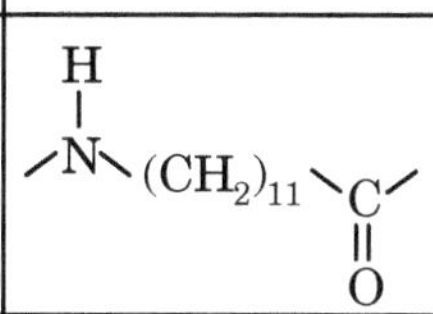

Two concepts we have to apply here :

1. Presence of polar group increases the intermolecular attraction, increases the crystalline and melting point.
2. Increase the length of (–CH_2) in the structure provides the free rotation to the main chain so required less energy to melt the polymer. Reduces the melting point.

Nylon 66 have higher melting point because presence more amide group than the Nylon 6, Nylon 10 & Nylon 12.

Nylon6> Nylon 10> nylon 12; due to increase in the chain length,

13. **Differential scanning Calorimetry :** Tg, percentage of crystallinity & Melting point

Thermo gravimetric : Degradation temperature, Weight loss, Ash Content & Ratio of blend

TEM & SEM : Internal structure of the surface-Morphology

FTIR : Functional Group

14. 1. Tackifiers are low-molecular weight compounds (oligomers) that are added to adhesive formulations to improve tack and peel adhesion. The three most important groups of tackifiers are hydrocarbon resins, rosin esters, and polyterpenes. Hydrocarbon resins are based on petroleum feedstocks whereas terpenes and rosin esters are gained from pine trees.

2. Extender oil, also often referred to as "process or softening oil", is added to rubber compounds inthe production process for tyres and other rubber goods to achieve an acceptable processability. Petroleum oils are useful with nonpolar elastomers. Petroleum oils, usually called extender oils, are further classed as either paraffinic, naphthenic, or aromatic.

3. Accelerator - An accelerator is defined as a compound that increases the speed of vulcanization and that enables vulcanization to proceed at lower temperature and with greater efficiency. Many of the sulfur-based vulcanization systems require activators. For example, dithiocarbamate and thiazole accelerators are activated with *zinc oxide* and *stearic acid* which also increase the speed of vulcanization.

4. Retarder- To avoid premature vulcanization during processing, retarders are often added to the cure system. A compound that meets both requirements is *N-(cyclohexylthio) phthalimide* (CTP). Other important (acidic) retarders/inhibitors include benzoic, salicylic, and phthalic anhydride when used with thiazoles.

15. Where no stoichiometric imbalance $r = 1$

X_n (degree of polymerization) = N_o / N

Number average molecular weight = $M_o * X_n$

$M_o = M_A + M_B /2$

So Number average molecular weight

$$= N_0 (M_A + M_B)/2N$$

16.

$$\delta = 45°$$

$$E^* = E' + iE''$$

$$= E'(1 + i \tan \delta)$$

$$E^* / E' = (1 + i \tan 45°)$$

$$= 1 + i$$

17. 1. Generally fillers incorporated in rubber composites can be divided into two categories, reinforcing and non-reinforcing fillers. The reinforcing fillers play a significant role in increasing or at least maintaining the strength of rubber composites, while the non-reinforcing fillers are added to reduce cost. **Carbon black (CB) and silica** have been used as the main reinforcing fillers that increase the usefulness of rubbers.

2. Non-reinforcing fillers include **particulate alumina** (its trihydrate is of use for flame retardation), calcium carbonates and silicates, clay (hard or soft), talc (platy talc is uniquely pure), thermal carbon, wollastonite (very white and abrasive), zinc oxide (now mainly used as an activator of the vulcanization.

3. Plasticizer is necessary in rubber formulations for improving the processing of the rubber by lowering the compound's viscosity, and also for aiding in low temperature flexibility of the formulated rubber. The most common plasticisers include esters such as adipates, azelates, citrates, benzoates, ortho-phthalates, terephthalates, sebacates, and trimellitates.

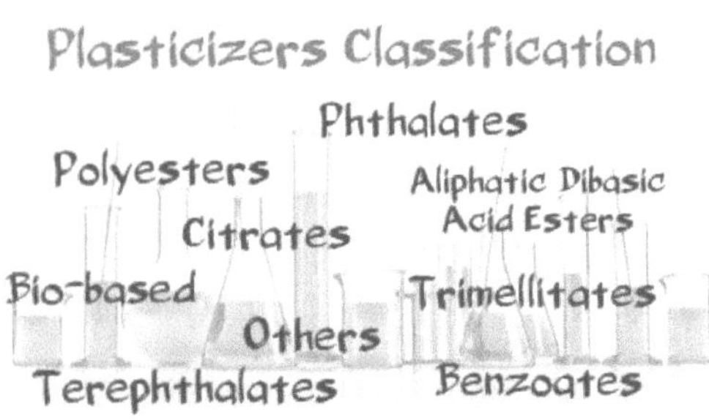

4. Flame retardants (FR)are chemical compounds added with an objective to inhibit/retard the ignition/burning of the plastic. Brominated (BFRs), Chlorinated (CFRs), Phosphorous (PFRs), Alumina Trihydrate (ATH), Magnesium Hydroxide (MDH), Antimony Oxide etc

18. P. **Flexural Strength**

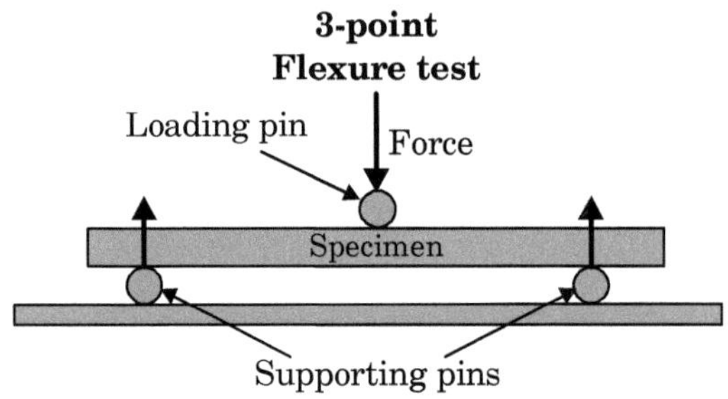

Q. **Impact Strength**

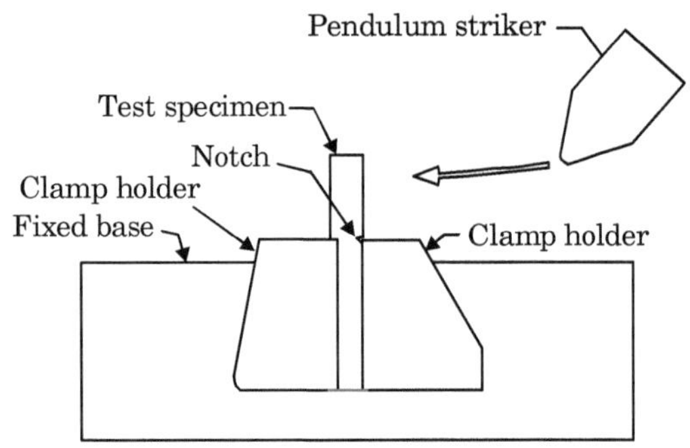

Notched izod impact test

R. **Hardness**

Durometer hardness test

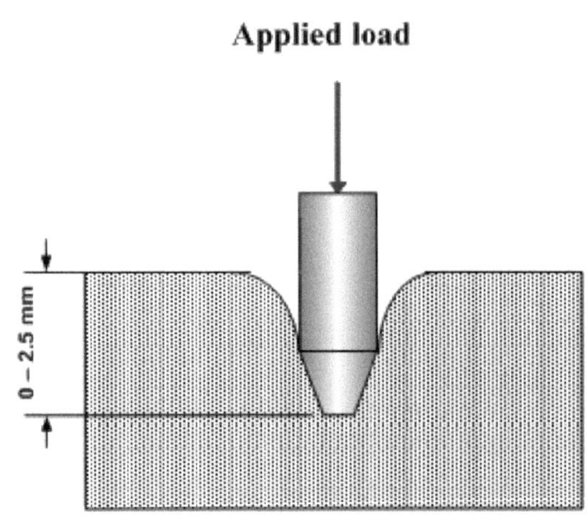

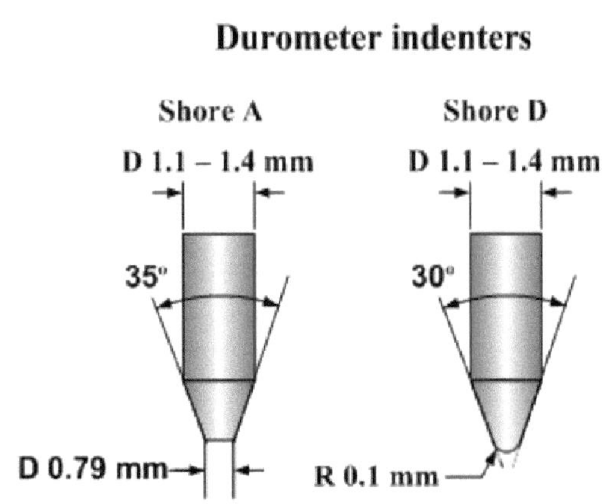

S. **Tensile Strength**

Testing the Tensile Properties of Rigid and Semi-rigid Plastics (ASTM D638 and ISO 527).

19. Modulus of the composite

$E_{cl} = E_m V_m + E_f V_f$

$E_{cl} = 0.6 * 35 + 0.4 * 100 = 121$ GPa

20. Critical fibre length

$$L_c = \frac{\sigma d}{2\tau_c} \qquad \tau_c = \frac{\sigma d}{2L_c},$$

$$\tau_c = \frac{1240 \times 5 \times 10^{-6}}{2 \times 12 \times 10^{-3}}$$

= 0.258 MPa

21. Shear stress distribution in the Hagen-Poiseuille equation;

$$\tau = \frac{R}{2}\frac{dp}{dx}$$

$$\tau = \frac{10}{2} \times \frac{100}{100} = 5\text{MPa}$$

22. Power = volumetric rate * pressure drop

$$\dot{W} = \dot{V}\Delta P$$

Power = $0.1 * 10^{-3} * 100 * 10^{6} = 10$ kW

23.
$$\phi_C = \frac{\rho - \rho_a}{\rho_c - \rho_a}$$

(volume fraction of material in the crystalline state)

ρ : density of the sample

ρ_a : density of amorphous polymer

ρ_c : density of crystalline polymer

Crystallinity fraction by volume (Φ_c)

= 1.407 –1.335/1.515 – 1.335 = 0.4

24. The crystallinity of the polymer sample can be calculated from the enthalpy/heat of fusion values with the following equation:

$$X = \frac{\Delta H_f}{\Delta H_{f,c}}$$

ΔH_f = melting enthalpy of the crystals in sample (J/g)

$\Delta H_{f,c}$ = melting enthalpy of the completely crystalline polymer.

Crystallinity fraction by volume = X = 0.4

$\Delta H_f = 54.6$ J/g

$$0.4 = \frac{54.6}{\Delta H_{f,c}}$$

$\Delta_{f,c} = 136.5$ J/g

SOLVED PAPER - 2008

1. Among the polymerzation methods listed below, the one that is likely to give a polydispersity close to unity is
   (*a*) anionic polymerization
   (*b*) cationic polymerization
   (*c*) condensation polymerization
   (*d*) radical polymerization
2. The end-groups in a polymer sample prepared by using ROOH/Fe^{2+} (where R = alkyl) as the initiator system is
   (*a*) Fe^{2+} (*b*) –OR
   (*c*) –OH (*d*) Fe^{3+}
3. Most polymers exhibit Newtonian behaviour at
   (*a*) high temperature
   (*b*) low shear rate
   (*c*) high molecular weight
   (*d*) low filler content
4. The shear rate of a typical injection molding process is
   (*a*) 1 s^{-1}
   (*b*) 10 s^{-1}
   (*c*) 100 s^{-1}
   (*d*) 1000 s^{-1}
5. Which of the following monomers is used in the synthesis of poly (vinyl alcohol)
   (*a*) CH_3CH_2OH
   (*b*) $CH_2 = CH(OH)$
   (*c*) $CH_2 = CH - O - CO - CH_3$
   (*d*) $CH_2 = CH - CO_2H$
6. The extension ratio of an elastomer deformed to 10 times is
   (*a*) 2 (*b*) 5
   (*c*) 9 (*d*) 11
7. Most plausible value for the Gibb's free energy change for a miscible blend of two polymers is
   (*a*) +5 $kJmol^{-1}$
   (*b*) +1 $kJmol^{-1}$
   (*c*) 0 $kJmol^{-1}$
   (*d*) –0.01 $kJmol^{-1}$
8. The glass transition temperature of raw natural rubber is
   (*a*) – 70°C (*b*) – 10°C
   (*c*) 0°C (*d*) + 30°C
9. 2,2'-azobisisobutyronitrile (AIBN) is an initiator used in the free radical polymerization of methyl methacrylate (MMA). When the concentration of AIBN is doubled maintaining MMA concentration unchanged, the rate of propagation
   (*a*) is doubled
   (*b*) increases by a factor of √2
   (*c*) is reduced by half
   (*d*) decreases by a factor of √2
10. A polymer sample has 3 molecules with molecular weights 1×10^5, 2×10^5 and 3×10^5 $gmol^{-1}$ respectively. The weight average molecular weight of the sample is
   (*a*) 2.99×10^5 $gmol^{-1}$
   (*b*) 2.66×10^5 $gmol^{-1}$
   (*c*) 2.33×10^5 $gmol^{-1}$
   (*d*) 2.00×10^5 $gmol^{-1}$
11. Which of the following reagents is capable of effecting Group Transfer polymerization with methacrylates?
   (*a*) 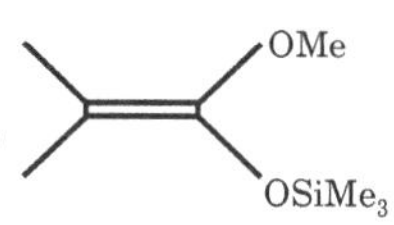

   (*b*) 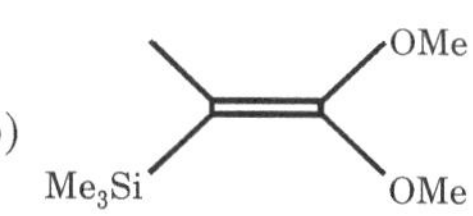

   (*c*) 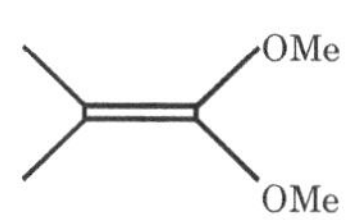

   (*d*) 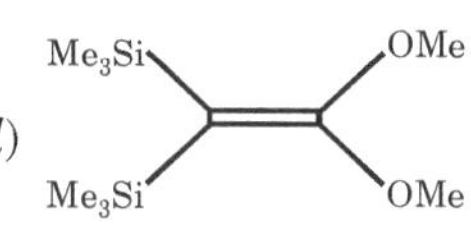

12. For the copolymerization of MMA with vinyl chloride, the monomer reactivity ratios were found to be 10 and 0.1 respectively. The resulting polymer is most likely to be
   (*a*) an alternating copolymer
   (*b*) an ideal copolymer
   (*c*) a block copolymer
   (*d*) a branched copolymer

13. Match the characterization techniques listed in Group l with the applications listed in Group 11 and select the correct answer from (A), (B), (C) or (D)

Group I (*Technique*)	**Group II** (*Application*)
P. X-ray Diffraction	1. Functional Groups
Q. Differential Thermal Analysis	2. Crystallinity
R. Infrared Spectroscopy	3. Morphology
S. Microscopy	4. Enthalpy &
	5. Power Factor

(*a*) P-5, Q-4. R-3, S-2 (*b*) P-2, Q-3, R-1, S-5

(*c*) P-3, Q-2, R-4, S-5 (*d*) P-2, Q-4, R-1, S-3

14. For a polymer, viscosity at 50°C and at 80°C was found to be 2.00 Pas and 1.00 Pas respectively. The value of viscosity at 60°C

(*a*) 1.65 Pa.s (*b*) 1.55 Pa.s

(*c*) 1.45 Pa.s (*d*) 1.35 Pa.s

15. For a viscoelastic material behaving as Maxwell model, the modulus at its relaxation time under constant strain reduces to

(*a*) 36.8 %of the initial value

(*b*) 63.2 %of the initial value

(*c*) 66.7 %of the initial value

(*d*) 33.3% of the initial value

16. The capacity of an extruder can be maximized by a combination of

(*a*) higher barrel diameter; higher screw diameter; higher helix angle; higher rpm

(*b*) higher barrel diameter: higher screw diameter: higher helix angle: lower rpm

(*c*) higher barrel diameter; higher screw diameter; lower helix angle; higher rpm

(*d*) higher barrel diameter; lower screw diameter; higher helix angle; higher rpm

17. Match the raw materials in Group I with the polymer processing operation in Group II and select the correct answer from (A), (B), (C) or (D).

Group I (*raw material*)	**Group II** (*processing operation*)
P. polyethylene granules	1. Injection molding
Q. polycarbonate granules	2. Film extrusion
R. polystyrene sheet	3. Calendering
S. plasticized poly(vinyl chloride)	4. Thermoforming &
	5. Rotational molding

(*a*) P-1, Q-2, R-3, S-4 (*b*) P-2, Q-1, R-4, S-3

(*c*) P-2, Q-5, R-3, S-1 (*d*) P-4, Q-3, R-2, S-5

18. The difference in the stress-strain curve for plastics, elastomer and metals can be represented by: (M = Modulus; ε = elongation at break)

(*a*) $M_{metal} < M_{plastic} < M_{elastomer}$ and $\varepsilon_{metal} > \varepsilon_{plastic} > \varepsilon_{elastomer}$

(*b*) $M_{plastic} < M_{elastomer} < M_{metal}$ and $\varepsilon_{plastic} > \varepsilon_{elastomer} > \varepsilon_{metal}$

(*c*) $M_{elastomer} < M_{plastic} < M_{metal}$ and $\varepsilon_{elastomer} > \varepsilon_{plastic} > \varepsilon_{metal}$

(*d*) $M_{plastic} < M_{metal} < M_{elastomer}$ and $\varepsilon_{plastic} > \varepsilon_{elastomer} > \varepsilon$

19. Match the following rubbers in Group I with their applications in Group II and select the correct answer from (A), (B), (C) or (D).

Group I (rubbers)	**Group II** (applications)
P. Butyl rubber	1. Gaskets in chemical plants
Q. Fluorocarbon elastomer	2. Petrol hose
R. Natural rubber	3. Hand gloves
S. Nitrile rubber	4. Roofing membrane &
	5. Tire inner liner

(*a*) P-5, Q-1, R-3, S-2

(*b*) P-1, Q-3, R-2, S-5

(*c*) P-2, Q-3, R-l, S-4

(*d*) P-3, Q-5, R-1, S-4

20. A carbon fiber-epoxy bar of dimensions (0.5m × 0.04m × 0.04m) gave a breaking load of 784N in a three point bending test. The flexural strength of the material is

(*a*) 15.8 MPa (*b*) 9.2 MPa

(*c*) 0.3 GPa (*d*) 108.1 GPa

21. Match the polymers in Group 1 with their crystalline melting point (m. p.) in Group II and select the right answer from (A). (B), (C) or (D).

Group I (*polymers*)	**Group II** (*melting Point °C*)
P. Nylon66	1. 108
Q. PBT	2. 320
R. PP	3. 264
S. LDPE	4. 165 &
	5. 220

(*a*) P-1, Q-3, R-5, S-2 (*b*) P-3, Q-4, R-2, S-5

(*c*) P-3, Q-5, R-4. S-1 (*d*) P-5, Q-1, R-3, S-4

22. Match the additives listed in Group I below with their function listed in Group II and select the right answer from (A), (B), (C) or (D).

Group I *(additives)*	**Group II** *(function)*
P. Sulfur	1. Age resistor
Q. Zinc oxide	2. Accelerator activator
R. Paraphenylene diamine	3. Vulcanizing agent
S. Dioctyl phthalate	4. Plasticizer &
	5. Accelerator

(*a*) P-1, Q-3, R-4. S-5 (*b*) P-3, Q-2, R-1, S-4
(*c*) P-3, Q-1, R-5, S-4 (*d*) P-2, Q-4, R-5, S-1

23. Match the ingredients in Group I with their amount in parts by weight in Group II in a typical recipe and select the right answer from (A), (B), (C) or (D)

GroupI *(ingredients)*	**Group II** *(parts by weight)*
P. Polyvinylchloride	1. 0.5
Q. Plasticizer	2. 40
R. Stabilizer	3. 3
S. Calcium stearate	4. 100

(*a*) P-1, Q-2, R-3, S-4 (*b*) P-4, Q-3, R-2, S-1
(*c*) P-2, Q-3, R-1, S-4 (*d*) P-4, Q-2, R-3, S-1

24. The heat flow across the thickness to the opposite surface of a plastic slab of dimensions 0.1 m $\times$ 0.1 m $\times$ 0.05m is 19W. If the temperature difference between the surfaces of the slab is 10K, the thermal conductivity of the material will be

(*a*) 0.3 $WK^{-1}m^{-1}$ (*b*) 35.1 $WK^{-1}m^{-1}$
(*c*) 2.1 $WK^{-1}m^{-1}$ (*d*) 9.5$WK^{-1}m^{-1}$

25. A miscible polymer blend consisting of 60% of polymer X (Tg = 208°C) and 40% of polymer Y (Tg = 100°C) will show a glass transition temperature in the range of

(*a*) 100-120 °C (*b*) 145-165°C
(*c*) 200-220°C (*d*) 250-270°C

26. Crystallinity of the three different types of polyethylene (PE) follows the order

(*a*) HDPE > LLDPE > LDPE
(*b*) LDPE > HDPE > LLDPE
(*c*) HDPE > LDPE > LLDPE
(*d*) LLDPE > HDPE > LDPE

27. The notched lzod impact strength of acrylonitrile-butadiene-styrene polymer(ABS), polypropylene (PP), polycarbonate (PC) and phenol-formaldehyde (PF) resin follows the order

(*a*) PC < ABS < PP < PF (*b*) ABS < PF <PC< PP
(*c*) PP < PC < ABS < PF (*d*) PF < PP <ABS < PC

28. The properties of three polymers are as follows:

	Polymer X	Polymer Y	Polymer Z
Density (kg/m^3)	920	1130	900
HDT (°C)	40	110	55
Tensile(MPa)	10	85	35
Elongation at break(%)	600	200	400

Which of the following is true?

(*a*) Polymer X is Commodity and Polymer Z is Engineering Plastic
(*b*) Polymer Y is Commodity and Polymer X is Engineering Plastic
(*c*) Polymer Z is Commodity and Polymer Y is Engineering Plastic
(*d*) Polymer Y is Commodity and Polymer Z is Engineering Plastic

Common Data for Questions 29 and 30 :

For a polymer which follows the Mark-Houwink equation, the various parameters determined were as follows:

$K = 1.2 \times 10^{-4}$;
$[\eta] = 2.4$;
$a = 0.76$;

Huggins' constant = 0.33;
concentration, c = 0.3 gdL^{-1}

29. The molecular weight of the polymer is

(*a*) 4.5×10^5 (*b*) 6.1×10^4
(*c*) 3.2×10^6 (*d*) 7.9×10^5

30. The specific viscosity of the above polymer is

(*a*) 0.73 (*b*) 1.12
(*c*) 0.89 (*d*) 2.30

Statement for Linked Answer Questions 31 and 32:

Consider step growth polymerization of two bifunctional monomers with a monomer ratio of 0.99 and the number average degree of polymerization of 66.8

31. The extent of reaction will be

(*a*) 0.90 (*b*) 0.95
(*c*) 0.99 (*d*) 1.00

32. The polydispersity index at stoichiometric conditions would be

(*a*) 1.90 (*b*) 1.95
(*c*) 1.85 (*d*) 1.99

Statement for Linked Answer Questions 33 and 34:

A polymer composite of mica filled polypropylene contains 60% polymer by mass.

Tensile elastic modulus of polypropylene = 23 MPa

Tensile elastic modulus of mica= 30 GPa

Density of polypropylene= 900 kgm^{-3}

Density of mica = 2800 kgm^{-3}

33. The volume% of mica in the composite is

(*a*) 25.95 (*b*) 17.60

(*c*) 14.83 (*d*) 39.27

34. The modulus of elasticity of the composite is

(*a*) 12.8 GPa (*b*) 20.3 GPa

(*c*) 5.3 GPa (*d*) 31.7 GPa

ANSWERS

1. (*a*)	**2.** (*b*)	**3.** (*b*)	**4.** (*d*)	**5.** (*c*)	**6.** (*d*)	**7.** (*d*)	**8.** (*a*)	**9.** (*b*)	**10.** (*c*)
11. (*a*)	**12.** (*d*)	**13.** (*d*)	**14.** (*a*)	**15.** (*a*)	**16.** (*a*)	**17.** (*c*)	**18.** (*c*)	**19.** (*a*)	**20.** (*b*)
21. (*c*)	**22.** (*b*)	**23.** (*b*)	**24.** (*d*)	**25.** (*b*)	**26.** (*a*)	**27.** (*d*)	**28.** (*c*)	**29.** (*a*)	**30.** (*a*)
31. (*c*)	**32.** (*d*)	**33.** (*b*)	**34.** (*c*)						

EXPLANATIONS

1.

Polymerisation type	$\overline{M}_w / \overline{M}_n$
Free-radical chain polymerisation :	
(*i*) with precise temperature control (solution, suspension and emulsion systems) :	1.5-2
(*ii*) with moderate temperate control (Bulk system)	2-5
(*iii*) without temperature control (with autoacceleration)	8-10
Cationic/anionic chain polymerisation:	
(*i*) using homogeneous catalyst system :	<1.5
(*ii*) using heterogeneous catalyst system:	>10
Polycondensation, polyaddition and ring-opening polymerisation	2-3
Coordination polymerisation	> 10
Polymerisation system leading to chain-branching	> 20

2. The decompositionof hydrogen peroxide by a ferrous ion and that of a hydroperoxide by a cobaltous ion are other examples:

$$H_2O_2 + Fe^{2+} \rightarrow Fe^{3+} + HO^- + HO^\circ$$

$$R—O—OH + Co^{2+} \rightarrow RO\cdot + Co^{3+} + HO^-$$

$$R—O—OH + Co^{2+} \rightarrow ROO\cdot + Co^{2+} + H^+$$

3. Viscous fluids follow the Newton's law; Stress is proportional to the strain rate.

According to Newton's law, the response of a fluid to a shearing stress σ is viscous flow, given by

$$\sigma \,\alpha\, \frac{d\gamma}{dt}, \quad \sigma = \eta \frac{d\gamma}{dt}$$

Where η is viscosity and $d\gamma/dt$ is strain rate. But Polymer are not pure viscous or elastic. But at lower shear rate polymer behave like Newtonian behaviour.

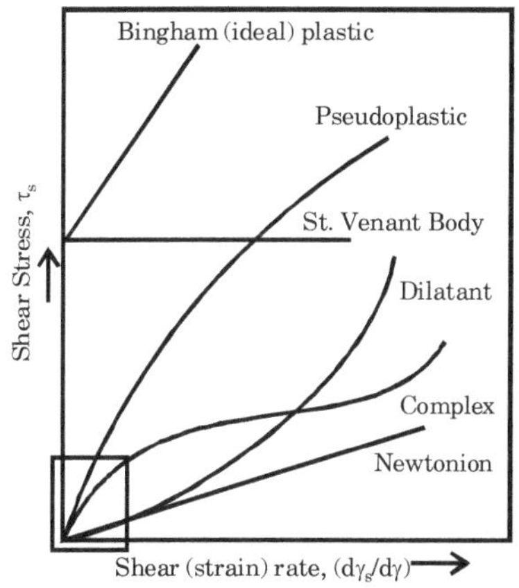

4.

Processing	Shear rate (1/s)
Compression molding	1 to 10
Calendering	10 to 100
Extrusion	100 to 1000
Injection molding	10^3 to 10^4
Fiber spinning	> 10^4

5. 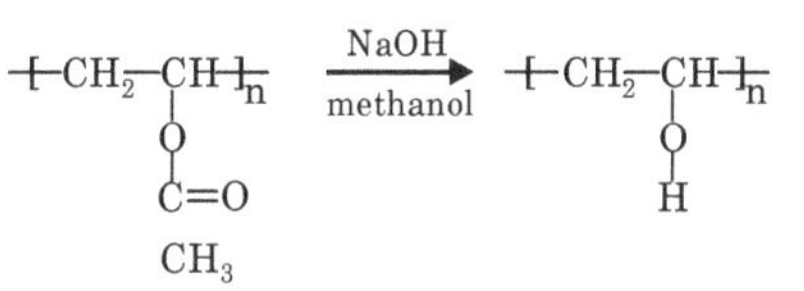

Poly(vinyl acetate) Poly(vinyl alcohol)

6. Extension ratio $\lambda = 1 + \delta 1/1 = 1 + 10 = 11$

7. For miscible of a blend Gibb's free energy should be less than Zero.

9. $$R_p = k_p \left(\frac{fk_d}{k_t}\right)^{1/2} [I]^{1/2}[M]$$

10. Weight average molecualr weight:

$$M_w = \frac{\sum N_i M_i^2}{\sum N_i M_i}$$

$$M_w = \frac{1 \times 100000^2 + 1 \times 200000^2 + 1 \times 300000^2}{1 \times 100000 + 1 \times 200000 + 1 \times 300000}$$

$Mw = 2.33 \times 10^5$

14. Viscosity and temperature assume a linear relation:

Equation $y = mx + C$

Find the m and C value by given condition viscosity at 50°C and at 80°C was found to be 2.00 Pas and 1.00 Pas.

Equation: $y = -1/30x + 110/30$

Value of viscosity at 60°C = (–1/30)* 60 + 110/30

= 1.65 Pa.s

15. $\sigma = \sigma_0 e^{(-t/\tau)}$

Where τ (relaxation time) = η/E

Time t is equal to relaxation time then stress is equal at t;

$$\sigma = \frac{\sigma_0}{e} = 0.37 \times \sigma_0$$

18. Elastic modulus is inversely proportional to the strain.

20. Flexural strength $\sigma_f = \dfrac{3FL}{2bd^2}$

Flexural strength $\sigma_f = \dfrac{3 \times 784 \times 0.5}{2 \times 0.04 \times 0.04^2}$

= 9.187 GPa

24. $$k = \frac{Q \times L}{A \times \Delta T}$$

$k = 19 * 0.5/(0.1 * 0.1 * 10) = 9.5$

25. $$\frac{1}{T_g} = \frac{W_1}{T_{g1}} + \frac{W_2}{T_{g2}}$$

$$\frac{1}{T_g} = \frac{0.6}{481} + \frac{0.4}{373}$$

$T_g = 158°C$

26. Density α crystallinity

27. 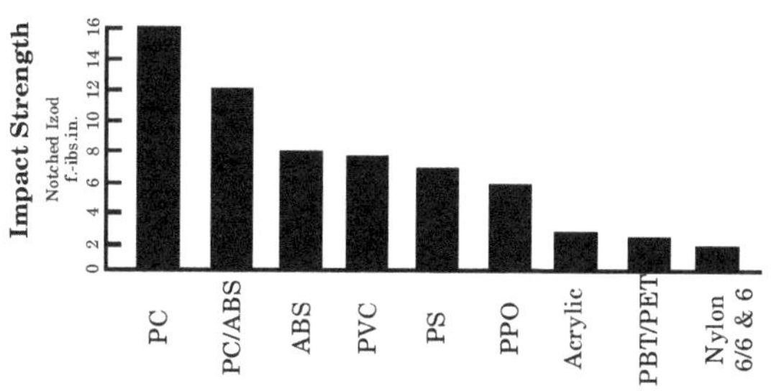

28. Tensile strength of the elastomer is 2-15Mpa, Commodity plastics 15-40 and engineering plastics above 40.

29. Mark-Houwink equation the relationship among the molecular weight and viscosity are given below

$$[\eta] = KM^a$$

Where $[\eta]$ is the intrinsic viscosity, M is Molecular weight, K and a are constants for a particular polymer solvent system.

$K = 1.2 \times 10^{-4}$ dl g^{-1}

$a = 0.76$ $\eta = 2.4$

$$\frac{[\eta]}{K} = M^a;$$

$$M^{0.76} = \frac{2.4}{1.2 \times 10^{-4}}$$

$$= 20000,$$

$$M = \sqrt[0.76]{20000}$$

$$= 456299.5$$

30. Intrinsic Viscosity $= \left(\frac{\eta_{sp}}{C}\right)_{C \to 0} = \left(\frac{\eta_r}{C}\right)_{C \to 0}$

$$= [\eta], dl/g$$

$$\eta_{sp} = 2.4 * 0.3$$

$$= 0.72$$

31. $X_n = \frac{1+r}{1+r-2Pr}$

$$66.8 = \frac{1+0.99}{1+0.99-2P*0.99};$$

$$P = 0.99$$

32. Polydispersity index = 1 + P = 1 + 0.99 = 1.99

33. Volume fraction of mica $= \frac{40/2800}{40/2800 + 60/900}$

$$= 0.176; 17.6\%$$

34. Modulus of the composite

$$E_{cl} = E_m V_m + E_f V_f$$

$$E_{cl} = 0.824*23000 + 0.176*30000000$$

$$= 5.3 GPa$$

9 789391 061586

Printed by Libri Plureos GmbH in Hamburg,
Germany